**Also by Joseph M. Giglio**

*Fast Lane to the Future: The Privatization Route*

*Mobility: America's Transportation Mess and How to Fix It*

*Driving Questions: Developing a National Transportation Vision*

*Judges of the Secret Court*

*Unspeakable Truths*

*Columns That Cut*

# CUTTING DEEPER

## NEW REFLECTIONS AND ARGUMENTS

JOSEPH M. GIGLIO

ISBN: 979-8-9940911-0-4

For Annie and Alfred

# Author's Note

## Redefining Myself (Once Too Often)

**THIS BOOK CONTINUES** where *Columns That Cut* left off—another collection of reflections written from the intersection of experience and observation, the real world and the academic one. If the earlier volume captured my first foray into redefining myself, this one chronicles the ongoing experiment—what happens when someone who once lived in boardrooms and briefing rooms tries to make sense of the world from a classroom.

After several decades navigating the corridors of power—first in government, then in investment banking—I found myself standing at the front of a university classroom, holding a piece of chalk like it was a foreign object. Teaching was supposed to be a graceful "third act," an opportunity to redefine myself. Judging by some of my students' expressions, I may have redefined myself once too often.

For them, I'm a strange hybrid: part professor, part practitioner, part museum exhibit from the analog age. They seem both amused and reassured that someone who once signed paychecks now grades papers. When I mention "closing a deal," they think I'm referring to late-night negotiations over group project deliverables.

Still, there's something wonderfully renewing about academic life. The university provides a vantage point from which to connect theory with the scar tissue of experience—the kind you can't acquire from a peer-reviewed journal. Students quickly sense when a professor has earned those scars. They appreciate instructors who've lived the volatility, made payroll in a crisis, or negotiated with someone who didn't read the textbook on rational behavior.

As a university professor for nearly thirty years, my job has been to prepare undergraduate and graduate students not just to excel on academic examinations but also to navigate the challenges of the business world with agility and insight. Teaching is about equipping students with the tools to apply theoretical knowledge to practical situations—to analyze, to adapt, and to innovate. The hard truth is that a business school is, at its core, a trade school—our trade just happens to involve judgment, ethics, and the ability to make decisions under uncertainty.

My decision to become a professor was not a fallback plan or a quest for job security. It was a conscious choice to engage in a profession that offers the rare opportunity to make a tangible difference in the lives of students—particularly those embarking on an educational journey without a family blueprint. Teaching allows me to be part of a transformative process that challenges, inspires, and supports students in their pursuit of knowledge, personal growth, and a meaningful career—one that enables them to contribute to building a better society.

Professors with real-world mileage often mentor as much as they teach. They sponsor the serious students—the ones who raise their hands not to show off but because they genuinely want to understand how the world works. These relationships are the quiet dividends of teaching.

The columns that follow delve into a variety of political, social, business, and economic issues, each examined through the dual lenses of theory and practice. They draw on my experiences in the high-stakes world of finance, the strategic arena of government policy, and the reflective domain of academia. These vantage points—complementary and occasionally conflicting—offer a way to understand how ideas meet reality and how principles bend (but shouldn't break) under pressure.

This collection of columns, written between 2017 and 2023, reflects the perspective of someone straddling those worlds. They were born of classroom debates, office-hour conversations, and too many late nights trying to turn experience into insight. They aim to connect the dots between theory and practice, between what we teach and what we learn the hard way.

If these columns provoke a chuckle, a thought, or even mild disagreement, I'll count that as success. After all the purpose of both teaching and writing is not to settle arguments but to start them—preferably with people still young enough to believe they can win one.

This is not a book that insists on being read straight through, cover to cover, in neat and orderly fashion—unless, of course, that's exactly how you prefer to read. In that case, carry on. The columns collected here appear in chronological order, reflecting the moment and the context in which they were written. But they were never meant to be consumed in one sitting, or even in sequence. Dip in and where a title catches your eye, skip what doesn't, circle back later, or jump ahead entirely. Think of this less as a single narrative and more as a conversation you can join at any point. And for those who do eventually reach the end—whether

sooner or later—there's a Postscript and Acknowledgments waiting, should you choose to keep going.

Boston, 2026

# 1

## 2017 Columns

### In Afghanistan, Little to Show for America's Longest War

1/7/2017

It is the longest war in US history, yet it hardly gets any attention. The public may be suffering from Afghan fatigue, especially when there is little to show for the expenditure of life and treasure.

It has been fifteen years since the United States invaded Afghanistan to hunt down the architects of the 9/11 attacks. The invasion was an integral piece of President Bush's hastily conceived "Global War on Terrorism." By the end of 2001, American forces had toppled the Taliban government. Mission accomplished.

Afghanistan is a country of about thirty million people, about the size of Texas, nestled between Pakistan, Iran, and several former Soviet republics. Its location has made it a source of significant geopolitical interest and tension since the nineteenth century.

The country has historically been wrought with turbulence, characterized by chronic instability and repeated bouts of civil war. Since 329 BC, when Alexander the Great came to Kabul, Afghanistan has been invaded by Arabs, Chinese, Mongols, mogul, the British, and the Soviets. As scholars have written, Afghanistan is the graveyard of empires.

The Taliban took over in 1996. This fundamentalist Islamic group formed from remnants of the mujahideen (holy warriors) who battled the Soviets for over a decade.

The United States has spent over $1 trillion on fighting and reconstruction, building an Afghan army, instilling Western values in a land of warlords and tribal hostilities, and establishing a functioning democracy in a place that has never been changed by a foreign power. More than 2,200 American lives have been sacrificed.

According to the Special Inspector General for Afghanistan Reconstruction, about $115 billion has been spent to support Afghanistan relief and assist the government. Yet the World Bank reports that it remains one of the poorest countries in the world, and three quarters of the population is illiterate.

While the United States and NATO formally ended the war in Afghanistan on December 28, 2014, a force of 8,500 Americans remains to train and support the Afghan security forces.

Since the Taliban fell, some progress has arguably been made in opening up the country and expanding democratic freedoms, especially among women. However, lack of security still impedes development, and corruption remains a significant barrier to progress. The 2015 Corruption Perceptions Index ranks Afghanistan 166th out of the 168 countries monitored. Taliban insurgency is on the rise, drug trafficking flourishes, human rights abuses continue, and the rule of law is weak. All the while the United States picks up the tab for the Afghan army and police and continues to provide foreign aid.

Billions have been wasted on fruitless projects that are awash in corruption and have little government oversight, according to the Special Inspector General. This office has documented a greatest hits compilation of waste, fraud, and abuse in US government-sponsored programs.

Among the more egregious boondoggles was importing rare blond male Italian goats to mate with female Afghan goats and make cashmere. The $6 million program included shipping nine male goats to western Afghanistan and setting up a farm, lab, and staff to certify their wool.

But the entire herd of female goats was wiped out by disease. As a result only two of the imported Italian goats are still usable; it could not be confirmed whether the others were dead or alive.

Another baaad idea. You *goat* to be kidding.

That was not the only example of wasting American taxpayer money. The Pentagon's Task Force for Business and Stability Operations spent nearly $150 million for employees to stay in private luxury villas with flat-screen TVs rather than bunking at military bases. Another $43 million was spent on a gas station that should have cost about $500,000.

America may have good intentions, but we know which road is paved with those. We will be mowing the grass in Afghanistan for the foreseeable future, like Sisyphus rolling his boulder up the hill for all eternity.

## Automakers Under Pressure to Reinvent the Industry
1/21/2017

Automakers face unprecedented technological changes and market trends that will ultimately force them, along with the

Cleveland Browns and the Democratic Party, to reinvent their business models. Sources of disruption include electric vehicles; connectivity; autonomous vehicles, including trucks; changing patterns of car ownership and use; and on-demand ride services.

Car companies face an array of new competitors. Besides their traditional rivals, new market entrants, including Google, Apple, Tesla, Uber, and Lyft, are fielding new technology vehicles.

Technology is but one of the threats that connected, automated, and autonomous driving is introducing to the industry. Connected vehicles are able to "talk" with one another through radio frequency devices or cellular technology.

General Motors plans to have connected vehicles on the street by the end of the year. The 2017 Cadillac CTS sports sedan will offer technology that allows sharing information about driving conditions such as weather, speed, sudden braking, and more. Other automakers are expected to follow suit.

Automated and autonomous driving is more complicated. Automated cars use onboard sensors and systems to aid the driver, while autonomous vehicles actually do the driving. It is unclear whether fully autonomous vehicles are ten or fifteen years away.

Autonomous vehicles may get the attention, but the notion of cars talking to one another is the real deal. Vehicle connectivity has generated great interest from the US Department of Transportation (USDOT). The holy grail of connectivity is vehicles talking with one another without human intervention. The feds have bet that such communication will prevent millions of crashes that result in thousands of fatalities. Last December, USDOT proposed rules requiring that all new cars and small trucks contain technology, allowing them to broadcast data to other vehicles within a 984-foot radius about their speed, location, and direction.

The proposed rules will standardize how one car talks to another and warns drivers, and eventually autonomous vehicles, about potential dangers. The carmaker determines what to do with the data, be it automated braking or a visual dashboard warning. At an intersection, vehicles would decide if you have enough time to make that right on red and who gets to go next at a four-way stop.

According to the National Highway Traffic Safety Administration, the vehicle-to-vehicle (V2V) equipment and supporting communications functions would cost about $350 per vehicle in 2020. If the rule is adopted, the feds say all new cars would have the technology in four years.

The rule would not require retrofitting existing vehicles. As technology evolves, automobiles will likely become more connected to people's home and mobile devices and integrated into the Internet of Things.

The deployment of V2V technologies faces a number of hurdles, such as data security and privacy concerns. If V2V communications get hacked, the possibilities for traffic accidents increase.

Then there is the question of the underlying technology that would enable V2V communication. The feds mandate the use of dedicated short-range communications (DSRC). Many believe that DSRC is obsolete and that newer technologies, such as 5G cellular wireless to power smartphone communication, will be released before DSRC market penetration is achieved.

Moreover critics argue that cellular networks have already built infrastructure in the form of cell towers, obviating the need for state and local governments to roll out dedicated short-range receivers on roadside infrastructure.

The other half of the communication network is vehicle-to-infrastructure (V2I). USDOT plans to issue guidance on V2I communications, which in theory should help transportation planners integrate the technologies to allow vehicles to "talk" to roadway infrastructure, such as traffic lights, stop signs, and work zones to improve mobility, reduce congestion, and improve safety.

No matter how the technology battle sorts out, the car of the future will be connected. Our transportation system is on the cusp of a transformation, with technology bridging the gap between vehicles and intelligent roadside infrastructure, creating a network that works like the internet and can prevent collisions, keep traffic moving, and reduce environmental impacts.

## Put a Money-Back Guarantee on Infrastructure Work
2/4/2017

Americans are told that the nation's most serious transportation infrastructure problem is a lack of funding. Perhaps people would be willing to pay more if they receive a money-back guarantee in return.

Today's roadway funding depends primarily on motor vehicle fuel taxes and state and local appropriations. But federal fuel tax revenues no longer keep pace with needs because of the self-serving assumption that it's become politically impossible to "raise taxes." Everyone wants better roads and bridges, but almost no one wants to pay for them.

All this makes finding adequate funding to rehabilitate the nation's highway system, add new lanes, and develop highway corridors a major challenge. Between 2005 and 2015, there were two five-year federal surface transportation reauthorization bills and thirty-four short-term funding extensions. To maintain the committed level of funding, the federal government was forced to raid the General Fund for an average of $10 billion per year to supplement the dwindling Highway Trust Fund.

Even so, Congress struggled to find the revenues to support a long-term bill without increasing the fuel tax, which has remained at 18.4 cents per gallon for cars since 1991. Congressmen have moved in unison to avoid dealing with an increase in the federal fuel tax.

In real terms, fuel tax revenue is actually projected to decline as the nation's motor vehicle fleet becomes more fuel efficient. It is safe to say that the fuel tax is like a marriage that dies long before divorce papers are filed.

At the same time, state and local government budgets are increasingly burdened with funding demands for education, fighting crime, better security against terrorist threats, and a host of other deserving services. Roadway funding inevitability gets shortchanged, which is relatively easy to do since it takes a while for the impact to become apparent.

A new US Department of Transportation "conditions and performance" report estimates that there is a $926 billion backlog of needed highway and transit infrastructure projects and that many more billions will be needed to keep up with demand over the next twenty years. The congressionally mandated biennial report identifies an $836 billion highway and bridge backlog.

The public can quibble about the size of these numbers, just as maritime historians do about the size of the iceberg that sank the *Titanic*. But their magnitude is so enormous that it scarcely matters whether the estimates are off by 5 or 10 percent. What matters is that the needs are enormous, and the longer you wait to address them, the worse they become.

Senate Democrats just unveiled a ten-year, $1 trillion infrastructure plan that includes $210 billion to repair "crumbling" roads and bridges, but they are vague about how to finance it other than through direct federal spending. During the campaign, President Trump also called for a $1 trillion infrastructure investment that proposed leveraging new revenues and using public-private partnerships to incentivize investment and spare taxpayers from bearing the burden.

At one end of the funding spectrum are people who think the public should pay for it via tolls. At the other end are those who argue that the benefits transportation infrastructure provides are not confined to users, so society as a whole should pay out of general tax revenues. Between these extremes lies a range of payment mechanisms.

But for American motorists to accept a plan, it must be perceived to deliver superior travel service with appropriate regard for equity and environmental considerations. One thought is to pair any increase in taxes or user fees with a money-back performance guarantee so customers can rest assure that they will get guaranteed travel time savings in return for paying for access to surface transportation such as highways. This gives the traveling public confidence that they are getting their money's worth.

The rapid introduction of intelligent transportation technologies facilitates an efficient way to implement a money-back guarantee. The result would be a dramatically transformed approach to transportation infrastructure.

## Widening Gap Between Rich and Poor a Challenge for Capitalism

2/18/2017

Capitalism is a well-known paradigm that attempts to answer the question of what constitutes an economically just society through the production and distribution of economic goods. It is a classic example of a paradigm that was developed by studying what was going on in the real world and reducing it to abstract theory.

As practiced in most societies, capitalism is an inevitable outgrowth of the human instinct to trade goods with each other. This instinct seems to be as strongly hardwired into the DNA of our species as the instinct to reproduce and has defied all attempts to suppress it. Various forms of capitalism have, over time and across countries, improved the lives of billions of people, especially since the collapse of the Soviet Union and China's adoption of a form of state capitalism in 1976. But how effective is it when it comes to the just distribution of goods among members of society?

A late-night television wag once quipped that paradigms were the last refuge of the intellectually challenged. Preconceptions can be a useful starting point for organizing great masses of empirical evidence, but it is prudent not to edit the evidence to fit our normative theories about what the real world ought to look like.

This was the mistake made by the medieval European philosophers who based their cosmology of an earth-centered universe on accepted Christian myths carefully propped up with Aristotelian logic. The result was the need for constant tinkering with their theoretical models to accommodate a growing body of astronomical evidence about how the known planets actually moved.

This does not even account for the centuries of embarrassment for the Roman Catholic Church after it forced Galileo to recant the evidence of his own eyes that supported the "heretical" sun-centered cosmology of Copernicus.

As capitalism matured and came to dominate Western societies during the last two centuries, it attracted the attention of various writers who developed paradigms to explain it. Beginning with Adam Smith and proceeding through John Stuart Mill to today's stained glass theorists of the Austrian and Chicago schools, these writers, with the regularity of Swiss trains, sought to purify their paradigms and give them a hard core of academic logic.

In Smith's world, competition among those who pursue their own interest promotes the general welfare of society more effectively than the efforts of any individual who might deliberately set out to promote it. As he simply put it, "It is not from the benevolence of the butcher, the brewer, or the baker that we expect our dinner, but from their regard to their own interest."

Critics argue that, as currently structured, capitalism disproportionately benefits the wealthy and powerful. They say it exacerbates both economic inequality and other pressing societal problems, such as environmental issues.

Stated differently, one downside of capitalism as currently practiced is that it results in the rich getting richer and the poor getting poorer. This has led to unprecedented stagnation in American social mobility and is a major factor in the anger many Americans are expressing.

This condition is a real challenge in a country where, just this past November, we learned just how deeply economic and demographic factors have divided the electorate. To paraphrase Florida Senator Marco Rubio, it is a country in which half the people absolutely hate the other half. The relationship between the haves and have-nots is dramatized by the media and by politicians firing up their base.

In any case the practical test of a vision's standing in the real world is whether it can consistently pass the French Revolution Test. That is, whether it can win acceptance by a sufficiently large majority of a society's members to withstand the inevitable assaults from those who find it objectionable and seek to replace it with their own visions—by force, if other means fail.

## Technology Transforming the Automobile Industry
3/4/2017

It's obvious that the automobile industry is on the cusp of a technological revolution. Manufacturers and technology companies are working together to reinvent the automobile, much like the way Apple reinvented itself from a computer company to a cultural force or even how Madonna has remained a media icon by constantly adapting to new trends.

Although new technologies and consumer markets are still in their gestation stage, Ford, for example, is making major investments that will transform it from a company that just makes cars to one that touches all aspects of mobility.

Technology companies see a driverless world of autonomous or robotic vehicles as a software and artificial intelligence play. For them, the car is a platform, a commodity, like a cell phone body. You can get the car body anywhere; the real smarts are in the software. The car may be the ultimate mobile device.

As the value of each vehicle becomes more dependent on the software it contains, tech companies may be in a better position to capture this value than the automakers. New technologies are redefining boundaries between software firms and the lumbering dinosaurs of the automobile industry.

Opinions differ about when widespread adoption of fully autonomous and commercially viable vehicles will occur. They could dot our roadways in five to ten years, but saturation will take several decades.

Market penetration may not be uniform; it could start in trucks, for example, before private cars, or even as part of an on-demand commercial ride-sharing fleet. In any case it is not too early to start planning for the roadway management challenges that will be created by autonomous trucks and cars sharing the roads with driver-operated vehicles.

Autonomous vehicle proponents claim they hold the potential to dramatically reduce traffic casualties by eliminating human error. Activities such as speeding and driving while texting are deadly. The National Highway Traffic Safety Administration says human error is a factor in 94 percent of fatal crashes. According to the National Safety Council, as many as 40,000 people died in motor vehicle crashes last year, a 6 percent increase over 2015. An estimated 4.6 million people were seriously injured.

When we begin seeing fully driverless cars hinges as much on the regulatory environment as on advances in self-driving technology. Autonomous vehicles operating without a steering wheel, brake pedals, and human intervention pose questions about whether regulations can catch up to technological advances.

Market participants argue that realizing the safety benefits of autonomous vehicles will require a single national standard, not fifty sets of rules. Automakers complain that states are moving ahead with their own regulations, creating the potential for a confusing "patchwork" of laws under which autonomous vehicles operate. As of December, California, Florida, Michigan,

Nevada, Utah, and the District of Columbia had enacted laws authorizing autonomous vehicle testing under certain conditions. Washington, Ohio, Pennsylvania, and Texas have active testing programs but no legislation.

On the same day Uber started to test its self-driving Volvos near its Bay Area headquarters, the state's Department of Motor Vehicles ordered the firm to stop because its cars did not have the proper registration for such testing. Uber loaded the cars onto a self-driving truck and sent them to Arizona.

Michigan now allows companies to test self-driving vehicles without steering wheels, pedals, or a human operator to take over in an emergency. In contrast California has a rule that self-driving vehicles can only hit the road with a safety driver.

It is uncertain how soon fully autonomous vehicles will enter the mainstream. When they do, avoiding the pushback that, for example, on-demand mobility firms such as Uber and Lyft have faced in various cities will require clarifying the proper role of all levels of government within the regulatory landscape. If autonomous vehicles are safer than their driver-operated counterparts, it is imperative that regulators not risk preventable injuries and deaths by unnecessarily delaying their deployment.

## Weighing the Risks in Responding to North Korea
3/18/2017

The Korean Peninsula has been divided since the 1953 Armistice Agreement that ended the Korean War. South Korea has always faced a hostile, antidemocratic, heavily armed nation just an hour's drive from its capital, Seoul. Now North Korea's pursuit of a functional warhead that can reach American shores is a major security threat to the United States.

North Korea is a highly centralized communist state with about twenty-five million people and almost no real gross domestic product (GDP) growth. According to the State Department, the North's annual military expenditures average about $4 billion, which accounts for around a quarter of the country's average $17 billion GDP. China is North Korea's most important ally, biggest trading partner, and main source of food and energy.

Take away North Korea's nuclear weapons and it would be regarded as a failed state. In contrast South Korea is a high-tech, industrialized economic power fully integrated into the global economy.

North Korea's nuclear threat to its neighbors, America's interests, and the rest of the world has escalated. Earlier this month it fired four ballistic missiles into the sea off Japan's northwest coast, provocatively landing about two hundred miles from the mainland. The country's missile program has progressed from tactical rockets in the 1960s and '70s to short-range and medium-range ballistic missiles in the 1980s and '90s.

The launches violate multiple UN Security Council resolutions and represent a direct challenge to the international community. The test launch apparently was a response to annual United States and South Korea military exercises that the North regards as a rehearsal for an invasion.

North Korea said its launches were training for a strike on US bases in Japan. It appears that North Korea is on a trajectory to launch an intercontinental ballistic missile capable of reaching the continental United States, something President Trump has vowed would not happen.

The day after North Korea launched the ballistic missiles toward Japan, the United States deployed missile launchers and other military hardware needed to create an antimissile defense system in South Korea to intercept and destroy short- and medium-range ballistic missiles.

The North's nuclear weapons and long-range missile development and testing program pose a security threat to the region and the global order. Decades of economic sanctions, diplomacy, and sweet words have failed to topple the neo-Stalinist hermit kingdom or force a rollback of its nuclear and missile programs.

The underlying assumption behind economic sanctions is that North Korea's leaders care about their country's economy and the deprivations endured by their civilian population. They understand that in chess, the pawns are always sacrificed first.

Tightening the economic noose around North Korea bought time without using American muscle but at the cost of delaying hard decisions and creating an unacceptable risk to America's national security. In turn the breathing space gave North Korea time to develop its weapons program. It's wise to remember soft power is irrelevant unless underwritten by hard power.

The North Korean mess is another example of US administrations kicking the can down the road, then discovering at the eleventh hour that they have run out of road. President Trump is dealing with a more dangerous North Korea than did any of his predecessors and has little room to navigate.

His options are limited, and they all involve risks, trade-offs, and hard choices. They include continuing to increase the use of sanctions and hoping the cumulative effect will work, engaging in high-pressure diplomacy with China to rein in its client state, or cutting a deal directly with North Korea. All should be weighed against the risk of a nuclear-armed North Korea.

Then there is the high-risk military option: a limited surprise attack on this rogue state. Or even allowing South Korea and Japan to develop weapons of mass destruction.

Sadly the most likely outcome may be learning to live with a clear and present danger to the United States and its allies in Northeast Asia.

## No Easy or Cheap Fix for America's Infrastructure
4/1/2017

Earlier this month the American Society of Civil Engineers' "2017 Infrastructure Report Card," which looks at sixteen categories of infrastructure from schools to airports to dams, gave the nation an overall grade of D-plus. Creative approaches can finance some of the needed improvements, but others will need to be paid for the old-fashioned way.

The report is yet another in a series of reports making the case that America has underinvested in infrastructure for decades. Such chronicles of wretched conditions are a national sport that is nearly as popular as the Kardashians. But although much of the material is familiar, infrastructure is a gift that keeps on giving; there always seems to be something new to chew on.

The report card projects that $4.59 trillion will be required to bring America's infrastructure to a grade of B. That is more than the nation's annual budget of about $4 trillion.

Americans can quibble about the actual size of these projections, just as maritime historians quibble about the size of the iceberg that sank the *Titanic*. But it scarcely matters whether the estimates are off by 5 or 10 percent, give or take. What matters are the general proportions of these needs and the risks for the US economy if they are not addressed. The longer we wait, the bigger the problem becomes.

Most who deal with this issue agree that the country's infra-structure is in a bad way, but there is much partisan disagreement over how to pay for the fix.

Using public-private partnerships to invest in infrastructure was one of President Trump's major campaign promises, but fiscal conservatives in Congress are reluctant to back massive spending that exacerbates the federal budget deficit and skyrocketing federal debt.

Democrats, on the other hand, are for more direct federal spending. By reducing taxes on overseas profits, they believe some of the estimated $2–$3 trillion companies have kept outside the United States could be repatriated. The result is that the political hills come alive with the sound of heated debates over proposals to address the infrastructure gap.

The permanent political aristocracy's failure to deal with infrastructure reflects the simple fact that talking about balancing the budget is easy, but doing the things you have to do to balance it is hard. By the very nature of the process, politicians are focused on the very near term.

Upcoming elections, like hangings, have a way of focusing the mind on the here and now. That is why the federal gasoline tax of 18.4 cents per gallon and the diesel tax of 24.4 cents per gallon, the most important sources of federal transportation funding, have not risen since 1993. During that time they have lost about 40 percent of their purchasing power because of inflation. Fuel tax revenues can no longer keep pace with needs.

This is not just a problem with politicians; it's also a problem with voters, who say the deficit is a major concern yet favor lower taxes, more benefits, and fixing our infrastructure. Put simply, they don't want to pay for the government they want.

It's time to get real. Nothing works without a funding source, and we will need hard cash to correct our underinvestment in infrastructure. The feds, state and local governments, and the private sector have plenty of access to capital markets to finance infrastructure; the real issue is identifying revenue sources such as user fees or taxes to repay the debt.

A partial solution is to minimize the need for scarce government dollars by recruiting private firms as partners to help start, fund, and run infrastructure projects that have predictable revenue streams, such as toll roads. But a larger universe of projects, such as schools, dams, and local roads, for example, cannot be monetized.

Infrastructure's biggest challenge is funding. In the real world, that comes down to a choice between taxes and user fees. There is no free lunch.

## Private Firms Offer a Route to Financing Infrastructure

4/15/2017

President Trump and his advisers have identified recruiting private firms as active participants as one solution to the choking shortage of money to finance critical infrastructure needs. He's right, but maximizing the private sector's impact will require the administration to think outside the box.

If properly structured, public-private partnerships could tap into billions of dollars of private capital hungering for low-risk investment opportunities that offer decent returns. Piles of dough would be deposited on the front steps of city halls and state houses with the steely hand of the private sector at the tiller, minimizing the need for scarce taxpayer dollars to get infrastructure projects underway.

This means designing such partnerships as overtly commercial enterprises able to demonstrate reasonable prospects for earning reliable income streams large enough to pay consistent returns to their private investors. Not a simple challenge to be sure, but scarcely one that's beyond the capabilities of Wall Street's more innovative investment bankers.

Making this work on a sufficiently large scale would require significant rethinking of how government deals with private firms (which may be overdue anyway) since some of these partnerships may require user charges to generate the necessary income streams. If approached creatively, this could actually enhance the likelihood that the activities of these partnerships would meet environmental goals and other regulatory mandates that serve the public interest.

In many jurisdictions the public may not sit still for turning over the responsibility to operate an infrastructure project to the private sector because they know a natural business instinct is to maximize profits. The government could set up some sort of regulatory commission to oversee the project like they do for utility companies. But a better approach might be to set up an independent commercial corporation fully funded by user fees to build, own, and operate the infrastructure asset so taxpayers can participate in any upside from the project.

The state or local government could solicit bids from private investors to buy shares of equity ownership in return for annual dividends paid by the corporation. That brings private equity capital to the corporate balance sheet, reducing the amount of debt capital it has to issue.

In theory the government's incentive is to offer the most service for the lowest cost. Private investors, on the other hand, have the opposite incentive: to charge the highest user fees the market can bear while providing the least service it can get away with.

But a second class of private investors would likely purchase equity shares in the enterprise mainly because they have a vested interest in ensuring better roadways or other transportation infrastructure in the area. These investors might be private utility companies, local banks, and other local firms whose future revenue growth depends heavily on rising levels of economic activity. This class of owners would push for user fees that make sense from a financial standpoint and service levels that meet public needs in a financially responsible manner.

This model may be a reliable way to ensure that, for example, the original cost of every facility is evaluated on a life cycle basis so customers and operators alike don't wind up being confronted by expensive ongoing maintenance nightmares. There would also be the certainty of long-term financial commitments so taxpayers never have to deal with orphaned facilities displaced by disruptive technologies such as autonomous ride-sharing vehicles.

This model holds owners responsible for sound asset management in a clear and unambiguous way. Opportunities for abuse by limited-life warranties, guarantees written by "paper companies" that melt into the woodwork when push comes to shove, and the kind of multiparty finger-pointing that only ends up enriching the legal profession would be minimized. These realities are unlikely to be lost on the relevant parties.

Alternative models based on elaborate legislative mandates might accomplish the same thing. That is, if you believe the necessary legislation could be passed without being riddled with compromises, trade-offs, escape clauses, and weasel language.

## Technology Turns Reality on Its Head
4/29/2017

Over the last decade, Americans have witnessed a breakdown of traditional industry boundaries. New industries are being created and existing ones restructured by the accelerating pace of technological innovation.

This shift is taking place in the context of a larger economic transition—from the Industrial Age, which began in the second half of the eighteenth century, to the Information Age—fueled by revolutionary technologies such as the digital computer, the internet, and related information technologies.

The increasing pace of technological change affects human capital markets. Today's children will grow up in a world unlike that of their parents, as technology transforms media, medicine, transportation, and every aspect of how people conduct themselves.

The nanotechnology revolution and gene sequencing, which are just beginning, promise significant upheaval for a vast array of industries, ranging from tiny medical devices to new-age materials for earthquake-resistant buildings. Recent service innovations include social media and online search engines that respond to voice commands.

Reality is getting complicated. Dealing with it will require taking some of the wealth created from the new industries and reinvesting it in skills development for displaced workers, as well as rethinking policies about work and education.

Two things are certain: Technological progress is relentless and accelerating, and today's technology becomes outdated almost as soon as it can be brought to market. Consider the multiple models of smartphones introduced each year.

Advances in technology are causing disruptive changes in mature industries by introducing substitutes or altering the industry landscape by opening up whole new frontiers. For instance, revolutionary change in self-driving technology has enabled even companies such as Alphabet, the parent of Google, to enter the motor vehicle market.

Every major car company is researching and building its own version of a driverless vehicle, and industry observers predict they will have autonomous, internet-connected vehicles without pedals and steering wheels, on the road in five to ten years. The vehicle may turn out to be the ultimate mobile device.

Cutting-edge advances in artificial intelligence will have an unequal impact on livelihoods depending on which industries and individuals can create or adapt to these breakthroughs and which are left behind. They could be as consequential for labor as the agricultural and industrial revolutions that preceded it.

Two and a half million people in the United States make their living from driving trucks, taxis, or buses, and all are vulnerable to displacement by driverless cars. These jobs are just the tip of the iceberg.

For example, it is likely that children born today will never drive a car and may have a job in a career that does not yet exist. Robots have displaced manufacturing jobs in electronics, metal products, plastics, and chemicals by performing activities such as welding, painting, packaging, and even operating heavy machinery.

These changes are disorienting and more than a little scary for the ordinary American already dealing with a sense of economic insecurity. Meanwhile recent developments in robotics, artificial intelligence, and machine labor are automating cognitive and nonmanual work. Robots are increasingly being used for a variety of tasks, from precision agriculture to robotic surgery—jobs that were largely immune to technological advances.

Automation will not happen overnight. It will take years to play out fully and will vary across industries, firms, jobs, and activities. But the time is now to come to terms with the uncomfortable reality that in the future, just a fraction of the population may have the talent and education to work alongside machines, while everyone else will bear the brunt of the changes.

These discontinuities raise important public policy issues about the social framework that makes sure those who are losing their jobs can stay afloat long enough to pivot to new opportunities, and they force us to rethink issues such as providing a guaranteed universal basic income. The future is arriving sooner than we thought, and our country is unprepared.

## Rich Getting Richer Is No Accident
5/13/2017

The upward redistribution of income in the United States over the last four decades has been well documented. Many argue that there is little we can do about forces such as globalization, accelerating technological change, the transformation to a service economy, and taxes and government programs that have put downward pressure on wages for the ordinary American worker, but there are steps the government could take to address these changes.

Economic inequality is the result of conscious policy choices. This issue is especially relevant in light of President Trump's new tax blueprint and the health-care overhaul recently passed by the House of Representatives.

From the 1950s to the mid-1980s, the richest 1 percent of Americans earned a touch under a 10 percent share of the national income. By 2012 that number was about 20 percent.

Overall wealth is even more concentrated than income. In 2012 the top 1 percent of the population controlled about 42 percent of the wealth.

The promises many politicians make about material comforts are duplicitous since only a small minority have access to such comforts, and they come at great expense to the majority. Working-class Americans feel left behind, stewing in their resentment of economic hardships and being forced to make daily choices between things such as buying gas or putting food on the table.

They have come to believe the government is run by and for the rich, who are used to getting their own way and face none of the daily struggles they do. Much of the American working class lives in a provisional world where making it to the next day is a victory.

Average Americans were cut adrift from their former lives, given little help to build new ones, and disparaged as a "basket of deplorables." All this was largely happening outside the view of the media and the political class.

You don't have to have the psychological acuity of a self-important academic to understand the ironclad rage of the working class, which is proving to have the shelf life of radioactive waste. Is it any surprise that, when powerless to determine their own destinies and achieve the American dream, they backslide into anger and resentment?

This was not supposed to happen. In the optimistic period after the fall of the Berlin Wall in 1989 and the collapse of the Soviet Union in 1991, free-market capitalism, with its invisible hand miraculously transforming selfishness into common good, was seen as the way to usher in a period of prosperity and peace.

More recently one event after another has exposed this utopian narrative. The 2008 financial earthquake revealed fault lines running through the economic system that cost millions of Americans their jobs, homes, life savings, and hopes for a decent retirement. It unraveled communities, especially those where manufacturing jobs have disappeared, and the well-being of the working class has been marginalized by circumstances beyond their control. It was a cataclysm far worse than any natural disaster.

Troubling results from growing inequality include dampened economic growth, reduced social mobility, and a corrosive impact on democratic institutions. Another important consequence is weak consumer demand to support the economy.

It would be wise to recall how Henry Ford simultaneously created transportation for the masses and drove economic growth. He furnished consumers with reasonably priced cars while raising wages for his own workers to make the car affordable to them.

Rather than raising the federal minimum wage, a modern version of Ford's approach would be to expand the earned income tax credit to supplement low-wage workers' incomes, which would mean the government paying Americans whose earnings are below a certain level. The program was started under President Ford in 1975 and expanded once by President Reagan and again by President Clinton.

President Trump has proposed expanding the earned income tax credit beyond the twenty-seven million working families who currently benefit from it. Such a move would increase demand and economic growth by providing working-class Americans with the living wage they deserve.

# Whole Foods Feels the Pinch of a Changing Market
5/27/2017

Whole Foods Market, jokingly referred to as "Whole Paycheck" by consumers—who, as a late-night television wag quipped, love organic foods but can't stand parting with their money—has been fighting declining sales and increased competition, as basically every supermarket chain and other retailers enter the organic food market.

When it was founded in 1980, Whole Foods was one of the few natural food supermarkets in the United States. It enjoyed the benefits of a first mover and defined the organic grocery concept. Over the years it experienced rapid growth, positioned itself as the preeminent organic grocery brand, and charged premium prices. In June 2003 it became the nation's first national certified organic grocer.

But faced with declining sales in recent years, the firm is trying to reinvent itself as a lower-priced supermarket. The company has experienced six straight quarters of declining same-store sales, a key grocery industry performance metric, as consumers become less willing to pay a premium for the Whole Foods brand.

Organic and locally sourced offerings have increased at mainstream grocery store chains as organic food has become popular among American consumers, especially millennials. According to the Organic Trade Association, organic sales increased 209 percent between 2005 and 2015 and totaled about $43 billion in 2016.

As the American organic and sustainable foods market has grown, competitors have repositioned their brands to enter this segment of the grocery store business. In recent years Whole Foods has seen increased competition from chains such as Trader

Joe's, Bfresh, Wegmans, and Kroger; discount natural food operators such as Sprouts and Fresh Thyme; and big-box retailers such as Walmart and Costco, which cater to socially and environmentally conscious customers at lower price points.

According to a 2016 research report by Wedbush Securities, Whole Foods is about 15 percent more expensive than conventional supermarkets such as Kroger, Wegmans, and Safeway. The same report found that Whole Foods was about 19 percent more expensive than specialty grocers, including Trader Joe's and Sprouts Farmers Market.

Meal kit firms such as Blue Apron and HelloFresh add another layer of competition. On top of that, growing online grocers such as Amazon Fresh and FreshDirect appeal to the same affluent customers as Whole Foods. Earlier this year it was rumored that Amazon.com, Inc. considered buying the company. Big-box retailers are also diversifying their food offerings, aggressively courting the health food market to capitalize on consumers' growing interest.

To make matters worse, Whole Foods is facing pressure from activist investor Jana Partners, an $8.5 billion hedge fund. In April, Jana, which owns 8.3 percent of the company, unveiled a list of complaints about the firm's "chronic underperformance for shareholders," its management, operations, and strategy.

To enhance growth prospects and combat sliding sales by positioning itself as a competitively priced grocer, the firm has announced a plan that includes cutting more than $300 million from operating expenses, closing 9 stores, and abandoning its goal of reaching 1,200 stores. Earlier this year the firm eliminated its dual executive leadership structure and demonstrated a stronger commitment to shareholders by increasing the quarterly dividend and authorizing a new share repurchase program.

The firm plans on expanding its new "365 by Whole Foods Market" store format aimed at "value conscious" consumers. The danger here is that this expansion will cannibalize demand from the higher-end Whole Foods stores rather than take consumers from competitors.

Closely related, the firm has cut prices to shed its "Whole Paycheck" image and plans on offering direct discounts to those enrolled in a new customer rewards program by the end of the year.

These actions convey a sense of urgency and represent steps in the right direction that should boost stock prices. Still, Whole Foods will have difficulty shedding its costly image and getting consumers to understand the new value proposition in an increasingly crowded market while dealing with the "perennial gale of creative destruction." If they don't succeed, they may yet be acquired by one of their competitors.

## Tax Code Needs Lower Rates, Broader Base
6/10/2017

Washington is again engaged in a tax debate. Each year lobbyists and political contributors persuade politicians to insert new loopholes. As a result the four-million-word, seventy-four-thousand-page Internal Revenue tax code is riddled with special interest provisions.

The mind-boggling complexity of the tax code is a money machine for lawyers, accountants, and huge corporations. Americans spend six billion hours and $10 billion annually preparing and filing their income tax returns.

This is the exact opposite of the broad tax base with low rates that would best serve the American people. A broad-based income tax is one in which whatever you earn is taxable. Taxpayers lose their deductions but get a simpler and fairer code, and much lower rates. If the tax rate is low, economic decisions will be based on business and personal considerations, not tax implications.

In April the Trump administration released a broad outline of proposed tax changes that would reduce the corporate tax rate from 35 percent to 15 percent and include a one-time tax of 10 percent on overseas profits designed to bring the estimated $2.6 trillion stashed abroad back to be invested in the United States.

The plan cuts individual tax rates and reduces seven brackets to three. The top rate falls to 35 percent from 39.6 percent, and the lowest rate starts at 10 percent. The plan also doubles standard deductions. It does not specify to which income levels each bracket would apply. It also eliminates the federal income tax deduction for state and local taxes, except for mortgage interest and charitable contributions.

The Trump administration promises that 3 percent annual GDP growth would make up for potential revenue losses. On the other side, Democrats argue that the White House and Republicans would exacerbate income and wealth inequalities by throwing money at the rich at the expense of the middle class.

Republican deficit hawks argue that the plan will add trillions to the national debt over the next decade. They argue that deficit-financed tax cuts usually impede growth. For example, increased government borrowing drives up interest rates and reduces the financing available to the private sector. They want revenue-neutral reform, under which tax cuts are offset by closing loopholes.

Among the risks is that Americans may not spend the money they get from tax breaks, instead saving it or using it to pay down debt. Corporations could also decide to use the money to increase dividends, juice up executive pay, and generate a fresh wave of mergers and acquisitions.

Tax cuts are often confused with tax reform, which restructures the code to make it simpler, fairer, and more efficient. Cuts are easier than reform, which is a tough sell because there are winners and losers.

The United States needs a completely new tax code, one that reduces rates, broadens the tax base, and eliminates backdoor spending in the form of exemptions, exclusions, and tax credits.

This kind of reform was accomplished in the Tax Reform Act of 1986, which reduced the top marginal rate for individual taxpayers from 50 percent to 28 percent, eliminated about $100 billion in loopholes, and taxed labor and capital at the same rate. It also cut the basic corporate tax rate from 48 percent to 34 percent and eliminated many corporate deductions.

But since then lobbyists and political contributors have succeeded at restoring tax breaks, which narrowed the base. As a result rates had to increase to generate the same amount of revenue.

What needs to happen is clear, but don't hold your breath waiting for it to pass. Congress and the White House are distracted by the investigation into possible ties between former Trump aides and Russia, and the Senate health-care debate could drag on through the summer.

Meanwhile momentum for major tax cuts or major infrastructure investments has stalled. This time next year, leaders in Washington will likely still be arguing about tax reform.

# The Marshall Plan and China's "Belt and Road"
6/24/2017

In 1945 Europe lay in ruins. Its cities were devastated, its industries destroyed, and millions of its people homeless. The key to the recovery of Western Europe lay with the Marshall Plan, a decisive tool for the United States to rebuild Europe after World War II.

Seventy years later history may be repeating itself. Only this time China is the strategic benefactor, with the United States playing the role of the postwar Soviet Union, on the outside looking in as China strategically uses its largesse to develop lucrative new markets.

In June 1947 Secretary of State George C. Marshall gave a speech at Harvard's commencement announcing a plan to provide economic assistance to all European nations, including the Soviet Union. Although Russia and its Eastern satellites predictably rejected the plan, sixteen Western European nations eagerly participated.

The Marshall Plan, the largest peacetime foreign aid program in US history, channeled over $13 billion of American aid (some $150 billion in 2017 dollars) into sixteen Western European countries between 1948 and 1952 to help them rebuild their economies and normalize their societies. The Congressional Research Service estimates the plan's 1949 appropriation accounted for 12 percent of the entire federal budget.

But the Marshall Plan was more than economic and financial aid; it was a way for the United States to promote its anticommunist agenda, rebuild the economies of the recipient countries, and make them prosperous enough to buy large quantities of American goods. By the end of 1950, European industrial production had risen 64 percent, communist strength was declining in Western Europe, and opportunities for American trade had revived.

The Marshall Plan boosted American exports, manufacturing, and employment, and it helped the economies of the participating countries surpass prewar levels. In the two decades that followed, Western Europe achieved unprecedented growth and prosperity.

American goods flooded eastward, and political and economic ties with Western Europe grew even stronger. One unintended consequence is that it later made it possible for Western European companies to compete against American business in the automobile and other industries.

Some observers have compared China's ambitious new endeavor, the so-called Belt and Road Initiative unveiled in 2013, with the Marshall Plan as a game-changing effort to revolutionize trade and recast many long-standing relationships. The multitrillion-dollar proposal is China's largest economic and foreign policy undertaking since the founding of the People's Republic. The infrastructure plan that spans more than sixty countries, about 65 percent of the world's population, and about one-third of the global economy would spread Chinese investment and influence across Asia, Europe, and Africa.

The "belt" refers to a land route from western China through Central Asia to Europe; the "road" links to Europe by sea, connecting the country with Southeast Asia, the Middle East, and North Africa. The initiative has gained momentum, thanks to the decline of American influence in East Asia in the wake of withdrawing first from the Trans-Pacific Partnership and then the Paris Climate Agreement.

After World War II, the United States needed to export excess capacity. Today China's economic growth is slowing, and it is also looking for new markets. And just as the Marshall Plan was a blueprint for undermining the influence of the Soviet Union, so can the Belt and Road Initiative marginalize US influence by improving relations with traditional American allies.

As German Chancellor Angela Merkel, Europe's most influential leader, said after three days of transatlantic meetings, "The times in which we can fully count on others are somewhat over." She was referring to America's positions on NATO, Russia, climate change, trade, and its apparent relinquishing of a leadership role in world affairs contributing to a posthegemonic era in which no country has a dominant role.

If she's right, it could mark the end of seventy years of American world leadership.

## A Professor Who Made His Mark
7/8/2017

Distinguished Professor Daniel J. McCarthy left the academic teaching treadmill on June 30 after fifty-two years of legendary contributions to the D'Amore-McKim School of Business at Northeastern University.

Ralph Waldo Emerson wrote, "An institution is the lengthened shadow of one man." By any measure you would be hard pressed to find anyone who has so selflessly served the university and students as Professor McCarthy. Everyone at the university has been rewarded with his efforts.

His contributions to the institution go far beyond longevity. He was always welcoming and gracious to those who interacted with him without a tint of academic snobbery. The quintessential gentleman. Those who worked with him understand full well that he valued loyalty to the institution in the true sense of the word. It only matters when there are ten reasons not to be loyal.

Professor McCarthy is an internationally renowned scholar, outstanding teacher, and generous benefactor to the university. He is academically prolific with crazy energy levels. He is fiercely competitive, and when he puts his mind to getting something done, nothing will stop him unless a machine is attached to it.

As a scholar, since 2007 Professor McCarthy has authored or coauthored twenty-eight articles in academically refereed journals and ten book chapters, as well as presented his papers at over fifty conferences. And if those were not enough, he was in the top 5 percent of scholars globally who published in the leading international business journals from 1996 to 2000.

As a teacher, he was always giving students more than they asked for or even wanted. He was always present—listening, counseling, knee-deep in student engagement—and touched scores of students in meaningful and memorable ways. He deserves praise for pushing students to ask hard questions, omnivorously driving them to consider diverse perspectives, encouraging them to get to the bottom of things, and nurturing their intellectual growth without wounding their egos. He never avoided demanding excellence while always being fair. Unlike many he was not in love with the sound of his own voice.

Professor McCarthy has an almost unfair writing style with a gift for clarity. Unlike many academics he does not visit cruel and unusual punishment on the language. He makes the language work for the reader. His words travel well.

We should remember that he has enjoyed success in business as well as in the academy. Unlike many academicians he has a deep understanding of business. He knows whereof he speaks.

He understands that when there is a disparity between theory and facts, the flaws are not with the reality on the ground.

It goes without saying—but it goes better with saying—that Professor McCarthy and his wife, Margaret, have generously given personal treasure to the university over the years while also motivating others to give. For example, Professor McCarthy and venture capitalist Jeff McCarthy (unrelated) jointly invested $1 million to fund the university-wide venture mentoring program in 2012.

It is not hyperbole to acknowledge that Professor McCarthy played a key role in Richard D'Amore and Alan McKim making the largest philanthropic investment in the school's history of $60 million in 2012. In 2005 these two benefactors endowed the Distinguished Professor of Global Management and Innovation chair held by Professor McCarthy, who had mentored both when they were students at Northeastern.

While Professor McCarthy will no longer be formally teaching, fortunately for the school, he will continue to be intensely involved in the university-wide Venture Mentoring Network and IDEA, the student-run venture accelerator, both of which are housed within the university's Center for Entrepreneurship Education, where he chairs the board.

To paraphrase an anonymous author, while faculty, students, and staff may not remember all the things Professor McCarthy has done and said, they will always remember how he made them feel.

## Too Big to Jail
8/5/2017

The war on drugs is back in fashion. The Justice Department announced a tough new stance that requires prosecutors to pursue the highest charges possible, including those that carry mandatory minimum sentences, for low-level drug users and distributors as the United States continues to supersize the modern prison complex.

But you could combine every gangbanger selling crack on a corner in America, and they couldn't generate as much ill-gotten cash as the bankers who engaged in the widespread malfeasance that led to the 2008 financial crisis, which triggered the worst economic crisis since the 1930s.

Despite the gravity—and depravity—of their actions, the number of top Wall Street executives who were prosecuted for fraud related to the financial meltdown is exactly zero, even though they cost millions of Americans their jobs, homes, life savings, and hopes for a decent retirement and forced the government to hit up those very people to pay for the bailout that saved the country from a financial apocalypse of truly biblical proportions.

It is hard to believe, but the truth often is. Meanwhile the ordinary American is still dealing with the consequences of the financial meltdown, scoring, hustling, and struggling to make it in America.

There are many reasons no bankers were jailed, including the complexity of the cases and lack of criminal referrals from regulatory agencies. Prosecutors didn't want to put executives of "too big to fail" banks in prison, often because they feared that indicting the executives would drive their firms out of business, eliminating jobs and causing serious problems for financial markets and the economy.

In addition, the argument goes that investigating top executives of large firms is difficult because they insulate themselves from day-to-day decision-making. In the end the Department of Justice choked in the clutch. The ordinary American catches the joke that doing the right thing is always harder than simply doing what's convenient. You would be right to conclude that Lady Justice is blind because she can't stand to watch what's happening on the ground.

Those responsible for indicting and prosecuting Wall Street executives seemed to believe that just as there are banks that are too big to fail, there are also people who are "too big to jail." Instead of targeting individual corporate executives with trial and imprisonment, they almost exclusively settled with corporations for money. Corporate settlements were easier than identifying and prosecuting culpable top executives. Firms could pay the settlements with shareholders' money; it's even easier than locking up someone for dealing drugs on a street corner.

It shouldn't be overlooked that too many in the political elite shill for the top bankers, who come bearing large campaign contributions in both hands. As Illinois Senator Richard Durbin said in 2009, "They own this place."

More than a century ago, Pres. Theodore Roosevelt noted that concentrated economic power tends to capture political power, which undermines democracy. After 2008 the financial crimes committed with impunity gave rise to a tsunami of anger that washed away normal inhibitions and unleashed the Tea Party and Occupy Wall Street.

Wall Street still exerts inordinate influence over the economy; inequality is near all-time highs, and for the majority of

Americans, economic opportunity is close to an all-time low. We send some gangbanger from the hood to prison, but the United States appears to have reached the point where the government is afraid to prosecute a Wall Street executive for stealing millions, crashing the economy, and wreaking havoc upon millions of people.

A more aggressive response followed the savings and loan crisis of the 1980s and '90s, when hundreds of small banks across the country failed because of reckless real estate loans. Back then the Department of Justice prosecuted over one thousand people, including top executives at many of the largest failed banks.

These episodes bring to mind Honoré de Balzac's provocative and memorable line: "Behind every great fortune lies a great crime."

## Hero CEOs Need to Look in the Mirror About Economic Inequality

9/2/2017

In a strong rebuke to President Trump's response to the recent violence in Charlottesville, Virginia, a chorus of masters of the universe, titans of industry, and corporate rock stars lined up like soldiers to take headshots at the president, criticizing him by name for his handling of the violence.

Many were so appalled by what the president did and did not say that they resigned from his business advisory councils. The media certainly milked it for all it was worth, some characterizing senior executives as heroes for speaking truth to power.

Nothing stokes cable ratings like a sustained campaign of outrage that feeds into the attention-deficit disorder of the

American news cycle. But perhaps some of that outrage should be directed at the crusading corporate giants themselves.

Perhaps it is only a matter of time before chief executive officers show the same passion and anger when it comes to speaking out against the economic inequality that has risen so sharply since the mid-1970s. For example, CEOs could voluntarily take less compensation and use their concentrated political and economic power to support a national living wage.

After all the Gods of Fortune have continued to smile down on corporate executives with outsize payoffs. The average CEO earns something close to three hundred times the pay of the median American worker, whose real wages have been stagnant for decades. This ratio is up from roughly forty to one in 1980. In contrast to this growing gulf between the haves and the have-nots, the ratio of CEO to average worker pay in Japan is sixteen to one. In Denmark it is forty-eight to one and in the United Kingdom eighty-four to one.

CEOs do not have to worry about saving for retirement or their children's college education as they enjoy expensive perquisites ranging from country-club memberships to second homes a little smaller than Rhode Island to the personal use of corporate jets.

Is it any wonder that the public is mad as hell? They make the connection between business executive pay and growing economic inequality.

A few decades ago, executives were paid mostly in cash. Much of the story of executive compensation in recent decades comes down to two words: stock options.

To align incentives between shareholders and management, boards of directors use equity compensation by granting stock options. Today they comprise two-thirds of the typical executive's pay.

Stock options give the executive the right to buy a company's stock at a predetermined price sometime in the future. If share prices rise above the negotiated strike price, the executive stands to reap significant gains. If the options become worthless, the CEO breaks even, having paid nothing for them.

The result is a win-win for executives, especially when supplemented through the use of stock buybacks and the labyrinthine of accounting shenanigans such as excluding depreciation and amortization in calculating earnings for performance-based compensation.

The stock buyback binge of $4 trillion since 2008, much of it with borrowed money, thanks to low interest rates since the Great Recession, has resulted in firms reducing the number of outstanding shares by which profits have to be divided. So the share repurchases lift per-share earnings, improving a key metric for determining CEO compensation.

Solutions to the CEO compensation issue include tightening the cap on tax deductibility of CEO pay and disallowing deductions for excess salary, stock options, and perks. Fat chance, these reforms will happen when the positions of too many politicians closely reflect those of their big-money donors.

Cynicism about those in positions of power seems to be confirmed afresh each day by the latest tweets, pandering, and headlines. As a general rule, assume the worst about elected officials and the thinly veiled plutocracy. That way you will not be disappointed.

# Hold Wall Street Managers to Account
9/16/2017

At 1:45 a.m. on Monday, September 15, 2008, Lehman Brothers Holdings Inc., the fourth-largest investment bank, sought Chapter 11 protection in the biggest bankruptcy proceeding ever filed. There are many reasons why Lehman failed, and responsibility is shared among auditors, government officials, regulators, and credit rating agencies.

Looking back, much of the blame for Lehman's failure and the ensuing financial meltdown that led to the Great Recession resided with senior executives, a.k.a. professional managers, in the financial markets, who did a poor job of allocating capital and managing risk. They acted less like stewards of their firms and more like the keepers of a guild, accountable only to themselves and focused on short-term results at the expense of long-term performance.

The failure to understand that there are huge risks associated with the pursuit of high returns was a major contributor to the financial meltdown. One way to avoid repeating this disaster would be to require top managers in industries that are important to the public welfare to earn government licenses that testify to their qualifications, just like physicians and lawyers, who must pass tough state exams, and accountants, who must also demonstrate a certain number of years of successful professional work in their field to gain a certified public accountant license.

Why not have the same rigorous licensing requirements for professional managers before they are permitted to hold top management jobs in critical industries and public sector positions? It has become clear that the challenges of managing large organizations have grown to such a level of complexity that only individuals with the right mix of skills can effectively meet them.

One way to begin professionalizing management is to require anyone graduating with a management degree to pass a comprehensive federal or state exam that tests their mastery of the fundamental body of knowledge they allegedly learned, including accounting, finance, statistics, data analysis, and organizational behavior.

During the financial meltdown, Lehman's top executives could have, by no means, been described as competent. Ditto for Merrill Lynch, AIG, and so many other firms. Finding incompetent executives among this crowd was like finding sand on the beach; they were clueless to the real dangers of excessive risk-taking in the form of the lack of protective equity capital and massive use of leverage built around short-term borrowings.

Despite earning more than managers in any of the world's other major industries, they were like irresponsible children who had somehow gained access to Cold War missile-control rooms, playing with the shiny buttons that could launch nuclear warheads against an unsuspecting world.

They ultimately did, wiping out more than $11 trillion of wealth in the process and leaving the American taxpayer to clean up the mess.

In addition to core technical skills, a management licensure test should measure the ability to think critically and consider the moral consequences of decisions. Is it too much to expect a management graduate to be educated about how to leverage the power of markets to create a better world rather than serving only their own selfish interests? Or to possess the ability to think critically, which allows them to solve problems beyond those addressed by their functional training?

For sure, such an examination would increase employers' faith in a graduate's competence. It might be wise to make passing the test a periodic requirement to ensure that managers stay current in their knowledge and the ethical challenges posed by an ever-changing business world.

To paraphrase the philosopher George Santayana, those who fail to learn from history are destined to repeat it. The incompetence of senior managers was a driving force behind the 2008 financial meltdown from which many Americans still have not recovered nearly a decade later. The time has come to hold managers to the same standards as other professionals whose competence affects the well-being of society.

## Reforming Federal Flood Insurance in Wake of Hurricanes

9/30/2017

The federal government's flood insurance program is facing billions of dollars in claims after the recent monster hurricanes, with those who live in flood-prone homes applying for government buyouts through the Federal Emergency Management Agency (FEMA). Why not? American taxpayers have already bailed out the banks and automobile companies, among others.

There was a time when people who assumed increased risks as a result of where they chose to live would pay for those risks themselves. But in 1968 Congress enacted the National Flood Insurance Program, another product of the Great Society, to provide affordable insurance after private insurers stopped selling flood policies or began charging very high premiums for them because the business had become too risky. FEMA administers the program, which covers about five million properties worth more than $1.25 trillion.

The flood insurance program borrows from the US Treasury because paying out more in damages than it collects in policy-holder premiums has it drowning in $24.6 billion of debt. Congress must decide whether to reauthorize the program by the end of the year.

Since the value of the insurance exceeds the premiums being charged, taxpayers who reside inland foot the bill for the high-risk lifestyles of those who plant themselves in the path of hurricanes. The problem is only growing as sea levels rise and intense weather events become more frequent.

While originally designed to be self-funded through policy-holder premiums, about 20 percent of flood insurance program policyholders pay premiums that are about 60 percent lower than they would be if they reflected the true likelihood of flooding, according to government estimates.

The program places no restrictions on the number of times a property can be rebuilt, and repetitive loss properties have accounted for 30 percent of flood claims paid since the flood insurance program began. As *The Wall Street Journal* recently reported, one Texas house has flooded twenty-two times. The homeowner made claims each time, and the resulting payments exceed the value of the house.

Why fret about rebuilding when the American taxpayer is there to foot the bill? It would be impossible for even the Angel Gabriel to make a program work when it encourages people to build in harm's way.

A flood insurance program should discourage development in flood-prone areas by using risk-based premium pricing rather than encouraging people to use taxpayer money to build in flood zones. Those who face little risk of flooding should pay less for flood insurance; people at great risk should pay much more. The government may provide subsidies for the poor, but the flood coverage program should otherwise operate like other types of property and casualty insurance.

Encouraging development in vulnerable, low-lying areas also increases the damage caused by these storms, which further increases taxpayer costs. It's cheap for US homeowners to build in harm's way but not for American taxpayers.

Despite the program's rising costs, reforming the national flood insurance program will not be easy. It will require swimming upstream against the real estate lobby, homebuilders, and other development interests. The value of these littoral properties would decline if people were made to bear the true cost of their lifestyle choices, and that means a lot of coastal development would come to an end.

It is ironic that the 1 percenters who are affluent coastal dwellers and don't like government programs enjoy the subsidized flood insurance premiums. Depending on others to bail them out is an addiction that knows no economic class.

Back in the day, the American way was that you could live wherever you wanted, but you must assume the risks of your choice. The philosopher Joseph de Maistre wrote that people get the government they deserve. When it comes to federal flood insurance, ours is composed of politicians mainly interested in staying in office and using taxpayer dollars to do so.

## Equifax Brass Betrays America, Walks Away with a Windfall

10/14/2017

Just when you think nothing can surprise you when it comes to corporate incompetence, along comes the massive data breach at the credit reporting agency Equifax.

The breach may have given hackers the names, birth dates, driver's license numbers, Social Security numbers, and other personal, intimate data of 145.5 million Americans, about half the country's adult population. This data is what allows people to buy or rent homes, get auto loans, and have credit cards.

Failing to secure consumer information puts Americans at risk of identity theft, tax return scams, and financial fraud for the rest of their lives. The extent of the pain and expense people will endure as a result of the breach is not yet fully understood.

Equifax is one of three primary national credit reporting bureaus. The firm collects, processes, maintains, and sells the sensitive and personal data of more than 820 million consumers worldwide. Simply put, they harvest your information, sell it without your permission to companies who want to sell you stuff, and do not pay you. Consumers are not the clients under this business model; they are the product, so the firm has no incentive to prioritize them.

By relying on an open-source code that it knew was subject to hacking, Equifax left data exposed beginning at least on March 7, 2017. Free patches to the vulnerable software were available and well-known to the firm by that date. The following day the Department of Homeland Security alerted Equifax that its software was vulnerable to hackers, but the company failed to take precautions that would have protected the personal data of millions of people.

As a result information was compromised between May 12 and July 30. The company learned of the breach on July 29 and "rushed" to get the word out to the public—six weeks later. They did not notify each consumer affected by the hack, so individuals learned that their information was stolen long after the crime occurred.

The firm initially asked consumers to provide the last six numbers of their Social Security numbers to gain access to an unworkable website. While Equifax might have been unsure about whether a consumer was victimized, it was clear that everyone could sign up for a supposedly free credit monitoring service that required customers to provide credit card numbers.

After a year Equifax could start charging unless consumers canceled the service. Those who signed up for credit monitoring were also asked to give up their rights to sue the company.

The firm, where victims were being asked to pay for protection, was the same one that could not protect their information in the first place. Equifax's senior managers must be graduates of Trump University. The firm changed the terms after the media attacked the story like white blood cells ganging up on a diseased organ.

Consumer anger has been further intensified by the actions of three senior Equifax executives, including the chief financial officer, who sold shares worth $1.8 million in the days after the breach was discovered, according to Bloomberg. The firm said the executives were unaware of the breach when they sold the stock. This does not pass the smell test.

The miscreants being punished and doing time in the near future are about as likely as finding a clean politician in New Jersey.

Richard F. Smith stepped down as CEO and won't get the $5.2 million in severance he would otherwise have received, but he will collect a lavish pension estimated at $18.4 million. Compare that with the tens of millions of victims who may be haunted by the breach for the rest of their lives.

Equifax's senior management was criminally negligent. They put the firm's self-interest before their duty to the public, betrayed the public trust with impunity, and displayed contempt for consumers.

Once again, a big financial institution screws up. The CEO walks away with a golden parachute, and millions of Americans are left holding the bag.

## Transformation Takes the Fast Lane for Automakers

10/28/2017

Recently the Ford Motor Co.'s new CEO outlined plans to aggressively cut costs and funnel the savings to electric self-driving cars. The company plans on increasing its production of profitable trucks and SUVs while de-emphasizing less profitable cars and sedans.

What a difference a few years makes in the fast-changing automobile business. Car companies all have big plans to transform from mere sellers of vehicles to businesses that touch all aspects of mobility.

There are now multiple sources of innovation in an industry that has seen relatively little change. For over a century, the business model was how many vehicles a firm sold. Now companies are looking at how to reconcile disruptive innovations with traditional products and services.

The transformation is being driven by a succession of innovations—the internet, the cloud, big data, 3-D printing, robotics, machine learning, artificial intelligence, autonomous vehicles, connectivity, the Internet of Things, electric vehicle power trains, and shared mobility, as well as changing car ownership preferences. Each reinforces the others and accelerates disruption.

China, the United Kingdom, and France are talking about banning the internal combustion engine by 2030. Moreover China's government has implemented aggressive incentives for electric vehicles that favor local companies, which could give Chinese firms significant advantages and economies of scale in the world's largest consumer market.

These innovations are causing automakers to rethink the way they do business. Given how central the automobile is to the economy and to people's daily lives, it's not a stretch to suggest that these innovations will change how Americans live.

In addition to traditional automakers, changes in mobility will affect industries such as energy, insurance, retail, public transit, and health care. For example, the National Highway Traffic Safety Administration reported earlier this month that total traffic deaths on US highways rose 5.6 percent in 2016 to a decade high of 37,461. This is roughly the same number who die from breast cancer, gun deaths, and opioid overdoses combined. The Centers for Disease Control and Prevention estimated that in 2010–2011, there were an average of 3.9 million annual emergency room visits caused by motor vehicle traffic injuries.

Driverless technology creates a potentially accident-free future with drivers exiled to old-fashioned leisure trips on Sunday afternoons. What are the implications for reducing health-care costs as emergency rooms lose millions of patients each year and hospitals have hundreds of thousands fewer patients who need to stay overnight?

Automakers face a number of existential threats. Besides traditional rivals, a wide range of players have been racing to get in on the action, including tech companies, ride-hailing firms, logistics companies, and auto parts suppliers. Tech companies view the car as a platform, like a cell phone body. They see the vehicle of the future as software on wheels, enabling drivers and passengers to devote their time to personal activities. As Elon Musk once said, "Tesla is a sophisticated computer on wheels."

On the other hand, automobile companies think of it as a car with extra software. The only certainty is that it is uncertain who will come out on top: traditional players or new entrants? The hardware or the software folks? Western or Asian firms? Product or service companies?

Automobile companies are making big strategic bets on autonomous technology, electric cars, and transportation services. Financial decisions have to be made in light of the need to serve two worlds: the traditional automobile industry and disruptive technology-driven trends that will ultimately take over the mobility industry. Defining the right balance will be critical.

In a pervasive modern view, the past is a burden that must be shed to give way to a new kind of life. This is the fundamental challenge facing so many industries that are being disrupted by a succession of innovations. While it is debatable when driverless cars will be available to the masses, there is no doubt that a driverless future will profoundly change society, even in ways we are not yet even considering.

## Capping Retirement Accounts Is a Worrisome Tax Cut Notion

11/11/2017

Tax cuts often look like free lunches for taxpayers. Such is the case with the recent federal tax reform proposal. But tax cuts eventually have to be paid for with tax increases, closing of tax loopholes, or spending cuts, and that's why average Americans need to pay attention to the unfolding debate on Capitol Hill.

The first red flag came several weeks ago, when it was reported that House Republicans were thinking of drastically slashing the tax deduction for 401(k) contributions—from the current annual $18,000, or $24,000 for workers over fifty, to as little as $2,400—and mandating the use of after-tax Roth accounts for retirement savings.

Retirement income in the United States comes primarily from three sources: Social Security, pension plans sponsored by public and private employers, and individual savings in taxable and tax-advantaged accounts. There are generally two types of employer-sponsored pension plans: defined benefits and defined contributions.

Back in the day, workers could depend on defined benefit pensions in which retirees received a predetermined monthly annuity, either for the rest of their lives or those of their spouses. The benefit amount was usually based on an employee's wage, years of service, and age at retirement. The employer was responsible for contributing assets sufficient to fund the promised benefits.

But employers claimed that these plans left them overburdened by pension obligations and that defined contribution plans were much less expensive.

Now defined contribution pensions are the most common employer-sponsored plans.

Around fifty-four million American workers participate in about 550,000 so-called 401(k) plans, named after the section of the tax code that created them in 1978. These plans hold more than $5 trillion in assets. Tax-deductible contributions to defined contribution plans are predetermined, but the amount of benefits received upon retirement is not guaranteed.

Workers pay taxes when they withdraw the funds, manage the money themselves, and hope the market doesn't crash just when they retire. While in a defined benefit plan the employer bore the risks associated with investing assets in the plans, the employee is responsible for bearing those risks under defined contribution.

When news filtered out that the deduction for 401(k) contributions might be slashed, retirement experts, Vanguard, Fidelity, and other large mutual fund companies that manage assets in the lucrative 401(k) business joined together and howled like a pterodactyl. President Trump tweeted, "There will be NO change to your 401(k). This has always been a great and popular middle-class tax break that works, and it stays!"

Fortunately the long-awaited GOP tax plan unveiled last week leaves current contribution limits in place and abandons the notion that American workers are saving too much for retirement.

What were these Mighty Mendicants thinking? Cooking up a raiding party on workers' 401(k) plans was a way to pay for the middle-class tax cuts lawmakers claim they want to provide. They also want to significantly cut corporate taxes to catch up with the rest of the world, which has already done so.

The proposal was pure budget chicanery. Capping what the average American can place in these pension plans would force workers to pay more in taxes now rather than when they make withdrawals from their pension account. In effect the proposal would have helped pay for tax cuts by pulling future tax revenues forward.

Equally important it would have undermined workers' retirement security since the up-front deduction is an important incentive for workers to participate in retirement plans. Millions of Americans depend on the favorable tax treatment of 401(k)s, IRAs, and other savings vehicles to build long-term financial security.

The fate of House Republicans' tax proposal is uncertain; the twists and turns ahead will surely provide first-rate entertainment. And taxpayers had best pay close attention to the tax legislation as it makes its way through Congress to ensure that the notion of capping 401(k) contributions is not resurrected as lawmakers scramble to find ways to pay for the tax cuts.

## Ugly as It Is, Pay Attention to Tax Bill
11/25/2017

Otto von Bismarck, the Prussian statesman and architect of German unification, was reputed to have said, "Laws are like sausages. It's better not to see them being made."

This cliché is relevant today as Congress plays politics with tax legislation. The House has passed a $1.4 trillion tax cut package, while the Senate will consider its version after Thanksgiving.

Comparing sausage making to how lawmakers do their work may be insulting to sausage makers, whose process is transparent and predictable. In contrast, when the intricacies of the tax legislation get too sensitive, politicians demure by claiming "it's all part of the sausage making." The implication is that the public would be better off not knowing the details of the legislative process.

As tax reform negotiations enter the final stage, the so-called carried interest loophole, which provides preferential tax treatment for hedge funds and private equity firms, remains largely untouched. When legislators are asked about closing this loophole, they change the subject and recount the other loopholes they are ending.

Carried interest represents the share of profits that hedge funds, private equity, and other investment managers collect from clients. At issue is how much investors should be taxed on these profits. The managers typically take a 2 percent fee from investors and claim a share—generally 20 percent—of whatever profits they generate.

The 20 percent in profits that these managers pocket, known as carried interest, is currently treated as a long-term capital gain and taxed at 23.8 percent—the capital gains rate of 20 percent plus the Obama health-care surcharge of 3.8 percent on their income. That is well below the 39.6 percent rate plus the 3.8 percent surcharge they would pay if the money were treated as ordinary income.

As a candidate, President Trump repeatedly promised to close this loophole. He said, "The hedge fund guys didn't build this country. These are guys that shift paper around and they get lucky."

The carried interest provision is worth billions to superrich Wall Street folks. Congress's Joint Committee on Taxation has estimated that changing the treatment of carried interest could raise about $16 billion over the next decade. Academics claim that the figure is more like $180 billion. Regardless of who is right, this is not chopped liver, so these wealthy financiers have pushed back with an army of lobbyists and sprinkled enough dollars around Washington to preserve their beloved tax break.

They argue that the lower long-term capital gains rate affords them an incentive to take investment risks that benefit the economy. This defies logic since many of these managers are managing a pool of assets, not putting their own funds at risk.

Regardless of the merits, their efforts have yielded a handsome return. The House bill extends the period over which firms must hold an asset before it is eligible for the long-term capital gains rate from one year to three years. While that might bite some hedge fund managers, it will not touch the vast majority of private equity, venture capital, and real estate investment managers.

They would still pay 23.8 percent on their income, roughly the same as someone making between $37,450 and $90,750 annually. The financiers pay taxes at a rate that is well below those that apply to much of the middle class, once again validating the influence Wall Street and wealthy investors exert in the congressional sandbox. The strong take what they want, and the weak suffer.

Meanwhile the struggling middle and working classes could really use the help. After adjusting for inflation, household incomes have not risen since the 1970s.

Instead the discrepancy between rich and poor has widened. Forty years ago the richest Americans had more than 8 percent of the nation income; today it is about 20 percent. This is why it's so important for citizens to pay attention to the details of the legislative process.

## Imagining *It's a Wonderful Life, 2017*
12/9/2017

The holidays would not be the same without watching *It's a Wonderful Life* and feeling every moment of struggle as George Bailey discovers that riches are not measured in dollars and cents. The film highlights the importance of family and love and celebrates civic and familial virtues.

Those who have seen the classic 1946 movie will remember one of its most famous scenes. George Bailey runs a small community bank with a mortgage business. One day, as he is headed out on his honeymoon, George is confronted by a group of depositors wanting to withdraw their savings because they are nervous about the bank's solvency.

He explains that he doesn't keep their savings lying in the bank safe. Instead he has invested most of the money in affordable mortgages on the homes they own.

Sam's money is in Chuck's house. And Chuck's money is in Dick's house. And Dick's money is in Sam's house.

So it goes, with customers able to own their homes instead of having to pay rent to Old Man Potter, the predatory capitalist villain who owns the leading commercial bank in Bedford Falls—and most everything else in town.

In George Bailey's day, a lending institution would keep a home mortgage on its books until it was fully paid off. The default risk was held by the bank, which sought to protect itself by granting mortgages only to clearly creditworthy borrowers with stable incomes sufficient to meet monthly mortgage payments and the ability to invest a significant portion of their own money in a down payment.

In a modern *It's a Wonderful Life*, Dir. Frank Capra could have contributed to an understanding of the financial crisis by turning George Bailey into a rapacious mortgage broker willing to do almost anything to maximize his mortgage origination volume.

A modern-day Capra would present a series of fast-paced sequences showing how George converted low-income homebuyers with nonexistent credit into qualified subprime mortgage applicants.

No money for a down payment? "Not a problem," George reassures the applicant. "You can take out a small first mortgage to cover the down payment, then a larger second mortgage to cover the rest of the purchase price."

"But won't that mean high monthly payments?"

"Not with adjustable rate mortgages that charge interest only for the first two years."

"But after two years, when the much higher monthly payments kick in...?"

"Nothing to worry about. The way house prices are skyrocketing, you'll be able to refinance with a single bigger mortgage to pay off both original mortgages, and give yourself enough extra cash to cover the monthly payments for several years."

"And after that?"

"As long as home prices keep going up, you'll be building equity in your house, which you can tap for ready cash by refinancing yet again."

"So the house keeps paying for itself?"

"That's what it amounts to."

"Sounds great. What's next?"

"Let's fill out the mortgage applications together right here on my PC. I know how to word the answers to give banks what they're looking for."

"Do I need documentation for my income?"

"Nah. It's all streamlined these days. The banks run your applications against their crazy computer models to see if you qualify for the mortgage. And you will. It's just a formality."

"A formality?"

"Banks are mainly interested in generating new mortgages to sell to Wall Street. Each mortgage they sell increases their servicing fee volume, so they approve as many applicants as possible."

Just then, George gets a phone call from Old Man Potter, George's hungriest lender, for the subprime mortgages he sells to his Wall Street buddies.

"Hi, Mr. Potter," George says, leaning back in his desk chair with a big smile. "Just going to call you....No, a first and second mortgage this time....Yeah, I thought you'd like that....Great. I'll see you at the club around six."

A wonderful life indeed.

## Corporate America Needs a Twenty-First-Century Dragon Lady

12/23/2017

While successful female business leaders have made headlines in recent years—a Mary T. Barra, Virginia M. Rometty, and Indra K. Nooyi all come to mind—just 5.2 percent of S&P 500 CEOs are women.

To reduce this imbalance, we need a modern incarnation of the Dragon Lady, a protagonist who is surely among the great characters in American literature. Unfortunately her real significance has become obscured by the passage of time since she starred in the comic strip *Terry and the Pirates*, set in turbulent

China during the 1930s and '40s and is now regarded as something of a masterpiece.

It began as a standard newspaper comic strip that followed the adventure story traditions of its time. Terry Lee was a plucky adolescent who ran around China under the watchful eyes of his adult mentor, Pat Ryan. Pat was a two-fisted Black Irish soldier of fortune, assumed to be an appropriate guardian for Terry because he smoked a pipe, talked in terse ambiguities, played football in college, and never displayed any discernable sense of humor.

But all these conventions went out the window when the Dragon Lady appeared.

These days people think of her as the quintessential Asian temptress, luring men to perdition with her irresistible female wiles, embodying in full-blooded glory all the primal male fears of women that they have woven into elaborate horror stories to tell each other in locker rooms, sports bars, or their equivalent ever since Old Testament times.

Many contemporary women find this stereotype offensive, and rightly so. But it has nothing to do with the remarkable character Caniff created. Unfortunately newsprint is highly perishable, so few people today can see for themselves what the Dragon Lady was really all about.

Yes, she was awesomely beautiful. But she never let this genetic accident define her character. She paid no attention to the standard male view that a woman's physical appearance is the most important thing about her.

Yes, she spent most of her life engaged in various illegal activities. But this was more an expression of her clear-eyed pragmatism than evidence of any moral depravity inherent in her female nature. From her perspective, living outside the law gave her more freedom to be herself than she could ever have enjoyed in any of the conventional roles assigned to women. The Dragon Lady had no patience with this.

It is worth mentioning that Terry and Pat were not above reproach either since they were seeking a lost gold mine that was obviously not their lost gold mine.

She was a brilliant and sophisticated woman, whose Chinese English ancestry had made her an outcast to both societies. Highly educated in Eastern and Western cultures, she was wise in the ways of the world and the frailties of its people. Most of all she chose to live entirely by her own existential set of moral principles that gave no quarter to anyone. All of which made her more than a match for Caniff's irredeemably wicked multiethnic villains.

He introduced her in 1934 as the strong-willed leader of a pirate gang preying up and down the South China coast. This kind of dominating role in command of an all-male crew was scarcely common among female characters in the American literature of the time. But Caniff made it seem like the most natural thing in the world by emphasizing her cool intelligence, emotional toughness, and Wall Street trader's ability to balance risks and rewards.

The behavior of many members of the masters of the universe club would suggest that they have limited talent. Many organizations are directed by the can-do-no-wrong man of the extended moment, who leaves no indelible trace and will be forgotten long before he is remembered.

You will know women have finally arrived when there are as many incompetent women in the C-suite as incompetent men. Ain't it de troot?

# 2

## 2018 Columns

### Sham Tax "Reform" Proves More than Ever That Money Talks

1/6/2018

The imperfect tax bill President Trump signed into law on December 22 is further evidence of the rot in Washington. The tax bill isn't about tax reform; it's about money and influence.

Consider the giveaway known as the carried interest rule. It's another outrageous example of the powerful getting what they want, as they always do. This will come as no shock to anyone over age five.

The term "carried interest" derives from the share of profits that twelfth-century shipowners and captains were given as an interest in the cargo they carried, usually a 20 percent commission to provide an incentive to keep an eye on the cargo.

Today carried interest is the 20 percent of profits from their funds with which private equity firms, venture capitalists, and real estate partnerships compensate themselves. These proceeds are taxed at a capital gains rate of 20 percent, about half the top individual income rate, which will fall to 37 percent under the new tax law. Critics argue that this money is effectively income and should be taxed at individual income tax rates. The constituents for the deduction argue that removing the incentive would reduce entrepreneurial risk-taking.

The reason for the loophole's survival comes down to campaign contributions to key lawmakers and intense lobbying to maintain the favorable tax treatment. As Gary D. Cohn, director of the White House National Economic Council, said, "The reality of this town is that constituency has a very large presence in the House and the Senate, and they have really strong relationships on both sides of the aisle."

The American Investment Council, a Washington trade association that represents private equity firms, reported some $970,000 in lobbying expenditures for the first three quarters of 2017. This is in addition to the smart investment made by way of campaign contributions targeted to key lawmakers. For example, employees of the private equity firm Blackstone Group LP contributed $212,000 to Senate Majority Leader Mitch McConnell in 2017 alone. In turn politicians serve their contributors by protecting the carried interest preference.

Private equity firms have the means and vanity to get what they want. It is further proof that money is the mother's milk of politics and that big money gets its way in Washington, DC.

During the presidential campaign, both President Trump and Secretary Clinton gave a pitch-perfect populist performance, wanting everyone to know that they were militantly opposed to this loophole, a form of welfare for the wealthy. When a politician says something like that, sports fans, try inserting a negative and you will likely hit pay dirt. Political rhetoric is as unrelated to the truth as an advertising campaign.

The power of money seems eternal. Politicians love it like a child loves Christmas, and all are working hard to avoid reading their own political obituaries. Knowledge that it has always been this way is no consolation.

They tell pro forma lies to the public and the media and then begin to believe what they read. Not laying blame, just putting truth into words. So House Ways and Means Committee Chair Kevin Brady (R-Texas), with a truly magnificent smile, said on the *Morning Joe* talk show, "Carried interest, we can talk about that for the next hour if you like, but for most Americans they could care less about that."

In its pursuit of a free lunch, the public is often a bit too eager to accept the things they want to hear at face value, even though they should know that truthfulness is not a long (or short) suit for elected officials, who spin untruths with the same gusto young Abraham Lincoln supposedly split logs.

You can't bring about change by wishing upon a star. You can run with that.

## Next Up, Entitlement Programs
1/20/2018

With the so-called tax reform bill behind him, House Speaker Paul Ryan wants to reform and modernize the big three entitlement programs: Social Security, Medicare, and Medicaid. It's something that needs to happen, but it won't be easy, especially in an election year.

The speaker is under pressure from conservative House members and deficit hawks, who supported the tax reform legislation that added a whopping $1.5 trillion to the national debt in exchange for a commitment to address entitlements and deal with debt and deficits.

Entitlement costs are rising as the population grows older and sicker. Even if you assume that cutting the corporate tax rate will unleash economic growth, the tax cuts are highly unlikely to pay for themselves. We cannot grow our way out of the looming entitlement crisis.

But the speaker's plan to overhaul entitlement programs may run into the harsh political reality that not all Republicans are on board in an election year in which control of Congress is up for grabs.

Looking to preserve the GOP's narrow Senate margin, the Senate Majority Leader Mitch McConnell has thrown cold water on the idea of entitlement reform. He would prefer to focus on the long-awaited infrastructure funding plan, which is more of a bipartisan exercise.

During his campaign President Trump repeatedly promised not to cut Medicare, Medicaid, or Social Security. Of course, Democrats say that the Republicans plan to pay for the tax bill with cuts to entitlements and the social safety net.

There is no strong constituency for the tough budget cuts needed to limit the size of government or reduce the national debt.

Broadly speaking entitlements are government financial benefits to which beneficiaries have a legal right. The most important examples of federal entitlement programs include Social Security, Medicare and Medicaid, unemployment compensation, and food stamps. And don't forget agricultural support programs.

You can debate the merit of these programs, but one thing is clear: Entitlements are expensive, and for a long time, the cost has either been ignored or passed on to future generations.

Nearly half of all US households benefit from at least one federal entitlement program. Entitlement spending today is about a tenth of US gross domestic product, meaning one out of every ten dollars that Americans earn goes to pay for Medicaid, Medicare, or Social Security. As the government struggles to pay for these programs, the number of recipients grows as people live longer, thanks to advances in medical care.

This means they are drawing more benefits over their lifetimes than the funding systems were ever designed to generate. Since Americans are having fewer children, fewer workers are paying into the system. The Affordable Care Act also increased the number of people eligible for Medicaid.

According to the Center on Budget and Policy Priorities, about half the federal budget is spent on Social Security and health-care programs such as Medicare.

Another 16 percent goes to national defense and 6 percent to paying interest on the national debt. That does not leave much, especially as entitlement costs rise. If these programs are not fixed, they will consume the entire budget, leaving nothing to clean the environment, repair roads and bridges, and address countless other needs.

Nobody, including Speaker Ryan, is talking about actually cutting entitlement programs. The goal is to restrain increases and make the programs sustainable. On a positive note, there are approaches that enable the United States to fix the programs while exempting current beneficiaries.

For example, consider containing health-care costs by focusing more on preventive care and improved management of chronic conditions such as obesity and diabetes. As for Social Security, consider gradually raising the full retirement age and eliminating the current payroll tax cap.

If these choices don't seem palatable, it's important to remember that the biggest threat to the big three programs is to continue down the path of least resistance and do nothing at all.

## Irresponsible Behavior on Immigration Reform
2/3/2018

President Trump was hoping to mark his first anniversary in office at his Mar-a-Lago estate in Florida, but then the federal government shut down for sixty-nine hours. The high-stakes game of chicken that began January 20 ended when Democrats and Republicans in the Senate reluctantly came to an agreement that will keep the federal government paying its bills until February 8.

Unable to pass a federal budget for the fiscal year that began October 1, Congress has repeatedly resorted to these "continuing resolutions."

The latest stalemate ended when Senate Democrats woke up, smelled the coffee, and relented on their demand for immigration reform in return for assurances from Majority Leader Mitch McConnell that the Senate will consider immigration proposals in the coming weeks and take up the plight of Deferred Action Childhood Arrivals (DACA) recipients, often referred to as "Dreamers."

Poll after poll has shown that most Americans want the Dreamers, who were brought to the United States illegally as children, protected. But a recent CNN poll also showed that when given a choice between keeping the federal government open and passing DACA legislation, most said they don't want the government to shut down.

Americans understand that attracting hardworking legal immigrants has been an important reason for the nation's prosperity.

They also understand that promised entitlements such as Social Security won't be around in a few decades unless we have more workers paying into them.

President Obama introduced DACA in 2012 as a stopgap measure to avoid deportations. President Trump rescinded Obama's executive order creating the program last September but delayed implementation until March 2018 to give Congress the opportunity to develop a replacement. As a practical matter, Dreamers are not in immediate danger of being deported because any action would trigger legal challenges.

While the media was salivating over the prospect of an extended federal shutdown, this three-day version was uneventful. Unlike the twenty-one-day instance in 1995–1996 and the sixteen-day shutdown in 2013, the fight was not over raising the federal debt ceiling or health-care policy. Instead it was about Senate Democrats trying to pressure their Republican counterparts to ensure that about eight hundred thousand immigrants, mostly from Mexico, who came to the United States as children could remain.

Before you know it, February 8 will be upon us. There is no end to the suspense.

All this political posturing and blame gaming is about one part of a much larger immigration issue and the president's insistence on building a wall on our southern border.

Moreover both parties dance around an unspoken yet reasonable question: Once DACA recipients are addressed, how long before pressure mounts to accommodate the Obama administration's Deferred Action for Parents of Americans and Lawful Permanent Residents, which was designed to defer deportation for about five million parents of children born in the United States and also of children brought to the country legally?

"Deferred action" is Washington speak, which, in plain English, means ignoring the law.

The evidence with entitlements suggests that each extension of benefits establishes a new base for future expansion. As time passes, more groups of undocumented immigrants come forth, claiming they are no less deserving, and political pressure is brought on their behalf to again expand protection. The process repeats itself until a program's original intention is virtually unrecognizable.

Immigration issues have defied compromise for decades. Americans have a wide range of opinions on the subject, many of which don't add up to a coherent point of view. These conflicted emotions have blocked comprehensive immigration legislation and skirted the issue of enforcing existing laws.

Not to be overlooked is the political imperative to be reelected, which incentivizes politicians to follow Scarlett O'Hara's approach from *Gone with the Wind*: "After all, tomorrow is another day." Given that we elect politicians, the lack of a well-conceived immigration policy is the price the electorate must pay for their irresponsible behavior.

## For Big Banks, Crime Pays
2/17/2018

Last month federal authorities fined three European banks and arrested eight traders they say tried to manipulate the market in gold, silver, and certain financial products. This allegedly included a practice called "spoofing," or placing thousands of bids to buy or sell a stock for the sole purpose of moving the stock. The orders are then quickly canceled.

As usual the case against Deutsche Bank, HSBA, and UBS was settled for a total of $46.6 million in fines, without any of them admitting guilt. The money comes from shareholders, not individual bankers.

While the full extent of the wrongdoing is unknown, these and others of the world's largest banks have broken the law over and over again, settling with the government each time. Fines don't deter big banks, which are still out of control almost nine years after the financial crash.

The shameful legacy of the 2008 financial crisis continues. If a bank is "too big to fail," the worst thing that will befall its senior executives is a comparatively minor fine, which will be paid with shareholders' money.

The 2008 financial crisis devastated the global economy and cost American workers their jobs and homes. After the financial meltdown and subsequent Great Recession, the government did not charge any top bankers or pursue corporate prosecutions for the widespread malfeasance and mortgage fraud that fueled the bubble and led to the crisis.

Some believe bankers control the government. Others believe the banks did nothing wrong. Still others believe there was insufficient evidence to prove beyond a reasonable doubt that any specific individual committed a crime.

Then there are those who believe that prosecuting big banks will result in "collateral consequences" to financial markets and the economy. They argue that too-big-to-fail banks had to be rescued by the government to stave off total economic collapse, and this should be considered in deciding whether to file charges. The latter view has prevailed, with the government settling for cash rather than seeking prison sentences. Softball tactics.

In addition to being paid for by shareholders, the settlements lack transparency. They are sealed. The government does not spell out what the company did wrong or how the amount of the fine was determined. How can the public ever know how tough the government really was?

This was not always the case. After the savings and loan scandals of the 1980s, when hundreds of banks failed because of reckless real estate loans, the Department of Justice prosecuted and convicted over a thousand bankers for their transgressions.

But if you are a small, family-owned bank in Chinatown, that's a different story.

Abacus Federal Savings Bank—a small Chinatown-based bank wedged between two noodle shops and catering to poor immigrants in New York, New Jersey, and Connecticut—along with nineteen of its former employees, was charged by the Manhattan District Attorney in a massive mortgage fraud scheme. It was the only bank indicted for mortgage fraud related to the 2008 financial crisis. The 240-count indictment handed down in 2012 alleged that the bankers falsified loan applications to secure hundreds of millions of dollars in loans for unqualified borrowers through the Federal National Mortgage Association, also known as Fannie Mae.

At the time Abacus was the nation's 2,651st largest bank with about $300 million in assets. During the trial it was learned that the bank's default rate was 0.3 percent during the period covered by the indictment, from May 2005 to February 2010, far below the national average.

After a four-month trial in 2015 that cost the bank more than $10 million, a jury found Abacus and its senior officers not guilty of grand larceny, conspiracy, falsifying business records, mortgage fraud, and other charges.

You don't have to be Sherlock Holmes to conclude big banks get away with their crimes for a pittance. No one goes to jail, and no one ever gets prosecuted. The fines are just a cost of doing business.

## Time to Reform the Civil Service
3/10/2018

The American people are rightly fed up with an accelerating cascade of government failures. Just as one recedes from the headlines, another pops up.

Most recently Americans learned that law enforcement, including the FBI, failed to act on several detailed, credible tips about Nikolas Cruz, who went on a killing spree on February 14, killing seventeen and wounding another fourteen at a Parkland, Florida, high school. This was a perfect example of see something, do something, but government workers did nothing.

Their behavior validates the public's opinion that too many government workers are just plain incompetent and sometimes decide to ignore the public—the very people they are supposed to protect—knowing full well they will never be held accountable.

Surely it will not be long before these agencies are asking for more money and an expanded role.

The Parkland school shooting is just the latest in a series of high-profile institutional failures. They began with the September 11 attacks, when 2,977 people lost their lives because America's intelligence and law enforcement agencies missed warning signs. Then came botched efforts to deal with the devastation of Hurricane Katrina, the inadequate financial regulation that contributed to the 2008 financial meltdown, the National Security Agency letting Edward Snowden walk away with its crown jewels, the IRS's targeting of conservative political groups, Russian spies being allowed to meddle in US elections in the midst of Cold War 2.0, and the beat goes on.

These notable public failures contribute to the unhealthy divide between citizens and their government. With evidence of failure all around, is it any wonder that the public has become disillusioned, angry, and frustrated with all levels of government?

The scandal-plagued Veterans Administration (VA) is a glaring example of how government hurts the very people it purports to help when agency employees, not the nation's veterans, become its most important constituency.

The Veterans Health Administration, which is part of the VA, is charged with providing medical care to those who have served our country. In 2014 Americans learned that VA hospitals were making military veterans wait far longer than the targeted 14-day period to receive services.

Some died while waiting for care, and some hospitals falsified records to make it look like they were meeting their targets. The Phoenix VA Hospital reported that the average waiting time for medical appointments was 24 days. According to the VA inspector general's report, the actual time was 115 days.

Instead of being disciplined for mismanagement after the VA paid out over $200 million in wrongful death settlements over a decade, VA officials received generous bonuses.

In the most recent scandal, at the VA Medical Center in Bedford, Massachusetts, an employee allegedly steered several hundred thousand dollars in contracts for landscaping services and supplies to her brother's landscaping business. The supplies never showed up, and the work was never done. The employee was demoted one pay grade but kept her job.

If the American public wants the government to stop repeating stupid mistakes, it must recognize that civil servants act within a bureaucratic system that rewards the status quo. For decades, reforms have failed to fix a bureaucracy that is far too large to manage and adequately oversee.

Studies describe the sources of failure, including fragmentation of authority, misaligned political incentives, and the government's size. What is often overlooked is that federal workers are almost never fired for poor performance or misconduct. They have strong civil service protections, and firing processes are riddled with complex regulations and confusion over how to apply rules designed to preserve fairness and diversity.

It's time to get real. Civil servants enjoy a level of job security that the ordinary private sector employee can't begin to imagine. Nothing much will change until the civil service system is reformed and the notion of accountability accentuated.

To quote Plato, "What is honored in a culture gets cultivated there."

## The Eye-for-an-Eye Approach to Trade
3/22/2018

On March 8 America's populist-in-chief signed an executive order slapping a 25 percent tariff on steel imports and a 10 percent tariff on aluminum imports. President Trump said he did it to protect the nation's economic and national security. It came a little over a month after Trump said he would impose tariffs and quotas on imported solar panels and washing machines.

The United States has had the world's largest trade deficit ever since 1975. In 2017 imports were about $2.9 trillion, and exports were just over $2.3 trillion, as Americans continue to consume more than we produce.

The steel and aluminum tariffs have aroused little enthusiasm and much criticism. Naysayers argue they will do nothing to strengthen America's economy or national security and will instead spark a global trade war. They say the tariffs will result in higher prices as steel users pass costs onto consumers.

Supporters claim that there already is a trade war underway, and China is waging it. That country accounts for more than two-thirds of America's current trade deficit. We import $506 billion—mainly consumer electronics, clothing, and machinery—from China but export only about $131 billion in goods.

China has been blocking high-value exports from the United States. For example, it charges a 25 percent import duty on cars, ten times the 2.5 percent levy the United States puts on imported vehicles.

China also imposes steep tariffs on imported automobile parts. As Elon Musk tweeted, "No US auto company is allowed to own even 50% of their own factory in China, but there are five 100% China-owned EV auto companies in the US." Obviously engaging in tough trade talks with China is long overdue.

It will take years for the United States, China, and the global trading system to work out imbalances on a wide range of goods. America's prosperity depends on a robust approach to correct failed trade policies, with a focus on the industries of the future. It makes no sense for America to excel at innovation without securing the domestic and foreign markets for its products.

It merits mentioning that instances in which American companies ship raw materials to China for assembly at a lower cost, then sell the finished products count as imports. American multinational companies are happy to hire foreign workers from emerging markets with lower standards of living to keep their labor costs low and profits high. They figured out that to make income redistribution work on a global scale, American workers have to be less well-off so their overseas counterparts can be less poor.

But the new tariff on steel imports will not affect China. The United States is the world's biggest steel importer, buying 35.6 million tons in 2017. Nearly 17 percent come from Canada, 13.2 percent from Brazil, and 9.7 percent from South Korea. Unless the Chinese are routing their steel exports through American allies, the United States only imports about 3 percent of its steel from China.

After pushback from Canada, wiser minds prevailed within the administration, and tariff sanctions were suspended indefinitely, pending renegotiation of the North American Free Trade Agreement.

The tariffs may trigger reprisals. The day after President Trump signed the tariff executive order, the European Union published a ten-page list of American products that would be targets for retaliation, including peanut butter, grains, and motorcycles.

While steel and aluminum account for only a small portion of trade, the president's rhetoric indicates that this is just the opening salvo from the White House bunker after years of benign neglect. The primary target is China. Trump has already called its unfair trading practices "an assault on our country."

As the head of the World Trade Organization, one of the guardians of the global trading system noted after the tariffs were announced, "Once we start down this path it will be difficult to reverse direction. An eye for an eye will leave us all blind and the world in a deep recession."

## Trade Tariff Battle Will Not Lead to Any Long-Term Damage

4/7/2018

President Trump's views on trade have never been a secret. Trump finally delivered on his campaign promises by announcing unilateral tariffs on steel and aluminum imports, coupled with the imposition of about $60 billion in new tariffs on China. The moves generated frightening headlines, with experts predicting dire consequences for the global trading system, but such claims are exaggerated.

Trade is a competitive game, and every country plays hardball. The Trump policy is supposedly designed to counter a series of unfair Chinese trade practices, such as its long-standing restrictions on American companies, the forced transfer of American intellectual property, and many cases of patent and trademark infringement. The administration has demanded that China shave $100 billion off its record $375 billion trade surplus with the United States.

US firms have been unable to sell advanced goods and services to China's rapidly expanding middle class. It is widely acknowledged that in many market segments, China requires foreign firms to share proprietary technology as a condition of market access. The firms provide innovation, and their Chinese counterparts imitate foreign design.

Many of the president's media antagonists say these actions threaten to unleash a trade war, that the moves appease the president's Rust Belt constituency but are unlikely to end America's trade deficits or bring back manufacturing jobs. They also warn of rising consumer prices and are convinced that the United States would lose a trade war with the emerging market giant.

Yet it is unclear whether the president and the economic nationalists in his administration will govern as tough as they talk. It is quite possible that actual tariffs will fall short of the threats. For example, the tensions with American allies generated by the steel and aluminum tariffs are likely to be resolved through cosmetic concessions.

After the president's tariff announcement, China initially targeted tit-for-tat tariffs to put pressure on politically sensitive states that voted for Trump, hitting him where it hurts the most ahead of midterm elections later this year. China's Ministry of Commerce quickly said that it would impose a 15 percent tariff on $3 billion worth of American fruit, pork, wine, seamless steel pipes, and more than one hundred other products that represent about 2 percent of total American exports to China.

But soon after all this huffing and puffing, China's Premier Li Keqiang, at a conference that included global chief executive officers at the Great Hall of the People in Beijing, pledged to open markets to avert a trade war with the United States and to ease access for American businesses. Also, China offered to buy more American-made semiconductors and allow foreign financial firms to take majority stakes in Chinese securities firms.

Then on April 1, the Chinese Finance Ministry said the previously announced tariffs will take effect immediately.

China is reliant on foreign trade for growth and job creation and needs to retain access to the US market. The country certainly doesn't want to engage in a trade war with its best customer. China's exports to the United States are equal to about 4.5 percent of its GDP. In contrast US exports to China are equal to about two-thirds of 1 percent of GDP. Although less important to the economy than it was, trade accounts for almost 40 percent of Chinese GDP versus less than 30 percent in the United States.

America's decline relative to other countries is an old story. First the Russians were going to leave the United States in the dust, then the Japanese. But consider the strong and intrinsic advantages America enjoys. These include functional energy and agricultural independence, more favorable demographics, and a consensual society. Drug dealers still prefer suitcases full of dollars, not yuan, and global investors still seek Treasury bonds as a safe haven in times of crisis.

President Trump's trade moves may temporarily roil US markets, but there is no need to panic or bet against the United States.

## China Flexes Its Muscle in the Pacific
4/20/2018

Just as Imperial Japan did in the 1930s, China is developing and asserting its own version of the Monroe Doctrine in Asia so it may enjoy the same continental hegemony America does. The new reality is reflected in the South China Sea. China maintains that it has sovereignty over almost all of the South China Sea. The United States should respond by fostering closer ties with its allies in the region.

Beijing continues to militarize artificial islands in the South China Sea. It was reported earlier this month that China had installed antiship cruise missiles and surface-to-air missile systems for purely defensive reasons on fortified outposts in the hotly contested waters of the South China Sea. Taiwan, the Philippines, Vietnam, Malaysia, and Brunei are also contesting at least part of the chain of islands, reefs, and their surrounding waters in the South China Sea.

Each year a third of the world's shipping passes through the South China Sea, carrying around $3.4 trillion in trade. In 2016, 21 percent of all global trade passed through it. Any conflict in the South China Sea would likely have serious consequences for global commerce.

Following the logic of the Monroe Doctrine, which opposed European colonialism in the Americas, Communist Party leadership believes China's security would be better served by muscling the American military out of the Asia-Pacific region.

After all the Chinese remember what happened in the century between the First Opium War (1839–1842) and the end of World War II, when the United States and European powers took advantage of a weak China. The current generation of Chinese Communist Party leaders are so bitter about the one hundred years of humiliation that they can taste it.

In 1823 Pres. James Monroe, in his annual message to Congress, wrote, "The American continents, by the free and independent condition which they have assumed and maintain, are henceforth not to be considered as subjects for future colonization by any European powers."

The United States put European nations on notice that it would consider any foreign challenge to the sovereignty of existing American nations an unfriendly act.

The Monroe Doctrine, sweeping in scope and proclaiming hegemony over an entire hemisphere, was an expression of a growing spirit of nationalism in the United States in the 1820s. In short it warned everybody to stay out of the Americas; this is a United States preserve.

China's assertiveness in the South China Sea echoes the Monroe Doctrine. It wants to dominate Asia the way the United

States dominates the Western Hemisphere. Why should anyone expect China to act differently than the United States?

China's actions are not catching the United States at its best. The United States has been busy chasing bad guys in the Greater Middle East. Is it too late to contain and deter China as it did with the Soviet Union in the Cold War? Or is China just too big and powerful? It should be remembered that the United States did not have deep economic relationships with the Soviet Union, so Cold War–era policymakers did not have to contend with powerful American multinational corporations' economic interests as they managed foreign relations. Lawmakers in Washington, special interest groups, and the business elite eat at the same table.

China's moves in the South China Sea can be regarded as a threat. But it also represents an opportunity to deepen relationships with American allies in Asia and leverage their resources to serve as an effective counterweight to China's moves before it absorbs these countries into its economic orbit. The president may want to reconsider his decision to withdraw the United States from leadership of the Trans-Pacific Partnership. Keeping America secure means having partners and allies to magnify US power and extend US influence.

This approach merits consideration as long as the United States can avoid its usual perfection of getting things wrong when it comes to foreign affairs.

## Iraq and the Consequences of an Ill-Conceived War
5/6/2018

American troops are still in Iraq on the fifteenth anniversary of an invasion, the pretext for which was the entirely trumped-up claim that America's iconic foe Saddam Hussein had weapons of mass destruction. The failure of the 2003 invasion and continuing presence of American troops illustrate the importance of aligning ends with means.

The stated objectives of the invasion were to end the Hussein regime; eliminate the weapons of mass destruction; drive out Islamist militants; secure Iraq's petroleum infrastructure, which was to cover the cost of the war; and create a liberal, representative government that would spark a new age of freedom in the Middle East.

The invasion did change the region; it made things worse. It began on March 19, 2003, and the military campaign was quick and decisive. Baghdad fell on April 9.

But unlike in Las Vegas, what happened in Iraq did not stay in Iraq. The war opened a Pandora's box in the Middle East, releasing many demons.

The abrupt fall of Baghdad was accompanied by a full-scale collapse of public order and helped incubate and reinvigorate radical Islamist militants in the region. The invasion contributed to the civil war in Syria, helped create a vacuum that ISIS filled, and caused massive refugee flows to Syria, Jordan, and Europe; other than that it was a complete success.

In retrospect it is hard to overstate the damage the Iraq War did to America's global prestige, badly damaging America's Godzilla-like unipolar credentials and offering the world a pitiless example of the limits to American power. The magnitude of this disaster can also be measured in lives and money.

From 2003 until the formal withdrawal of troops in 2011, the war took the lives of 4,500 Americans and over 150,000 Iraqi civilians. Its direct cost has been estimated to be almost $1.7 trillion, with an additional $490 billion in benefits owed to war veterans.

The Ronald Reagan question is appropriate here: Is the Middle East better off today than it was before the Iraq War? Is the United States in a better place than before the invasion? In short, unintended consequences resulted in a shattered Iraq, an emboldened Iran, and a Middle East where many regional and international powers are engaged in a number of deadly conflicts.

Then there is the question of opportunity cost—the extent to which the war distracted America from a slew of other challenges, such as emerging nuclear threats from Iran and North Korea, China flexing its muscles in East Asia, completing the Afghanistan operation, and other global trouble spots.

Fundamentally the cleavage between the invasion's ambitious goals and its actual results boils down to the fact that President Bush and his hawkish advisers failed to establish a proper relationship between end and means in their prosecution of the war. The year before the invasion, Army Chief of Staff General Eric Shinseki made the point that American troops were already stretched too thin around the world. In February 2003 he told the Senate Armed Services Committee that it would take "several hundred thousand soldiers" to secure and pacify Iraq.

Two days later Defense Secretary Donald Rumsfeld said the postwar troop commitment would be less than the number of troops required to win the war, and the "idea that it would take several hundred thousand U.S. forces...is far from the mark." The Bush administration sent 150,000 American troops into Iraq.

Successful strategy in military affairs and business requires the proper alignment between potential goals and resources. The Bush team aroused sky-high expectations without sufficient resources to meet them.

President Bush and his advisers failed to understand the words of Prussian military theorist Carl von Clausewitz, who wrote, "Everything is very simple in war, but the simplest thing is difficult." Even great powers operate in a world in which resources are not always sufficient to exploit all opportunities and neutralize all threats. There is never enough of anything to go around.

## On D-Day, the Eyes of the World Were on the Allies
6/3/2018

In the first days of June 1944, BBC transmitters beamed to the forces of the French Resistance the prearranged signal that indicated the start of the long-awaited naval, air, and land invasion of France, which would open a critical second front against Germany.

The seventy-fourth anniversary of the Normandy landings is a useful moment to pause, reflect, and ensure that the memory of this historic event doesn't slip away. The date June 6, 1944, became historical shorthand for a generation of Americans, one that needs as little explanation as "September 11" does for their progeny.

As General Eisenhower wrote in his June 6 Order of the Day, "You are about to embark upon the Great Crusade, toward which we have striven these many months. The eyes of the world are upon you."

The plan for Operation Overlord was code-named D-Day. The *D* in D-Day is a general term for the start date of any military operation. The Allies selected Normandy as the landing site because it provided the best access to France's interior.

Operation Overlord was the greatest technical feat of the war. The challenges of mounting a successful landing were daunting. Herculean preparations requiring remarkable coordination among the Allies for Operation Overload had been going on since 1942.

The forces assembled constituted the greatest amphibious force in history. An armada of more than 5,000 ships and landing craft were waiting to transport more than 150,000 British, Canadian, and American troops; 1,500 tanks; and thousands of guns, vehicles, and supplies to five beachheads along a fifty-mile strip of the heavily fortified Normandy coast. Leading the way were over 300 minesweepers that cleared a path through a minefield that stretched across the English Channel to the Normandy beaches.

The Americans landed to the west on Utah and Omaha beaches, while the British and Canadians landed on the east at Gold, Juno, and Sword beaches. Allied casualties on D-Day have been estimated at 10,000 killed, wounded, and missing in action, 60 percent of them American. The first twenty minutes of the movie *Saving Private Ryan* captures vividly the horrible realities of the landing and the price paid by the soldiers.

They were supported by 12,000 planes, some of which had been systematically destroying bridges and access routes to seal off the invasion area from the interior while others—transports and gliders—prepared to drop paratroopers and demolition teams well behind the beaches to complete the job.

The invasion was a high-risk operation, the outcome of which was by no means certain. The defenders had been preparing their reception for four years, building a formidable Atlantic Wall of concrete, wire, machine guns, mines, and artillery. SS Panzer divisions lurked in the wings. As General Rommel famously remarked, "[T]he first twenty-four hours of the invasion will be decisive, the fate of Germany depends on the outcome...for the Allies as well as Germany it will be the longest day."

Despite furious German resistance, the Allies carried the day on June 6 and established a precious beachhead. Once the

Wehrmacht recovered from its surprise, resistance was fierce. The Americans could not take Cherbourg, the principal port of the invasion coast for three weeks. The British, who should have entered Caen on the evening of D-Day, fought their way in on D+34 (July 9).

Finally caught in the decisive Battle of the Falaise Pocket, the Germans had nothing to do but run. After that the road was clear for the race to Paris and the drive for the Rhine. Rommel was right—eleven months later Nazi Germany crumbled onto the scrap heap of history.

D-Day, June 6, 1944, paved the way for the liberation of Europe through countless acts of sacrifice by the men and women of the armed services that still resonate today. Success on the "longest day" marked the beginning of the end of the war in Europe.

## Lessons from the Great War Still Apply
6/16/2018

On June 18, 1914, the Austrian archduke Francis Ferdinand, nephew of Emperor Francis Joseph and heir to the throne of the Austria-Hungary empire, and his wife, Sophie, were assassinated by a Bosnian Serb in Sarajevo, the capital of Bosnia-Herzegovina. The assassination was the flash point that triggered a global conflict.

The Great War had a kaleidoscope of causes, including mutual defense alliances, imperialism, militarism, and nationalism. Its origins have eerie parallels to the present and hold important lessons for the future, especially for China and the United States. The emergence of China as a major power trying to assert itself has echoes of Germany's rise in the late nineteenth and early twentieth centuries, which was viewed as a threat by Britain, so the theory goes.

The two bullets fired in Sarajevo precipitated an international crisis, as various military alliances were activated, dragging everybody into a devastating global war. At the time of the royal murders, nobody believed it to be the "shot heard round the world," but Europe went from peace to war in five weeks. As British Foreign Affairs Minister Sir Edward Grey said, "The lamps are going out all over Europe; we shall not see them lit again in our lifetime."

Germany backed Austria after it declared war on Serbia, which was supported by Russia. When Germany then declared war on Russia, France was committed to Russia, and Germany attacked France through Belgium, pulling Britain into the war. Later Japan and the United States entered on the side of Britain, France, and Russia, along with Italy, which switched sides in 1915. As Henry Kissinger explained, "[T]he Great Powers managed to construct a diplomatic doomsday machine." The war to end all wars (until it didn't), later known as World War I, broke out in the summer of 1914 and was expected to be over by Christmas. Kaiser Wilhelm told his troops, "You will be home before the leaves have fallen from the trees."

But it lasted until November 11, 1918. Like the 2003 invasion of Iraq, it was to be swift, easy, and victorious. Those who plan on fighting short wars often end up losing long ones.

By the time World War I ended, nine million had been killed, including over one hundred thousand American soldiers. Eight million were prisoners or simply missing. Twenty-one million had been wounded, and who knows how many were damaged psychologically.

When the guns went silent, the Ottoman, Habsburg, and Russian empires had collapsed, a new German empire was foiled, and France and Great Britain were greatly weakened. The war sowed the seeds of the Great Depression, the rise of fascism and communism, and World War II. The dismemberment of the Ottoman Empire created the modern Middle East and laid the foundation for the chaotic conflicts that continue to plague the region. The Great War was also the catalyst for the coming American century.

China is an economic superpower and is translating economic might into military capabilities roughly in the same league as the United States. It is making a run at dominating Northeast Asia through various territorial disputes with Asian neighbors over claims in the contested East and South China Seas. By themselves, these neighbors are not powerful enough to check China.

The historical lesson for leaders in both China and regional rivals such as Japan is to recognize that growing political and military tensions are potential flash points.

Given the network of bilateral and collective defense agreements the United States has in the region, supporting its allies could draw it into disputes with China.

A clash between China and the United States is hardly remote. As recently as 2014, President Obama reaffirmed America's bilateral defense agreements with South Korea, Japan, and the Philippines. A lesson from World War I that seems so relevant today is that local conflicts can escalate into a great war.

## Strategy Defies Description
6/30/2018

In a famous Hindu parable, three blind men encounter an elephant for the first time and try to describe it, each touching a different part. "An elephant is like a snake," says one, grasping the trunk. "Nonsense; an elephant is a fan," says another, who holds an ear. "A tree trunk," insists a third, feeling his way around a leg.

Similar confusion surrounds the notion of strategy. The word is tossed around promiscuously. The many competing conceptions of strategy suggests that the concept is subjective and ambiguous enough to defy any singular definition.

Strategy is important, but it is also wickedly hard to deal with complexity, ambiguity, and uncertain outcomes in a competitive landscape. Getting it right is an uphill struggle, whether in business, athletics, military affairs, politics, or other human endeavors. Strategy is an art, not a science.

The confusion surrounding the subject of strategy presents a challenge, especially for students. It requires them to think in interdisciplinary terms, which invariably means finding connections. As historian Edith Hamilton put it, "[T]o see anything in relation to other things is to see it simplified." For example, business students struggle to integrate and coordinate various functional areas. They get caught between warring disciplines such as finance, accounting, and marketing. This is especially difficult in an academic environment with the pressure to specialize.

Strategy: The word is beguiling and elusive, but do we really know what it means? Is it as former Supreme Court Justice Potter Stewart said about pornography: "I know it when I see it"?

To put it simply, strategy is the link that connects resources with a set of realistic and prioritized objectives. Some theorists suggest that a practical way to think about strategy is that it is a bridge connecting means to ends and the present to the future. Scratch that. Because the metaphor is at odds with reality. Strategies are far from linear.

There are circles and waves and dead ends and the inevitable influence of chance. But they rarely form a straight line. Events seldom conform to expectations. To paraphrase Mike Tyson, everyone has a strategy until they get punched in the mouth.

The question that haunts every strategy is how. How do you get from means to ends? It's always the how before the who and why. Strategy is the relationship that unfolds at the intersection of means and ends.

Although your objectives may be infinite, available resources are finite. One challenge in developing a successful strategy is to keep goals within resources and not to confuse means with ends. That requires lining up feasible objectives in a queue and making hard decisions about trade-offs.

Strategy is more like having a map. It helps you navigate the distance between means and ends. It transports you from one place to another. It illuminates the competitive landscape with alternative routes. It traverses distance and time. Maps give you greater control over your surroundings. They help you see into the future—what you seek to accomplish and how you should go about it.

Strategy is not fixed; it's not a blueprint. It is an iterative, continuous process that involves seeking feedback, dealing with surprises, and correcting course when necessary, all while keeping the ultimate objective in view. It is not a three-act play but more like a soap opera—one thing after another.

Life often goes in a direction not of your choosing. That is why you need to adapt. No strategy is built to last forever. It is wise to allow for considerations of changing circumstances.

Changes in the external environment frequently are catalysts for strategy. If you are not growing and evolving, you're standing still while the rest of the world is surging ahead. It is Darwinism at its most refined; you develop the resources that allow you to survive, or you just hide. But even that will not last for long.

## No Doubt About It—China Doesn't Play Fair on Trade
7/14/2018

Trade issues are not everyone's idea of a good time. With so many demands on their attention, ordinary Americans are wary of the truth quotient in commentary on the subject. They are cautious about separating the genuine from the meretricious comments from corporate America, which is concerned about maximizing shareholder wealth rather than doing the right thing for the majority of Americans.

General Motors (GM) has warned that President Trump's threats to impose a 25 percent tariff on imports of cars and car parts are projected to cost the auto industry billions of dollars, could raise some car prices by nearly $6,000, and could result in fewer American jobs and a smaller GM. In contrast a Ford Motor Company spokesperson said they believe they are somewhat insulated from the proposed tariffs because their most profitable vehicles are built here.

Currently, vehicles imported to the United States face a 2.5 percent tariff. Cars built in America face a 10 percent tariff when they are shipped to the European Union and a 25 percent tariff when they head to China.

During the financial crisis, the feds put $49.5 billion of tax-payer money into the GM bailout, and the taxpayers ultimately lost an estimated $10.5 billion. The firm has remained profitable since then. In retrospect the bailout should have included provisions requiring that a portion of future profits go to fully repay taxpayers. Government Motors could also have been required to build automobiles and auto parts in the USA.

The automaker sold 4.04 million vehicles in China in 2017, a third more than the 3.02 million it sold in the United States. Last year represented the sixth consecutive year that China was GM's largest market.

GM and other multinational companies headquartered in America view China's emerging middle class as the world's largest market for their products. The firm's future growth relies as much on China as it does on how the automaker responds to emerging disruptive technologies, such as electric and autonomous vehicles, and changing patterns of car ownership and use, which will ultimately force the modification of its current business model.

Multinationals worry that the tariffs will cause the Chinese government to retaliate by imposing bureaucratic rules and regulations that could cause them to lose market share. China used this approach to roll back Japanese automakers' market share during a dispute with Japan over contested islands in the East China Sea.

When China was violating the World Trade Organization (WTO) rules on subsidies for wind turbines, General Electric and other firms that were in the business were reluctant to bring a dispute to the WTO for fear of Chinese retaliation. The United Steelworkers ultimately brought it to the WTO.

It is hard for multinational corporations to resist the temptation to placate the Chinese. China doesn't have to send lobbyists to walk the halls of Congress; they just have the multinationals do what they want.

It is implausible to argue that China does not engage in unfair trade practices. It is a one-party communist dictatorship. It is not bound by the political constraints of a democratic government with a constitution that imposes presidential term limits and secures the rights of free speech and association.

This political structure enables China to promote state-subsidized industries, such as steel, aluminum, and solar panels, that have flooded global markets, depressed prices, and forced hundreds of manufacturing plants to shut down, all in violation of WTO rules. Along with currency manipulation and stealing intellectual property, China's actions amount to a thumb on the scale.

"Free" trade is a concept that works in classrooms insulated from the harsh realities of unfair practices and policies. They ignore predatory practices by foreign governments who view trade as a competition between nations and play dirty to grab a competitive advantage for their industries.

Like that of multinational corporations, China's position on trade will be based on maximizing their own interest.

## A Safety Net for the Looming Trade War
7/28/2018

Much has been written about the continuous maelstrom of trade and tariffs. Articles are legion and lengthy, and the onslaught of words is entirely shorn of humor. Is the difference between trade and "free trade" the same as the difference between love and "free love"? Many of these articles fail the memory test.

Unlike academic arguments, debates about trade and tariffs are waged at a high-intensity pitch because the stakes are so high. Often overlooked is Trade Adjustment Assistance, a program with avid supporters and fierce critics.

Trade Adjustment Assistance is the primary policy response to dislocations caused by trade and globalization. This federal program provides assistance to workers who have involuntarily lost their jobs to foreign competition, either because their jobs moved outside the United States or because of an increase in directly competitive imports. It also assists those whose hours and wages are reduced as a result of increased imports, whether or not that had anything to do with a trade deal. Congress created the program as part Trade Adjustment Assistance of the Trade Expansion Act of 1962, but it was little used until the Trade Act of 1974 eased eligibility requirements.

Trade Adjustment Assistance offers eligible recipients a variety of benefits and reemployment services. It provides expanded unemployment insurance benefits, two years of job training, job search and relocation allowances, tax credits for health insurance coverage, wage insurance for workers over fifty years of age, and related subsidies.

Pres. John F. Kennedy initiated the legislation as a way of building domestic support for multilateral trade negotiations. The program has undergone changes through the years. Since free trade policies are expected to bring overall economic gains, there is a rationale for providing assistance to workers whose jobs are sacrificed for the greater good. Put differently, the benefits of free trade, which are diffused throughout the economy, exceed its costs, which are concentrated. The winners should compensate the losers and help train or retrain American workers to become more competitive.

The original legislation faced strong opposition, but with labor's backing, Trade Adjustment Assistance became law. It has been the necessary political price for keeping free trade on track, the sop to displaced domestic workers.

Critics of the program are wont to complain that despite its generosity, the program has been ineffective. For example, one study of Trade Adjustment Assistance recipients shows that their incomes after returning to work were no better than those of returning workers not eligible for Trade Adjustment Assistance.

Fairness is also an issue. Why should someone get special assistance after losing a job because of trade but not if they lose a job because of changes in technology and consumer preferences, domestic competition, or simple business failure? After all they still have bills to pay.

On the other hand, advocates argue that Trade Adjustment Assistance has provided badly needed assistance to more than 2.2 million workers who lost their jobs to globalization since the Trade Act of 1974 and is an essential complement to the broader trade agenda. They point to data showing that nearly 77 percent of program participants found employment within six months of completing their training. They are silent on the quality of the jobs and whether they have a positive effect on wages for program participants.

While the United States may gain from free trade policies at the macro level, the losses are concentrated and inflict real distress on affected workers. Free trade has cut consumer costs, reduced poverty around the world, and helped multinational corporations prosper; the United States should take care of workers who have paid the price.

Regardless of the dimensions of the coming trade and tariff wars and chaos in the international trading system, some version of Trade Adjustment Assistance is essential to provide a safety net, not just a fig leaf, for those who inevitably bear the cost of trade and tariff policies.

## Fiat's Sergio Marchionne Leaves a Legacy Worth Remembering

8/18/2018

Many CEOs know how to soar, but few know how to land the plane. One exception was Sergio Marchionne. The Canadian Italian leader was one of those dynamic, old-school executives who was grounded and anchored in reality, a rarity in the contemporary world. He died on July 25 at age sixty-six.

Marchionne first saved Fiat and then did the same thing five years later when Fiat took control of Chrysler from the United States government and turned the combination into a profit generator.

He took the driver's seat at a battered and indebted Fiat in June 2004, an accountant and tax specialist who described himself as a corporate fixer. He had no previous automobile industry experience and was Fiat's fifth CEO in less than two years.

Thus began his first remarkable turnaround. Fiat was near death when Marchionne became CEO. It was heavily indebted, had suffered huge losses, and was running out of cash. He took dramatic measures to get Fiat off its knees and return it to financial health, including shuttering factories, laying off thousands of employees, and cutting the time it took to bring new models to market from four years to just eighteen months.

A key issue for Fiat was its relationship with General Motors (GM). In 2001 the two had entered into a partnership, giving Fiat a put option to sell the 80 percent of the company it still owned to GM. Sergio Marchionne decided to play hardball, persuading GM to pay $2 billion to sever its ties and end its troubled alliance with Fiat. GM paid that huge sum not to buy Fiat.

Equally important he dismantled the bureaucracy and focused on developing leaders, promoting high-potential young managers to senior positions, creating a flat organizational structure, and linking and leveraging information and knowledge throughout the firm. He constantly reminded the organization that he could not make all the decisions and created an entrepreneurial environment. By 2005 Fiat had returned to profitability.

In 2008 the global automotive industry was in a deep crisis. The following year Mr. Marchionne found himself in a familiar situation. Fiat struck a deal with the United States government to take on the ailing Chrysler group and save several hundred thousand jobs in exchange for providing small-car technology. There was much skepticism about his ability to turn the firm around and grow the combined Fiat Chrysler into a profitable global automaker.

Marchionne chose an office in the industrial engineering department on the fourth floor of Chrysler's headquarters, sending a clear message that he was accessible and wanted to be where the action was. He understood that Fiat Chrysler Automobiles was too large and complicated for one person to lead and that human capital is a scarce strategic resource.

Just as he had done at Fiat, Marchionne fired most of the top management at Chrysler in 2009 and installed a dozen newcomers. By the end of the year, almost no one from the previous senior leadership team remained.

As he explained, "It is not a matter of how good they are at their jobs; it is a matter of change. I can spend twelve months arguing with them about what and how to change, but this won't work and will take a lot of time. I look for the youngster. They don't have seniority. They don't play the corporate habits; they're pure."

The chain-smoking, espresso-drinking CEO was direct and demanding, requiring his senior managers to be available 24/7 to match his own commitment. Like other successful executives, he focused on setting stretch goals, developing a clear strategy, constantly communicating it, and ensuring proper execution of the strategy—all while managing to stay cool.

The combined Fiat Chrysler Automobiles group's stock price nearly quadrupled over the past four years of his stewardship. Last year the firm posted $4.4 billion in pretax profits.

*Grazie mille.*

## 2008 Recession Is Anything but Ancient History
9/24/2018

If you think you have heard it all before about the 2008 financial meltdown, then you need to listen more closely. Enough is never enough when it comes to learning about what caused the crisis and the recession that followed.

This month marks the tenth anniversary of the financial crisis that devastated Wall Street and Main Street. While the autumn leaves were falling in September 2008, months of uncertainty crystallized to spark a financial panic.

The crisis, the worst financial downturn since the Great Depression, was triggered by the bursting of a housing price bubble that had been fueled by increased risk in mortgage lending. As a result millions of Americans lost their jobs, homes, or both.

The crisis had many causes, including too much irresponsible borrowing, foolish investments, the credit bubble that resulted from loose monetary policy, the housing bubble, national housing policies and nontraditional mortgages, relaxed mortgage lending standards, credit ratings and securitization, financial institutions' concentrated risk, leverage and liquidity risk, thirty years of deregulation, securities firms converting from partnerships to corporations, and perverse compensation incentives.

Scratch the familiar refrain of greed as a cause. Greed has been a constant in human affairs for millennia. It was not a new attribute in the lead-up to the crisis.

Today the economy is strong, according to official measures. The United States Bureau of Economic Analysis estimates that GDP growth reached 4.1 percent in the second quarter of 2018. Consumer confidence is high, and financial markets are flirting with records. The housing market, the epicenter of the crisis, has recovered in many places. Add low unemployment and things are looking good.

Wall Street has profited every year since the recession ended in 2009. Average Wall Street compensation, consisting of salary and bonus, hit $422,000 in 2017, 13 percent higher than the previous year, according to the New York State comptroller.

In contrast the latest Census Bureau data shows that the median income for American employees was $59,039 in 2016. Last month the average hourly wage rose 10 cents, to $27.16, according to the Bureau of Labor Statistics. While that was the largest gain since 2009, the increase was roughly equal to inflation, which eats away at purchasing power.

The crisis strikes some people as ancient history. Others, who saw their net worth wiped out, are still trying to recover. They want Old Testament justice for the financial institutions that got bailed out from their reckless behavior while ordinary people suffered and continue to tread water, thanks to ongoing wage stagnation. The hope is that as it gets hard to fill jobs with the country approaching full employment, wages will go up, and the average American will enjoy the recovery.

While many analysts hesitate to blame American families for contributing to the financial crisis, they did play a role, aided and abetted by bankers and mortgage brokers. To put their role in context, consider that highly risky mortgages were attractive, given that real wages in the United States had been stagnant since the early 1970s.

People came to understand the power of leverage, which had previously been available only to wealthy investors. No-down-payment mortgages with adjustable rates reduced their initial costs, providing the opportunity to improve their standard of living and enjoy wealth appreciation.

The assumption was that housing prices always increase. The rising value of the house would allow them to refinance and up-grade to a fixed-rate mortgage. When the housing bubble burst, many families were ravaged.

An economy that is strong for some continues to have harmful effects on the physical and emotional health of ordinary Americans. The results are a permanent state of outraged class warfare, declining social mobility, a shrinking middle class, and widening income inequality.

There is much to be mad about and plenty of blame to go around. Wall Street was the ultimate beneficiary of the Great Recession, not Main Street.

# Concentration of Power Benefits the Haves
10/13/2018

In the continuing controversy over economic inequality in the United States, the focus is on such factors as the decline of organized labor, tax cuts for the well-off, outsourcing of American manufacturing jobs overseas, and the substitution of capital for labor. But the lack of competition in many sectors of the economy is also a powerful driver of disparity, redistributing income and wealth from consumers generally to the affluent.

As with lengths of skirts, lapels on men's suits, and other more or less important customs, there are also fashions in markets. Over the last two decades, many firms have been consolidated across the US economy. Oligopolies are common, and concentration is increasing in numerous industries.

Many markets are now oligopolies, in which a small number of companies account for most sales. In major industries—from telecoms, social media, and internet search to retail, airlines, beer, pharmaceuticals, hospitals, and banks—the American public has seen a few giants come to dominate. What competition does exist is among just a few participants, not exactly the type described in textbooks.

These firms use their market power to increase prices, drive down wages, and assert greater authority over workers. They find ways to deter new firms by creating and maintaining barriers to entering the market, and they use economies of scale to exercise strong leverage over suppliers. In addition to raising prices relative to what they would charge in a competitive market, these powerful companies may also reduce quality or convenience, modifying product features and reducing customer discounts. All this leads to a transfer of wealth from buyers to sellers.

It should not be overlooked that consolidation of market power also concentrates political power, thanks to the lobbying muscle of oligopolistic companies. Economic and political power can be mutually reinforcing. As things stand, market power gives these companies the resources to protect their competitive advantages and leverage their advantages through the political process buying the all-important access.

Take the $2.5 trillion health-care industry, where rising prices are partially driven by increased consolidation. Consider the large number of hospital mergers that limit competition among hospitals. Today many Americans live in areas where there is little such competition.

The same is true in other economic sectors. Merger mania in the airline industry has resulted in eight majors combining to create four giant carriers over the past decade. Not to be ignored is that a handful of large institutional investors, such as BlackRock, Vanguard, Fidelity, and State Street, are among the top shareholders for all four major airlines. Given the huge extent of common ownership in the US airline industry, it is not surprising that the price wars of the 1990s have ended, and profits are on the rise as companies may refrain from competing aggressively when their competitors have the same large shareholders.

Consider the drastic increase in banking industry concentration, where too-big-to-fail banks, instead of getting smaller, are pretty much taking over the financial universe. The five largest banks in the United States—JPMorgan Chase, Bank of America, Wells Fargo, Citigroup, and U.S. Bancorp—have about $7 trillion in assets. That's nearly 45 percent of the industry's total. The other 55 percent of assets are divided among six thousand institutions, according to the Federal Reserve. The top ten banks' share of the deposit market has increased from about 20 percent to 50 percent from 1980 to 2010.

Looking beyond individual industries affected by excessive market power, the bad news is that this concentrated power leads to concentration of wealth and income and contributes to increasing economic inequality because the returns from market power go disproportionately to the wealthy, such as company shareholders and senior executives.

God love them, for they are reaping rewards to which ordinary Americans have no access. Amen.

## The Lesson of the Sears Bankruptcy
10/21/2018

Once the greatest retailer in the modern world, Sears, Roebuck and Co., now saddled by debt and declining sales, filed for Chapter 11 bankruptcy on October 15 after 125 years in business. The company was unable to pay $134 million in loans and announced it would close 142 unprofitable stores near the end of the year.

These closings are in addition to 46 others that were expected by next month. That will leave roughly 500 store locations. It is unclear whether the company will survive beyond the holiday season and the bankruptcy reorganization plan.

It was not always like that for the institution once regarded as America's Everything Store. At the top of its game for decades, Sears was regarded as one of the best-managed retailers in the world. It accounted for more than 2 percent of all US retail sales, selling everything from TVs to dresses to lawn mowers. The target customer was the average American, neither the richest nor the poorest 10 percent.

The often-overlooked thing about the company is that it was a technological wonder, the Amazon of its day. It pioneered supply chain management, store brands, catalog retailing, and credit card sales, all of which are critical to the success of today's most admired retailers.

Sears planted the seeds of its demise when it jumped from one strategy to another in the 1980s. For example, it acquired the financial services firm Dean Witter in 1981 and tried to sell investment products and power saws under the slogan "From Stocks to Socks." Customers could not reconcile the new image with the old. Inconsistencies such as these confused customers and undermined Sears's credibility and reputation.

While the firm shed Dean Witter in the 1990s, another big challenge loomed. It had to deal with heightened competition from big-box stores such as Walmart and Target throughout the 1980s. Sears was late to grasp the power of discounting and, later, the rise of online shopping. The company failed to understand that retailing was changing, and like other old-economy, big-name retailers such as Toys "R" Us and A&P, it failed to change with the times.

In 2005 the company merged with Kmart, which was headed by hedge fund manager Edward Lampert. He believed that merging the two firms, with a combined 355,000 employees and more than 3,500 stores in 2006, would make them strong. At the beginning of 2018, that workforce totaled less than 68,000 across fewer than 700 shops. The bankruptcy threatens to put these employees out of work and throw the financial security of its 100,000 pensioners into doubt.

Lampert's strategy was to run the company like a hedge fund, cutting spending on advertising, inventory, and store improvements, as well as spinning off many of Sears's best properties into a real estate trust he controlled. Over the past decade, the company sold or spun off many of its most valuable brands, such as Craftsman tools and Lands' End clothing, to stay afloat and pay the bills as it lost sales to Walmart, Target, Home Depot, and Amazon with its endless online catalog. All this hastened Sears's decline.

The story of Sears's demise is another cautionary tale about the ruthless process of creative destruction—new innovations driving out old ones. Once again an established company fell victim to the "creative destruction"—a term coined by Joseph A. Schumpeter, an economist working in the first half of the twentieth century—of new entrepreneurs.

Technology and customer tastes change and provide opportunities for competitors, especially those regarded as "too small to worry about," to develop new strategies that are better aligned with the altered industry landscape and ultimately eat established players' lunch (and breakfast and dinner).

All in all not a pretty story—one that once again proves that nothing is forever, not now, not ever.

## If the American Dream Isn't Dead, It's in Big Trouble
11/19/2018

The American dream is one of the country's most attractive founding myths. Ask Americans what the term means and they will provide various definitions that are neither true nor false; people are free to define their core concepts as they see fit.

There is no one American dream; there are many, based on specific circumstances. Historically, definitions have ranged from religious and political freedom to social equality and economic mobility in the hope that everyone would have an equal chance to succeed.

Sadly the idea that anyone who really wants to can make their way to the top in the United States may be dead. The ordinary working-class individual would have to be living in a commercial to still believe in the American dream. When you are poor, trying to get a fair share of the American pie can become a burden that only makes you angry and frustrated.

In 1931 the now obscure historian James Truslow Adams wrote *The Epic of America*, a book that gave one of the first recorded definitions of the American dream. He was not writing about consumption—buying things you don't need and can't afford with borrowed money. He focused on ideals rather than material goods. According to Adams, "[T]he American Dream is that dream of a land in which life should be better and richer and fuller for everyone, with opportunity for each according to ability or achievement....It is not a dream of motor cars and high wages merely, but a dream of social order in which each man and each woman shall be able to attain to the fullest stature of which they are innately capable, and be recognized by others for what they are, regardless of the fortuitous circumstances of birth or position."

He was describing a society that values equality and merit above all else; with hard work, everything is possible. It doesn't matter where you are from, what schools you went to, or how much money your parents have. What matters is that if you work hard, you can become anything you want. Everyone in America has a chance to pursue their personal vision no matter who they are.

Conversely, success is a choice. It's your own fault if you don't make it from rags to riches.

In the wake of the Great Recession and the 2008 financial crisis, many people believe the American dream is dead. The issue of economic inequality has captured the attention of groups across the social and political spectrum—the general public, policymakers, businesspeople, and academicians. Surveys show that more and more Americans believe income and wealth are distributed unfairly.

Few would deny that the growing gap between rich and poor in the United States is at historic levels. Wealth and income imbalances have been documented with monotony.

The inconvenient truth is that the richest 10 percent currently own nearly 60 percent of US wealth. The top 1 percent now earns about 30 percent of total income. The top 0.1 percent earns more than 10 percent. According to the Federal Reserve Board, 40 percent of Americans can't cover a $400 emergency expense.

A number of factors have been suggested as important contributors to the widening gap between the "haves" and "have-nots" and the increasing concentration of income and wealth. Among them are globalization, technological advances, crony capitalism, lower taxes on the rich, and government policies and programs.

Until these causes and consequences are addressed, there is no realistic hope for dealing with unacceptable levels of economic inequality in the world's richest country. America will continue to witness the erosion of the middle class and the creation of a permanent underclass that undermines the conceit of a democratic society in which all people have an equal and inalienable right to life, liberty, and the pursuit of their own happiness.

# A Day That Should Live in Infamy

*First published in 2014.*
12/5/2018

Early in 1941 the government of resource-poor Japan realized that it needed to seize control of the petroleum and other raw material sources in the Dutch East Indies, French Indochina, and the Malay Peninsula. Doing that would require neutralizing the threat posed by the US Navy's Pacific Fleet based at Pearl Harbor in Hawaii.

The government assigned this task to the Imperial Navy, whose combined fleet was headed by Adm. Isoroku Yamamoto. The Imperial Navy had two strategic alternatives for neutralizing the US Pacific Fleet: cripple the fleet itself through a direct attack on its warships or cripple Pearl Harbor's ability to function as the fleet's forward base in the Pacific.

Crippling the US fleet would require disabling the eight battleships that made up the fleet's traditional battle line. It was quite a tall order.

The most effective way to cripple Pearl Harbor's ability to function as a naval base would be to destroy its fuel storage and ship repair facilities. Without them, the Pacific Fleet would have to return to the United States, where it could no longer deter Japanese military expansion in the region during the year or so it would take to rebuild Pearl Harbor.

It soon became apparent that the basics of either strategy could be carried out through a surprise air raid launched from the Imperial Navy's six first-line aircraft carriers. Admiral Yamamoto had a reputation as an expert poker player, gained during his years of study at Harvard and as an Imperial Navy naval attaché in Washington. He decided to attack the US warships that were moored each weekend in Pearl Harbor. But in this case the expert poker player picked the wrong target.

The Imperial Navy's model for everything it did was the British Royal Navy. Standard histories of the Royal Navy emphasized its victories in spectacular naval battles.

Lost in the shuffle was any serious consideration of trying to cripple Pearl Harbor's ability to function as a forward naval base. So it was that, in one of history's finest displays of tactical management, six of the world's best aircraft carriers furtively approached the Hawaiian Islands from the north just before dawn that fateful Sunday, December 7, 1941; launched their planes into the rising sun; caught the US Pacific Fleet with its pants down; and wrought havoc in spectacular fashion. On paper at least, this rivaled the British Royal Navy's triumph at Trafalgar.

But so what?

The American battleships at Pearl Harbor were slow-moving antiques from the World War I era. As we know, the US Navy already had two brand-new battleships in its Atlantic Fleet that could run rings around them and eight more under construction were even better.

More importantly the Pacific Fleet's three aircraft carriers weren't at Pearl Harbor. American shipyards were already building ten modern carriers whose planes would later devastate Imperial Navy forces in the air/sea battles of the Philippine Sea and Leyte Gulf.

Most importantly, as the sun set on December 7 and the US Navy gathered the bodies of its 2,117 sailors and marines killed that day, all-important fuel storage and ship repair facilities remained untouched by Japanese bombs, allowing Pearl Harbor to continue as a forward base for American naval power in the Pacific.

So in reality December 7 marked the sunset of Japan's extravagant ambitions to dominate Asia. Admiral Yamamoto and the Imperial Navy's other tradition-bound leaders chose the wrong targets at Pearl Harbor.

The dictates of tradition are usually the worst guides to follow when it comes to doing anything really important. After all if they survived long enough to be venerated, they're probably obsolete.

## Short-Term Thinking Costs General Motors, US Taxpayers

12/22/2018

Just after Thanksgiving, General Motors (GM) made the jarring announcement that it was closing five factories in Ohio, Michigan, and Ontario, killing the production of several models—including the Cadillac CT6, the Chevrolet Cruze compact, the Buick LaCrosse, and the Volt plug-in hybrid—and cutting about 14,700 jobs. This is the firm's largest cost-saving plan since the taxpayer-funded bankruptcy bailout in 2009.

GM received more than $50 billion of taxpayer assistance through the Troubled Asset Relief Program during the financial crisis. While the feds recovered $39 billion, the firm's management failures cost taxpayers $10.5 billion. GM had racked up more than $40 billion in losses since 2005 alone, losses that had little to do with the financial crisis.

Many of the jobs to be eliminated are populated by those who are perpetually in debt, no matter how hard they work. And if you believe senior GM executives will not receive their annual bonuses, then you believe pigs can fly.

The automaker, the leading automobile manufacturer of the twentieth century, expects to free up $6 billion in cash flow by the end of 2020, which will enable it to double down on its investment in electric and autonomous vehicles to stay competitive in a fast-changing market and sluggish sales.

The automobile industry is simultaneously facing multiple disruptions. For example, young, environmentally conscious, technology-oriented urban residents increasingly shun car ownership in favor of more convenient, less expensive mobility options. Owning a car and getting a driver's license aren't the life milestones they once were.

For years GM has not been building the vehicles American consumers want. As a result their car lineup has had more misses than hits. It has been slow to respond to competitive pressures and to align firm resources with changing market demands. For example, the rapid rise of Tesla Motors in the electric vehicle market, Toyota gaining market share with its eco-friendly Prius, and the subsequent GM bankruptcy suggest that the firm made the wrong decision when it aborted its electric vehicle program in 2002.

In the ultimate irony, GM had a head start with electric vehicles. The firm introduced the "Impact," a concept electric car, at the Los Angeles Auto Show in January 1990. The Impact was met with immediate praise, and GM announced that it would become a production vehicle. Based on the proof-of-concept electric vehicle, the California Air Resources Board passed a zero-emissions vehicle mandate requiring all major automobile suppliers to develop them if they wanted to continue to sell in California.

GM became the world's first mass-produced electric vehicle retailer when, in a blaze of glory, it released the EV1 in 1996. The vehicle could only be leased, despite requests by many customers to purchase it.

But in 2002 the firm canceled the model that might have been its best hope for the future, citing high costs, a limited market for electric vehicles, and the lack of technology to make high-performance cars. GM recalled all the EV1 and, in one of its worst public relations moves, recycled them, meaning the recalled vehicles were taken to Arizona and crushed. The electric power train that powered Tesla vehicles was based on the prototype developed for the EV1.

Once again GM management demonstrated that short-term thinking is extremely costly in the long term. It reflects the firm's slow adjustment to changing consumer tastes and the failure to tailor the firm's resources and business strategy to rapidly changing market forces.

GM may have been a twentieth-century giant with a large past, but today its future may be getting smaller. The sands of time may well be running out for the firm to prepare for the automobile industry's still-uncertain future.

# 3

## 2019 Columns

### A High-Stakes Contest for Technological Supremacy

1/4/2019

Meng Wanzhou, chief financial officer of privately owned Huawei Technologies Co., was arrested by Canadian police at the behest of American law enforcement authorities seeking extradition as she changed planes at Vancouver International Airport. Wanzhou is the daughter of the company's founder, a former military engineer with China's People's Liberation Army.

She has been charged with conspiracy to defraud banks in connection with alleged violations of American sanctions on Iran. The December 1 arrest occurred on the same day that President Trump and Chinese President Xi Jinping agreed to a ceasefire in the escalating trade war between the world's two largest economies.

Huawei, China's smartphone and telecommunications giant, has long been at the center of drama between the United States and China. The United States has pressured allies to limit use of Huawei products and technology.

Huawei may not be a familiar name to Americans, but it is a global telecom behemoth, with about $93 billion in revenue in 2017, almost on par with Microsoft.

Based in Shenzhen, near Hong Kong, it has the biggest research and development budget of any Chinese company. The firm has benefited from Chinese government subsidies, contracts, and financing from the state-owned China Development Bank. These subsidies give Huawei a huge advantage over its competitors.

The company is the world's second-largest maker of smartphones, behind only Samsung. It is the world's largest provider of telecom equipment, including switches, routers, cell tower gear, cloud computing, and cybersecurity. It also sells personal computers and a wide array of wireless devices such as smartwatches.

Huawei is seen as a global leader in 5G, the ultrafast wireless technology that will soon allow all the objects around us to be connected. That is good for China but bad for the United States. The United States worries that if Huawei wins the race to develop 5G technology, Americans may someday be buying their equipment to connect factories, vehicles, homes, utility grids, and more.

Huawei is also seen as a cybersecurity threat. Washington has accused it of being a potential conduit for Chinese spying and cyber theft. The Justice Department, intelligence agencies, and regulators have long believed that the firm has violated American sanctions against Iran, that it works primarily for Chinese government interests, and that its equipment contains back doors that allow that government to spy on customers.

In 2012 the House Intelligence Committee released a report that tagged Huawei's products a potential security threat, accused them of engaging in intellectual property theft, and recommended a ban on the company's equipment. As early as 2003, Cisco Systems accused Huawei of infringing on its patents and illegally copying source codes used in its routers and switches. Other accusations have also surfaced. Motorola named the firm as a codefendant in a lawsuit, and T-Mobile alleged that Huawei stole technology from its headquarters.

The Committee on Foreign Investment in the United States, an interagency committee of the federal government, has blocked deals involving Huawei on grounds that it had possible ties to the Chinese government and that the strategic nature of the telecommunications industry made such deals potential threats to national security. This August a defense policy bill prohibited the federal government from using Huawei equipment.

President Trump is considering an executive order that would bar American companies from using telecommunication equipment made by Huawei and other Chinese telecom companies because the equipment poses serious national security risks. Of course, the company strongly denies stealing intellectual property or enabling Chinese espionage.

It is unclear how the arrest of Meng Wanzhou will influence ongoing trade talks between the United States and China. One possibility is that the US government will allow trade to trump national security concerns, as the president has suggested he would intervene on the Huawei issue if it would help secure an agreement.

Americans best stay tuned as this high-stakes contest for technological supremacy unfolds.

## Find an Intelligent Way to Deal with China and Economy

1/27/2019

Trade policy is a contentious issue in contemporary America. A common refrain in trade discussions is "all we want is a level playing field." President Trump portrays his tough trade sanctions, especially against China, as a confrontation aimed at remedying decades of America being ripped off in the global marketplace.

This represents a major reversal in America's China policy. Since President Nixon's opening to China in 1971 and across eight subsequent administrations, it was generally believed that engagement would induce China to work with the West and become a peace-loving democracy with no designs on regional or global power.

As a candidate, Trump stood out for his embrace of America-first policies and his promise to "Make America Great Again" by addressing the grievances of ordinary citizens who feel dispossessed. Once in office, Trump, a self-described dealmaker, has not been fond of large multilateral deals. He was quick to withdraw from the Trans-Pacific Partnership Agreement. After first threatening to void the North American Free Trade Agreement by executive order, his administration renegotiated it.

Countries often use protectionism tools such as tariffs and quotas to support domestic industries until they are able to compete internationally. Tariffs are taxes imposed by a country that make imports more expensive. Quotas amount to quantitative restrictions on imports. It helps to keep in mind who loses and who gains from a tariff or quota. Domestic producers and employees gain and consumers lose. Governments also benefit from tariffs because they generate revenue, but tariff revenues are typically not a big consideration in developed countries.

Countries can also impose stringent quality and safety standards on foreign products. A country can tailor the standards to the product descriptions at home, thereby giving domestic producers an advantage. Consider the continuing debate over stricter standards for antibiotics in the European Union versus the United States. Are these measures of safety or a way to protect a domestic industry? Then there are all kinds of red tape that delay exporters from gaining access to a country's market.

Still, there is another insidious tool that a country can use to promote its domestic industries. China and other countries build national champions with government funding of state-owned enterprises (SOEs). China is the world's second-largest economy, accounting for about 15 percent of global economic output. It has seen extraordinary economic expansion over an extended period, with double-digit growth for close to thirty years.

Its SOEs have facilitated that growth and are the backbone of the Chinese economy. The nation's about 150,000 SOEs control around $16 trillion in assets, constitute about 40 percent of China's gross domestic product and employ thirty-five million people in strategic industries such as energy, technology, and telecom.

China's government helped launch new and emerging industries by channeling capital into SOEs. For example, it flooded global markets, depressed prices, and literally shut down hundreds of US solar panel startups. China's SOEs are front and center in implementing its One Belt, One Road initiative, the nation's vision for massive development of trade routes between Asia, Africa, and Europe.

These government subsidies stimulate excess production, depress market prices, and enable SOEs to capture market share. Closely related is the theft of intellectual property and forced technology transfers, often by SOEs, which highlight the need to constrain these enterprises. Countries such as China hesitate to allow SOEs to fail for fear that it would unleash a tidal wave of unemployment.

While trade talks between China and the United States may be productive in dealing with tariffs, the Trump administration should also address less traditional tactics that amount to cheating. They include China's use of subsidies to key state-run companies to undercut their American competitors. What should be clearly understood here is that dealing with the Chinese is like engaging in unprotected sex.

## Automakers Face a Challenge in Managing the Future
2/9/2019

When businesses are initially established, their success largely depends on their value proposition and unique offering to the market. This success enables companies to grow and expand. But then what?

Large organizations often become so focused on current revenue streams that they lose sight of priorities such as imagining the future, identifying innovations, and making smart strategic choices about where to invest. Instead they move into survival mode, trying to maintain their current positions rather than taking the risk of transitioning into new ones.

Put differently, the challenge for companies is how to deliver on this year's goals while simultaneously trying to position themselves to be successful in the future. This dynamic is playing out big time in the transportation industry. There is perhaps no better current example of this dilemma than traditional automakers. These companies are facing disruptive technologies such as electric vehicles, connectivity, autonomous vehicles, a change from vehicle ownership to purchasing transportation as a service, and the global emergence of subcompact vehicles. They also face an unexpected wave of new competitors such as Waymo, Tesla, Uber, Lyft, and others from Silicon Valley, as well as BYD and LeEco from China.

The great challenge for senior industry executives is how to manage the decline in traditional vehicle sales until the return on new technology investments fills the void. In this way auto executives are facing a situation similar to what traditional entertainment companies faced with the switch to streaming or brick-and-mortar retailers with the rise of e-commerce.

The challenge presented is determining which strategic bets automakers should make and how they can modify current business models to maximize positive outcomes for all stakeholders. Companies are reengaging with fundamental questions about where and how they should compete.

Automakers aren't the only one faced with challenges by a changing transportation industry. For those born since the 1980s, owning a car and getting a driver's license aren't the life milestones they once were. Younger buyers are more interested in ease of transportation and mobility, and with often crippling student loan debt, they are thrilled not to have car payments. Students graduate from college with an average of about $37,000 in student loan debt. It all adds up to $1.5 trillion across the country.

Millennials are also killing the motorcycle industry. For instance, Harley-Davidson is struggling with declining sales and an aging demographic that is increasingly hanging up its boots. Being an "Easy Rider" is no longer easy for an aging customer base, and younger consumers are more interested in less expensive bikes that generate lower margins for manufacturers. To attract younger customers to the brand, Harley-Davidson is setting up riding schools around the country and is releasing an electric motorcycle called the "Livewire," which will be priced at just under $30,000. The manufacturer's suggested retail price for the entry-level Toyota Prius is about $23,500.

In the unlikely event you are not clear on this, everyone—individuals and institutions—is living in an age of disruption. The growing challenges of globalization and the rapid spread of digital technologies and artificial intelligence offer both existential threats and new opportunities. The younger generation will experience the consequences of these disruptions for many years to come and will witness industries in transformation through their own daily experiences as they change the way Americans live and work.

It once again shows that the late great author V. S. Naipaul was right when he said, "The world is always in movement."

## Shifts in Automobile Technology and Ownership Will Affect Public Transit

2/15/2019

The rise of shared electric self-driving cars and the transition from a world of ownership to one of consumers purchasing transportation as a service hold the promise of significant economic, environmental, and quality-of-life benefits. But it will also pose an existential threat to public transportation in general and commuter rail in particular.

The first recommendation in the December report from Governor Baker's Commission on the Future of Transportation is "[p]rioritize investment in public transit as the foundation for a robust, reliable, clean, and efficient transportation system." In broad terms the commission is right. But maximizing potential benefits from the unprecedented disruption of surface transportation that lies ahead will also require fundamental change at the Massachusetts Bay Transportation Authority (MBTA) and a hard look at which transit modes are positioned to compete in a brave new world.

The commission's charge was to look at the commonwealth's needs and challenges over the next twenty years. But if that horizon is extended to forty years, station-to-station service to the suburbs is unlikely to be very attractive in a world where shared electric self-driving cars will offer much faster door-to-door service at a price that won't be much higher.

Drivers are normally the largest expense for any transportation business. It currently costs about fifty-five cents a mile to operate a vehicle with a single occupant. But it's estimated that the cost could fall to fifteen cents a mile for autonomous vehicles carrying two or three passengers, which would significantly reduce public transit's price advantage.

Connected vehicles will also dramatically reduce human error, resulting in big increases in throughput, thanks to variables such as higher travel speeds, less space between vehicles, and less frequent braking in response to accidents and other travel events.

In the future, agencies such as the MBTA will probably subsidize trips that are currently taken on commuter rail rather than operate them. Even with the transportation transformation in its infancy, Florida's Pinellas Suncoast Transit Authority, which serves the St. Petersburg/Clearwater area, eliminated some bus routes further from the urban core, after it experienced an 11 percent overall drop in ridership, and replaced them with subsidies for Uber and Lyft rides. Since then over twenty-five US communities have established similar partnerships—and the disruption caused by ride-hailing services is minuscule compared with what is to come.

MBTA commuter rail ridership has declined. Nonetheless, it will remain with us for the next couple of decades. It still needs to be improved, but massive investments in new lines such as South Coast Rail or, even worse, Springfield, would be a fool's errand.

The biggest challenge for the future will be making transit work in congested downtown areas. One Boston traffic simulation model showed that while shared autonomous vehicles would reduce travel times and the number of vehicles on the road even as total miles traveled rose by 16 percent overall, downtown travel times would be 5.5 percent longer because the vehicles would substitute for transit use.

Rising to this challenge will require focusing more investment in the urban core. But success will require something more: changing the MBTA's priority from providing jobs and pensions to serving its riders.

During a three-year exemption from the commonwealth's costly antiprivatization law, the T dramatically improved performance in areas such as cash collection and reconciliation, as well as warehousing and logistics, saving millions. Despite this success, there was nary a peep about extending the exemption or making it permanent.

Few would argue that the MBTA is skilled at putting customers first. The question is whether—in the face of an existential threat to public transit and with far less margin for error—political leaders, bureaucrats, and unions can change the authority's culture and begin to lay the groundwork that will allow the T to perform the way we'll desperately need it to in the future.

Part of that culture change will be recognizing that commuter rail is poorly positioned to compete over the long term. When the Patriots win the 2060 Super Bowl, stories about a suburban rail network overwhelmed with riders are likely to generate the same reaction as when we tell our kids about having to get up and walk to the television to change the channel.

## All Strategy Is Relative
3/15/2019

The word "strategy" has undergone much inflation in recent years. There is no strategy deficit; today everyone is a strategist. The word is employed promiscuously as a value-enhancing qualifier—a strategy for tax preparation, for breastfeeding, for losing weight. The word has been drained of meaning.

In the business world, books about strategy are legion. For instance, airport bookshops, as any regular traveler knows, are replete with books on successful business strategies that make extravagant promises. The road to strategy is paved with platitudes in these popular books: *Think Outside the Box*, *Break Down Siloes*, *Move the Needle*, *Paradigm Shift*, *Low-Hanging Fruit*, and *Aim High*. So if you miss, you won't shoot your foot off.

When reading books on business strategy that offer prescriptions for managers, often one comes away with the uneasy sense that each author has defined the term in self-serving ways to support whatever management shtick they happen to be promoting, creating a strategic straitjacket, if not a cottage industry, with thoughts that don't extend much beyond the drabbest clichés.

In this context strategy may seem like nothing more than an impressive label pasted on an author's pet idea to boost book sales. As the late Peter Drucker, a widely noted management consultant, educator, and prolific author, once commented, "I have been saying for many years that we are using the word 'guru' because 'charlatan' is too long to fit into a headline."

Put simply, strategy is aligning means with ends, and the trick is getting the proportions right. The alignment, like beauty, is in the eyes of the beholder. The question that haunts every strategy is how. How do you get from means to ends? It is always the how before the who and why. Strategy happens in the space between means and ends. that the relationship unfolds at the intersection of the two.

Consider an example from the wide world of sports: Regardless of the quality of its players, no National Football League team can hope to reach the Super Bowl without an effective strategy to guide its performance. The ability to develop and implement a strategy is the secret to success for such coaching icons such as Bill Walsh, Tom Landry, Vince Lombardi, and of course, Bill Belichick.

They all understood the importance of beginning each season with a strategy that incorporates everything knowable at the time about the performance potential of their own players and how best to exploit these resources, plus the potential of opposing players and how best to defuse it. Not to be overlooked is that the competition gets a vote. And all this knowledge is written down (along with accompanying tables and diagrams) in thick playbooks.

But they also understood that no preseason strategy is ever carved in stone. It must be continually revised in response to the inevitability of events that can never be anticipated—such as injuries to key players and to those on opposing teams, the unexpected emergence of star rookies, and the mystical ability of battered old pros to somehow pull it together one more time as the season unfolds.

To quote the justly criticized former Secretary of Defense Donald Rumsfeld, "stuff happens." No meaningful National Football League strategy ever has a half-life of more than a week or so. Top coaches know this. They even welcome it because of the fresh opportunities it can bring.

The dirty little secret they understand is that you don't have to get your strategy perfectly right, as long as it's not so far wrong you cannot put it right quickly. If the competition has a poor strategy, your strategy only has to be less poor. Strategy is a relative venture.

Finally, it is always useful to remember Damon Runyon's advice: "Maybe the race isn't always to the swift. Or the battle to the strong. But that's still the way to bet."

## Market Boom Won't Float All Boats
3/29/2019

Forgetting history is an American pastime. The current bull market that ranks among the great rallies in stock market history began ten years ago this month, just about the time when Lady Gaga's "Poker Face" was the number one song in America.

The stock market party has been going on for a decade, but many Americans have not been invited. The Standard & Poor's

500 index has soared over 300 percent since March 2009, but the gains are heavily concentrated among the richest families.

The richest families are far more likely to own stocks than are middle- or working-class families. Eighty-nine percent of families with incomes over $100,000 have at least some money in the market, compared with just 21 percent of households earning $30,000 or less, according to a Gallup survey.

Overall, 62 percent of families owned stocks before 2008. That number has fallen to 54 percent, the Gallup poll found. The psychological and financial damage inflicted by the 2008 financial crisis and the subsequent Great Recession continues to weigh heavily on the average American, just as memories of the Great Depression influenced financial habits for decades.

In March 2008 the financial meltdown, financial apocalypse, financial collapse—call it what you will—began, with the feds arranging a shotgun marriage between Bear Stearns and JPMorgan Chase. In March 2008 Bear Stearns, the smallest of the five major Wall Street investment banks, was unable to fund its operations and was bleeding cash, having lost the confidence of the market. The feds were faced with a choice between letting the company fail or taking extraordinary steps to rescue it. They choose the latter.

Bear Stearns was sold to JPMorgan Chase, with the Federal Reserve providing $29 billion as an inducement to the acquiring bank. Bear Stearns may have ceased to exist as an independent firm, but it continued to haunt the financial world like Marley's Ghost for months thereafter. Its collapse signaled the real start of the financial crisis. Bear's demise started a banking liquidity crisis in which financial institutions became unwilling to lend to each other, and credit markets seized up.

A growing number of formerly solid financial institutions were turned into basket cases. After years of kindergarten management games, shooting up on short-term borrowings, extensively using leverage fueled by low interest rates, and binging on risky trades, it all blew up in their faces. Freezing their lending to businesses and individuals alike caused vast portions of the nation's business activity to grind to a halt, leading to the Great Recession.

The financial meltdown of 2008 was one of the most critical events in American history, a biblical-style plague that tanked the stock market by nearly 60 percent in the fall of 2008, killing off other financial and credit markets in the process. Banks and firms either vanished into bankruptcy or had to be rescued by taxpayers. The financial system nearly collapsed, triggering an economic crisis.

The deepest recession in decades wiped out some $11 trillion of wealth and vaporized more than eight million American jobs by September 2009. It froze up the nation's vast financial credit system, leaving many firms without enough cash to operate. It forced the federal government to spend $2.8 trillion and commit another $8.2 trillion in taxpayer funds to bail out crippled corporations such as General Motors, Chrysler, Citigroup, AIG, and a host of other too-big-to-fail private institutions.

In addition to their jobs, it cost millions of Americans their homes, life savings, and hopes for a decent retirement. These Americans were in no position to invest in stocks and benefit from the subsequent run-up in the stock market. By contrast, the wealthy have gotten even richer.

This was a cataclysm far worse than any natural disaster the nation has experienced, and its ripples continue to be felt today.

# Congestion Pricing Is Part of the Solution to Gridlock

4/12/2019

The problem of traffic congestion is reminiscent of Mark Twain's comment about the weather: "Everybody talks about it, but nobody does anything about it." It is no easy matter to deal with the congestion problem in major urban centers.

New York is getting ready to address the issue with a congestion pricing plan. After many years it may be an idea whose time has finally come, but there is even more governments can do to combat traffic bottlenecks.

Congestion pricing advocates point to an array of health, safety, and environmental benefits, including air pollution, pedestrian injuries, and unclogging city streets. They cite the success of congestion pricing plans in places such as London, Stockholm, and Singapore.

These cities use different methods to toll drivers in their respective congestion zones. London uses a video surveillance system to record car license plates. Singapore uses larger gantries with sensors to read license plates or directly charges E-ZPass-like units in cars. Stockholm has installed gantries and cameras at all entry points to the tolled zone.

Some New Yorkers claim congestion pricing is an unfair tax that disproportionately hurts poor people who lack access to public transit. While affluent motorists can pay for a quicker ride, the working class will struggle to pay the toll. Suburban commuters, of course, see the plan as benefiting the city at their expense.

After years of hesitation, New York is on the verge of becoming the first US city to charge motorists for driving into a central business district. The program is expected to be implemented in 2021, once the necessary infrastructure is in place.

The congestion pricing plan will help pay for badly needed repairs to the city's transit system and reduce gridlock. The goal is to generate $1 billion annually to secure the issuance of $15 billion in municipal bonds.

Drivers could pay $12 for cars and $25 for trucks to enter the heart of Manhattan. Prices may vary based on time of day and traffic volume and potentially offer exemptions and credits to certain travelers, such as discounts for buses, taxis, and motor-cycles. For example, residents in the congestion zone who earn less than $60,000 annually will be eligible for credits.

Not surprisingly politicians avoided making many of these difficult decisions. Instead they will be made by a six-member Traffic Mobility Review Board.

The idea of road pricing was developed by Professor William S. Vickrey, the 1996 Noble Prize winner in economics who passed away four days after winning the prize. He argued that the con-sequences of not charging motorists for their rush hour usage could be "disastrously expensive."

Society pays a high price for congestion. When traffic flow nears maximum road capacity, each additional motorist imposes a delay on others (as density increases, speed drops, and travel time lengthens). The delays increase geometrically. Vickrey argued that only peak-load pricing could solve the congestion problem in urban transportation.

Major US cities, including Los Angeles, San Francisco, Seattle, and Boston, are exploring various forms of congestion pricing to unclog city streets and raise money for transportation. And the time may be right to consider tying price to performance.

Money-back travel time guarantees could be offered to help customers accept higher prices for transportation services.

For instance, a turnpike charge of ten cents per mile during a particular time of day would be linked to a minimum average speed. If the average falls below the minimum, customers are charged progressively less. Advances in technology make it possible to put customers first and introduce a new level of accountability for public transportation providers by offering these guarantees.

This would promote customer trust and acceptance of pricing changes and provide a turnpike operator with an incentive to ensure that the road is providing superior service. Former House Speaker Tip O'Neill famously said, "All politics is local." The same can be said for trust in government transportation agencies.

## Not Everyone Considers Socialism a Cracker Jack Idea
4/27/2019

Capitalism seemed untouchable several decades ago, but not today. Many politicians aspiring to high office, such as Sen. Bernie Sanders, a self-declared democratic socialist, are making the case for the inevitable and Darwinian triumph of socialism.

It is unclear what socialism means to them. It is a word that means many things to many people and has taken many forms. The modern version is different from the textbook variety of public ownership of the means of production, distribution, and exchange, leaving to individuals only the free discretion over consumer goods and creating a paradise on earth. Publicly owned property is preferable to private enterprise, with everyone acting virtuously and focusing on the greater good.

Is it the ideal commonwealth in Plato's *Republic*, with a ruling class that has no property of its own and shares all things in common? Or a more robust version of New Deal Liberalism, or perhaps Northern European social democracy? What about the path taken in Venezuela, North Korea, and Cuba?

Or is it a planned economy, with benevolent bureaucrats taking the place of free-market capitalism—playing the omniscient busybody in economic affairs—to create more opportunities for the underprivileged; open the horizons of education to all; eliminate discriminatory practices based on sex, religion, race, or social class; regulate and reorganize the economy for the benefit of the whole community; protect the environment; and provide adequate Social Security and universal health care for the sick, unemployed, and aged in a utopian ideal of total equality of opportunity and outcome?

The term has become a blank canvas as presidential candidates embracing some of these ideas become more outspoken about socialism as the solution to problems of social and economic equality and embracing a political wish list that includes Medicare for All, a Green New Deal, and free public college. All grand ideas if they work.

These proposals have great appeal to millennials, the term generally used to refer to people born after 1980 and before 2000. Millennials outnumber baby boomers as the largest generational cohort in American society.

Recent surveys of Americans aged eighteen to thirty-four find that 45 percent have a positive view of socialism. It gets even higher marks from Hispanics, Asian Americans, and African Americans. This attraction may have less to do with their understanding of socialism and more to do with their discontent with the current economic system. In contrast only 26 percent of baby boomers would prefer to live in a socialist country.

Why the generational disparity? Is it because many of these folks reached adulthood in a dismal job market with crippling student loans caused by the brutal 2007–2009 recession, which left them with less disposable income than their predecessors? They end up hating their own culture, even as millions around the world dream of coming to the land of milk and honey. Many agree with Governor Cuomo's comment that "America was never that great."

But these proposals also create agita for many politicians. That is why House Speaker Nancy Pelosi, in a recent interview with CBS's *60 Minutes*, said that socialism is "not the view of the Democratic Party" and that lawmakers on her side of the aisle "know that we have to hold the center." The Republicans are trying to paint Democrats with the socialism brush, using accusations of rampant amnesia about the failures of socialism as a 2020 campaign weapon.

Former President Ronald Reagan once mocked Fidel Castro's brand of socialism with a clever joke. He said Castro was immersed in one of his long speeches when a person in the crowd was heard shouting, "Peanuts, popcorn, Cracker Jacks." Castro continued on with his speech when a second voice was heard shouting the same thing. This time Castro became angry and screamed, "We will kick the tush of the next person I hear say that all the way to Miami Beach." At which point the whole crowd yelled, "Peanuts, popcorn, Cracker Jacks."

# Economic Inequality a Crisis for Capitalism
5/11/2019

Increasing economic inequality and decreasing mobility have entered mainstream consciousness and are identified as among the most pressing challenges of capitalist societies such as the United States in the twenty-first century. Today capitalism has a distinctly pejorative interpretation here in its free-market Mecca.

Increasingly Americans are questioning the ideology of capitalism itself. This crisis manifests itself prominently among the nuevo millennial socialists for whom capitalism is all about profit. For them, profit is a bad word. They ignore the reality that in any economic system people hope to gain more value from things than they put into them and that this is true in whatever you do in life.

According to a new Harris Poll, more millennials would prefer to live in a socialist country (44 percent) than a capitalist one (42 percent). The percentage of millennials who would prefer socialism to capitalism is a full ten points higher than that of the general population. What's more, this crowd rejects capitalism as an economic system because it benefits the wealthy and powerful, poses large social costs, and contributes to the obscene prosperity of a tiny, privileged minority.

Alternatively proponents of capitalism argue that it is the only system humans have developed that maintains both improvement in living standards and individual freedom. Despite criticism that it is morally bankrupt, capitalism has spread prosperity across the planet. Free markets have generated enormous wealth in recent decades, as documented by the World Bank, delivering millions of people out of poverty and raising living standards throughout the world. In 1990 about 40 percent of the global population lived on less than $1.90 a day, according to the World Bank; today it is less than 10 percent.

But the story is different for the average American. Since the 1970s, their wages have stagnated. Since the 1990s, cheap imports made available by the North American Free Trade Agreement and China's accession to the World Trade Organization have benefited consumers but depressed wages and robbed blue-collar Americans of the secure manufacturing jobs and the health and retirement benefits that went with them.

Technological advances certainly played a major role in worker displacement, but trade policy also contributed to the United States losing 7 million of its 19.2 million manufacturing jobs from 1980 to 2015. Yes, consumers have enjoyed lower costs for imported products, but displaced workers in the United States have paid the price and contributed to what has been labeled the crisis of capitalism: the growing gap between the haves and the have-nots.

How then to define capitalism? In theory it is another "-ism" that describes an economic way of life, a system that emphasizes private ownership of personal property and business assets, property rights that protect ownership, the sanctity of private contracts, the use of prices to allocate resources efficiently, reliance on competition and incentives, voluntary exchanges between consenting adults, profit maximization, an effective legal system, and limited state intervention.

In practice capitalism is not monolithic; it takes many forms. For instance, in the United States, government plays a more limited role in economic decisions than under China's form of market-driven state capitalism. There, the government has a substantial role in shaping the rules of the market and is a significant player in the economy. In the Russian style of state capitalism, the Kremlin relies on both direct government intervention in key economic sectors and control of politically connected businessmen to promote the interests of the Russian state and those who run it.

Like any economic system, capitalism is a human institution and, as such, is imperfect. It should be judged on the basis of whether it is the best system available, not the best imaginable. And it is capable of reform. As the saying goes, "Nothing is forever, not now, not ever, never."

Finally, it is worth remembering John Kenneth Galbraith's comment: "Under capitalism, man exploits man; while under socialism just the reverse is true."

## Putting Modern Monetary Theory to the Test
6/1/2019

An unconventional approach called Modern Monetary Theory (MMT), which suggests governments don't have to worry about debt, is gaining traction. Its basic starting point is that a government that can borrow in its own currency can take on much more debt than orthodox economics says is prudent. If you want to spend more on government programs, just print more money with a few key strokes on the Federal Reserve computer.

Governments can manage their economies through spending and taxes instead of relying on a quasi-independent central bank to do it via interest rates. If spending much more than it collects in tax revenue creates inflation, the government can deal with inflation by raising taxes.

MMT is the economic rationale coming from potential Democratic candidates for president and rising political stars such as Rep. Alexandria Ocasio-Cortez (D-NY), who argue that the nation can afford large-scale social projects such as the recently proposed Green New Deal, Medicare for All, free college tuition, massive public infrastructure projects, and a job guarantee program with the federal government becoming the employer of last resort.

The MMT enthusiasts acknowledge that ballooning deficits risk triggering inflation but claim the low inflation of the past decade leaves plenty of room to increase the budget deficit. Advocates of MMT suggest using taxes to pull money out of the economy before it overheats.

Voters punish politicians for tax hikes. Do you really trust them to raise taxes to pull money out of the economy? The theory says the government should stop trying to balance the budget because policies aimed at doing it hurt the economy, which forces cuts to social programs. They believe a budget surplus should be avoided at all costs.

This perspective is contrary to the conventional economic thinking that when the government spends more than it collects, it either has to borrow or raise taxes. Critics such as Warren Buffett say, "We don't need to get into danger zones, and we don't know precisely where they are." Other detractors jokingly refer to MMT as magical monetary thinking. They believe you cannot borrow endlessly without risking real economic harm, especially if the return on government investments is below the interest rate on borrowing.

And such policies may undermine the United States' standing as the world's reserve currency. When countries reject the dollar as a world currency and foreign buyers such as China do not want to buy US debt, increased government borrowing could eventually cause interest rates to rise as investors demand a better return on treasury bonds. MMT advocates respond that US borrowing costs and inflation have remained low despite our being waist deep in deficits and debt.

Yes, the federal government could print more dollars to pay off the debt if it ever came to that, but is the dollar in danger of no longer being the world's primary reserve currency and enjoying the lower interest rates and ability to fund budget deficits in perpetuity that goes along with it? Will rising debt and deficits cause foreign investors such as foreign central banks, sovereign wealth funds, and institutional investors to turn away from the dollar because they see increased risks from holding dollars as the government ratchets up borrowing to unprecedented levels?

The real world is much more complicated than ideological simplifications and abstractions. True to form, progressive politicians reveal good intentions, outsize ambitions, and a deficit of humility. Good intentions and grand ideas are frequently blind to the bothersome trivia of execution and to unintended consequences.

Whether you agree with MMT or not, it represents an important heterodox challenge to mainstream economic orthodoxy. Hedge fund king Ray Dalio has said the United States will adopt this economic philosophy to finance big government spending for more widespread growth.

After all economic growth is the religion of the modern world.

## Financial Sector Is Driving the Economy
6/15/2019

The contemporary rise of finance, promoted by both Republican and Democratic administrations, has changed America from an economy focused on sustainable growth to one dominated by the financial sector itself—a broad range of industries that includes banks, investment firms, insurance companies, and real estate firms that provide financial services to commercial and retail customers.

Since the 1980s, the financial sector has expanded to take up an extremely large slice of the US economy, a trend referred to as "financialization." Financial institutions have significantly increased in scale and profitability relative to what most see as the "real" economy—businesses that produce tangible goods—which has left the United States increasingly reliant on the financial sector to generate economic growth.

The growth is apparent when measuring the size of the financial sector as a percentage of gross domestic product. Finance and insurance alone represent about 7 percent of the US gross domestic product. Profits tell a similar story. The sector now takes around a quarter of all corporate profits yet creates only 4 percent of jobs, according to the Bureau of Economic Analysis. In short the financial sector has captured a larger and larger piece of the national economic pie.

Many say this has contributed to widening income inequality between a small pool of high earners and the rest of society, giving the financial elite ample resources to sway government policy in their favor. This political influence is quite unlike the 99 percent, whose choices are increasingly limited to making ends meet. Several Democratic presidential candidates have criticized the United States' reliance on the financial sector and lax government regulation. Sen. Bernie Sanders has made "breaking up the banks" a key plank in his presidential platform.

One factor that has contributed to financial sector growth is deregulation.

Before the Great Depression, the status and influence of financiers were so great that when Pres. Theodore Roosevelt filed the first major antitrust lawsuit against J. P. Morgan's

Northern Pacific Railroad, Morgan, the fabled Wall Street titan, at a February 1902 White House meeting, told the president, "If we have done anything wrong, send your man to my man, and they can fix it up."

Four years after the stock market crash of 1929, the United States passed the Glass–Steagall Act in 1933 and other legislation to rigorously regulate the financial sector and make it more stable and transparent. The Glass–Steagall legislation separated investment banking from commercial banking, forcing banks to choose one or the other. Little by little, over the last several decades, those laws that served America so well were rolled back, starting in the 1980s onward.

The financialization of the economy was jacked up in the 1980s, fueled by Reagan-era laissez-faire policies. For example, the 1982 tax reform lowered the capital gains tax. Deregulation from the 1980s onward encouraged banks to move away from their traditional role of supporting businesses and individuals and providing the liquidity and credit needed to lubricate the economy.

For instance, the repeal of the Glass–Steagall Act in 1999, a seismic moment in the story of financialization, triggered high-risk deals and trading by financial institutions by enabling them to use deposits collected through their commercial banking arms. Lusting for quick, short-term profits that kept the money within the financial sector rather than investing it in the real economy, banks began to focus on high-risk "financial engineering" such as subprime loans, collateralized debt obligations, structured investment vehicles, and derivatives, which Warren Buffett famously called "financial weapons of mass destruction."

Such activities are remote from the production of tangible goods and services. Finance has become a business unto itself, all about making money from money rather than making things and being a facilitator for real business. Populists from the left and the right say Wall Street has done better than Main Street—and that may be the truth of it.

## Labor Unions and Inequality
6/28/2019

In the wake of the Great Recession, economic inequality—the extent to which income and wealth are distributed unevenly across a population—has emerged as a major issue in the United States.

Since the late 1970s, there has been enormous change in the distribution of income and wealth in the United States. The gap between the "haves" and the "have-nots" has widened, with a small portion of the population reaping an increasingly larger share of the country's economic rewards. Warren Buffett got it right when he said, "There's been class warfare going on for the last 20 years and my class has won."

The average American has lost. Since the mid-1970s, wages have remained stagnant, and middle-class earnings have lagged the cost of living.

Several factors contribute to economic inequality, downward mobility among working-class Americans, and the dangerous fissures it has caused American society. These include government tax and regulatory policies, the acceleration of finance capitalism, culture, immigration, globalization, and the rate of technological change.

Frequently overlooked is the declining strength of private sector labor unions. In 1979 unions represented 24 percent of the private sector labor force; today only 6.5 percent of private sector workers are unionized.

The effects of this decline are fiercely debated. Conservatives argue that labor unions decrease competitiveness and business profitability. Progressives say that in an era of globalization, companies threaten to ship jobs to factories offshore to extract concessions from unions with impunity. For sure, unions raise wages, but that doesn't necessarily mean they reduce profitability or diminish competitiveness. Consider the success of unionized firms such as Southwest Airlines and UPS.

American manufacturing and wages suffered as US companies engaged in extensive offshore outsourcing of decent-paying domestic jobs to China and other low-wage countries under the banner of free trade, prioritizing short-term profits over long-term investments and the public interest. For example, from 2000 to 2016, the United States shed five million manufacturing jobs, a fact that supporters of free trade and globalization rarely mention.

The loss of traditional manufacturing jobs has contributed to income inequality and declining union membership. According to a report by the Washington-based think tank the Economic Policy Institute, if unions had the same presence in the private sector today as in 1979, both union members and nonmembers would be making about $2,500 more each year.

Many companies have built their business models around offshoring manufacturing to reduce costs without passing the savings on to consumers. They view the wages and benefits that once underpinned a middle-class lifestyle as obscenely excessive. That's why they support free trade and use their political power to generate the support of both major political parties, helping accelerate the demise of labor unions. Government turned a blind eye as corporations packed up good jobs and send them overseas, weakening private sector unions.

The American public has repeatedly been told that policies that restrain foreign competition are a form of protectionism that subsidizes inefficient domestic industries and raises prices. The issue of job losses is ignored. The benefits of free trade allegedly exceed the costs of lost jobs, especially for those who work with their hands. Assumed consumer benefits should be considered when it comes to trade policy, but so should giving working-class people a fair shot at the American dream. Americans need a more balanced way of thinking about free trade and the offshoring of American jobs.

Is it any wonder that President Trump's campaign slogan—"Make America Great Again"—resonated with ordinary Americans? This rhetoric is reminiscent of 1988 Democratic presidential candidate Rep. Richard Gephardt's slogan, "Let's Make American First Again."

Writing over 2,400 years ago, the Greek philosopher Aristotle captured the importance of inequality when he wrote, "A polity with extremes of wealth and poverty is a city not of free persons but of slaves and masters, the ones consumed by envy, the others by contempt."

## Deficits and Debt
7/13/2019

As chairman of the Joint Chiefs of Staff from 2007 through 2011, Adm. Michael Mullen was particularly vocal about saying that the greatest threat to US national security was budget deficits. He pointed out that interest on the debt will nearly equal the defense budget and jeopardize the ability to properly resource the military.

In economic terms the national debt—the sum total of annual budget deficits—now exceeds $22 trillion. The nonpartisan Congressional Budget Office (CBO) projects a deficit of $896 billion for 2019, about a 15 percent increase over the $779 billion deficit in 2018. The CBO predicts deficits will keep rising in the next few years, topping $1 trillion in 2020 and never dropping beneath that amount through 2029.

Federal debt held by the public is projected to grow from 78 percent of gross domestic product in 2019 to 92 percent in 2029 and 144 percent in 2049, which would be the most in American history. The prospect of such large deficits and debt poses substantial risks, sayeth the CBO.

In case you missed it, neither Democrats nor Republicans seem to care much. Putting the federal government's fiscal house in order currently commands the attention of few national politicos. They behave like Scarlett O'Hara in *Gone with the Wind*, who reacted to adverse circumstances by saying, "I can't think of this now…I'll think about it tomorrow."

Democratic presidential candidates have presented plans such as Medicare for All, Free College, and the Green Leap Forward. They advocate increasing taxes on the rich to address wealth and income inequality, social problems, and any number of other things but not to reduce deficits and debt. They don't appear to be worried by deficits and accumulating debt and seem to think a magic money tree will fund their spending initiatives.

Republicans also usher the idea of taming deficits out of the room rather quickly, accepting bigger deficits in exchange for tax cuts they argue will promote economic growth and fill budget shortfalls over the long term. The theory is that the debt is manageable so long as the economy grows at a faster pace than the feds' borrowing costs.

In 2016 President Trump campaigned on eliminating the then-$19 trillion national debt in eight years, but the White House spending plan for the next decade calls for adding another $10.5 trillion to the $22 trillion federal debt—and that assumes continued economic growth.

Doing nothing about government red ink shifts the burden to future generations. The theory is that it is wrong for the current generation to enjoy the benefits of government spending without paying for them.

The CBO estimates the federal government will spend more on servicing outstanding debt in 2020 than on Medicaid and more than on national defense by 2025. Many Democrats and Republicans deny this is a problem, arguing that the United States can simply borrow more to fund unrestrained spending. They appear unconcerned that the government's debt payments may crowd out a good portion of the spending they want.

The Treasury Department's Office of Debt Management forecasts that starting in 2024, all US debt issuance will be used to fund the US net interest expense, which will be anywhere between $700 billion and $1.2 trillion or more. If this happens, the United States will be engaging in the ultimate Ponzi scheme, in which new debt issuance is used exclusively to fund interest on the debt by around 2024.

Out-of-control spending will haunt the taxpayers for years to come. Obviously there is no political gain in being a good fiscal steward.

Nota bene what Edmund Burke wrote in *Reflections on the Revolution in France* in 1790: "Society is indeed a contract. It is a partnership…not only between those who are living, but between those who are dead, and those who are to be born."

# Demography Is Destiny
7/27/2019

The world is undergoing a dramatic transition because of the confluence of disruptive forces such as accelerating technological change and globalization. But another important factor that often gets overlooked will shape society and the global economy over the coming decades: The life expectancy of humans is increasing. Fertility rates are falling, and the world's population is growing gray.

This unprecedented demographic shift has major implications for US fiscal policy. Entitlement programs will be increasingly strapped as the number of beneficiaries increases and the number of working people who pay for the benefits shrinks.

Because of advances in medical science and technology, people—especially the well to do—expect to live longer, better lives than they might have imagined even three decades ago. According to the Census Bureau, the average American born today can expect to live to about eighty, up dramatically from the average of sixty-eight in 1950.

Additionally the Census Bureau notes that whereas the average American woman in 1950 had 3.5 children during her lifetime, the figure today has fallen below 2. The causes of declining fertility include the rising social status of women, widespread availability of birth control, and the growing cost of raising children.

French sociologist and philosopher Auguste Comte coined the aphorism "demography is destiny" with dubious finality almost two hundred years ago. But that does not suggest that destiny is immutable, nor is it inevitable. Just as aging individuals must adjust their lifestyles to maintain personal vitality, societies with aging populations must adjust policies to preserve and promote their economic prosperity.

Demographic trends can have big implications. This shift from a predominantly young to predominantly older population has both broad macroeconomic implications and important financial consequences. Consider that many US entitlement programs were created with the assumption that there would be a relatively small group of old people and a large number of working-age people, followed by an even bigger cohort of children.

According to the Census Bureau, 47.8 million Americans are sixty-five and over. This figure is projected to nearly double to 83.7 million by 2050. Just ten years ago, 12.5 percent of the population was sixty-five and over. Today it is 15 percent and is projected to reach 21 percent in just twenty years. By 2030, 1 in every 5 US residents will be over sixty-five. For decades this was the age when people were expected to end their careers and embrace a life of leisure, following Andrew Carnegie's advice to spend the first third of life getting educated, the second third getting rich, and the last third giving money away.

As the baby boomer generation retires, fertility rates keep falling, and life expectancy continues to increase, there will be too many beneficiaries and too few taxpayers. In 1950 the American economy had 8.1 people of working age for each person of retirement age. Recent figures indicate that this "dependency ratio," as the demographers call it, has shrunk to just over 5:1. By 2030 the Census folks estimate it will have fallen to 3:1.

Caring for large numbers of elderly people will put severe pressure on government finances. More specifically and painfully, the United States may be facing major tax increases, significant budget cuts, or most likely some combination of the two to secure the future stability of old-age entitlement programs.

In particular Social Security and Medicare, which provides health insurance to the elderly, will rise as a share of gross domestic product as the baby boomers retire.

With the retirement of the baby boomers and the rising number of elderly in the population, the nation will face a slow-motion train wreck absent changes in government fiscal policy. The good news is the slow motion part, which gives Americans enough time to take on the challenge of real entitlement reforms that will allow the country to successfully navigate this demographic transition.

## Let Them Eat Credit
8/16/2019

The Federal Reserve Bank cut interest rates by a quarter of a point on July 31, the first reduction in more than a decade. The twenty-five-basis points reduction was seen as an effort to stimulate the economy and counteract the escalating tit-for-tat trade war with China, which is seen as impeding global growth.

The Federal Reserve, the world's most powerful central bank, is again bearing the burden of keeping the economy growing and minimizing financial instability. What's more, they are pursuing pro-growth policies without any fiscal policy support from elected officials.

Just last month, President Trump reached a bipartisan two-year budget agreement with Democratic leadership in the House of Representatives and Republican leaders in the US Senate that raises discretionary spending caps by $320 billion and suspends the debt ceiling until July 31, 2021. The legislation will add $1.7 trillion to projected debt. It is a really bad idea to assume the future will look after itself. The good news is that they got on well together to pass the legislation. If you believe that, you can't be helped.

This budget deal avoids the risk of another partial federal government shutdown and a potentially catastrophic default on the nation's debt. The Republicans voting for it touted the increase in military spending while the Democrats talked up the additional domestic spending it includes. The federal debt has grown from about $19 trillion in January 2017 to more than $22 trillion now. Fear of debt and its potentially dangerous implications are nowhere to be found in 2019.

But it's not just the ruling class in Washington that has become addicted to debt; the whole country is waist deep in it. Taken together, all segments of US debt—federal, state, local, corporate, and household—are at 350 percent of the gross domestic product. American household debt continues to climb to record levels, reaching $13.54 trillion in the fourth quarter of 2018, $869 billion above the 2008 peak of $12.68 trillion, according to the Federal Reserve Bank of New York.

The Federal Reserve also claims to be tweaking the benchmark federal funds rate because it is worried that inflation is running below its target of 2 percent. According to the Fed, prices rose just 1.6 percent in the year through June, not counting volatile food and fuel prices.

Inflation, as defined and measured by the Fed, may be running pretty low right now, but bear in mind that the typical family's living costs may be nothing like the official stats. It is also fair to say that Americans want a bigger paycheck, not higher prices resulting from a 2 percent inflation target. On a daily basis, they experience the Dickensian nightmare of the accumulated high cost of several decades of low wages.

Don't forget that even modest inflation for a prolonged period can seriously erode purchasing power. For instance, inflation averaged 2.46 percent annually between 1990 and 2018. Sounds low, but you would need just about $2,000 today to buy what $1,000 would have bought in 1990. You don't have to be a socialist or an economist to understand that despite the strong labor market, today's wages provide about the same purchasing power as years ago—if you are lucky.

To compensate, households turn to debt. The average American now has about $38,000 in personal debt, excluding home mortgages. The average household carries about $137,000 in debt, and the median household income is about $59,000. So when the cost of living rises faster than household income, more Americans use credit to cover basic needs such as food, clothing, and medical expenses. When wage growth does not keep up with the cost of living, the government promotes cheap credit to grease the economic wheel, especially in an on-demand society that values the immediate over the remote.

Put differently, US economic policy has, for decades, been—paraphrasing the misquoted Marie Antoinette—"Let them eat credit."

## The Lehman Brothers Story
8/24/2019

Next month is the eleventh anniversary of the fall of the famed investment banking firm Lehman Brothers ("Lehman"), which froze up the nation's credit system when it collapsed on September 15.

The firm was founded as a dry goods business in 1850 in Alabama by brothers Henry, Emanuel, and Mayer. Lehman began focusing on cotton trading and moved to New York during the late 1850s. That office eventually became its headquarters.

By 1900 Lehman had begun moving into underwriting new issues of common stocks for corporate clients, as well as bond trading and financial advisory services. During the ensuing decades, it underwrote issues for corporations such as Sears Roebuck, RCA, and Macy's. In 1984 Lehman was acquired by American Express and merged with Shearson, the company's brokerage subsidiary. This lasted until 1994, when American Express decided to get out of the brokerage business and spun off Lehman.

The company saw considerable success in the years that followed, as it increased its net revenues more than sixfold, to $19.2 billion. By the end of 2007, it was the fourth-largest investment bank in the United States and seemed poised to continue its stellar growth.

But Lehman had become increasingly reliant on the subprime and commercial real estate markets. This went hand in hand with a 46 percent increase in its leverage ratio, from twenty-four to one in 2003 to thirty-five to one in 2007. Much of this leverage took the form of short-term debt with maturities as short as a single day. So Lehman had to continuously sweet-talk its lenders about the "solid value" of the assets it had pledged as collateral for these "here-today-gone-tomorrow" loans.

The sweet talk was undercut by the continued erosion of the housing and mortgage markets during the summer of 2007. Lehman's common stock price fell 37 percent from June to August, as the firm closed its subprime mortgage arm, wrote off $3.5 billion in mortgage-related assets, and laid off more than 6,000 employees by year's end.

Things got even worse in 2008. In January, Lehman closed its wholesale mortgage lending unit and laid off another 1,300 employees in a vain attempt to stem further hemorrhaging in its subprime mortgage operations. Then Standard & Poor's credit rating agency downgraded its outlook on Lehman from stable to negative on the expectation that its revenue would decline by at least another 20 percent, which caused Lehman's stock price to plunge an additional 48 percent.

Lehman attempted to counter by selling $4 billion in convertible preferred stock, but the fresh cash was quickly soaked up by more write-offs. Rumors flew that other firms were refusing to trade with Lehman.

The company contemplated "taking itself private," but financing wasn't available. Lehman's next move was to try to locate buyers for $30 billion of its commercial mortgages, whose actual market value couldn't be determined because their trading activity was virtually nonexistent. Talks with the Korea Development Bank, China's CITIC Securities, and the Royal Bank of Canada went nowhere.

The time had come for the federal government to step in if Lehman was to be saved. But public backlash against the earlier Bear Stearns bailout made such a rescue politically untenable. Voices from all sides of the political spectrum were screaming at the feds for using taxpayer funds to bail out big Wall Street firms that had caused this mess, while refusing to lift a finger to help American families in danger of losing their homes.

On September 15, 2008, Lehman had to file for Chapter 11 bankruptcy, leaving its viable businesses to be snapped up at fire-sale prices by sharp-eyed bottom fishers.

At the time it was the largest Chapter 11 bankruptcy in American history. In retrospect it's generally regarded as the most disastrous decision by the feds since the early 1930s, when the Federal Reserve chose to shrink the nation's money supply by one-third, which shattered the American economy for the rest of the decade.

## The Merrill Lynch Story
9/7/2019

The weekend of September 13 and 14, 2008, was one of the worst ever on Wall Street. And when Lehman Brothers went bankrupt on September 15, it triggered a global financial panic.

Also over that weekend, Bank of America and Merrill Lynch hammered out one of the biggest deals in Wall Street history in less than thirty-six hours. The feds pushed for a deal to prevent Merrill from becoming the next domino to fall. With Lehman preparing to file for bankruptcy after failing to find a buyer, executives at both Bank of America and Merrill knew they needed to act quickly, as Merrill's liquidity was evaporating.

Merrill Lynch was founded in 1914 by Charles Merrill and his friend Edmund Lynch. During the next thirty years, it grew by a series of mergers and acquisitions into the nation's largest and best-known retail brokerage firm. Just as Lehman Brothers had epitomized the "aristocratic German-Jewish culture" in the financial industry, Merrill Lynch became a symbol of "working-class Irish Catholic culture" (like New York City's police and fire departments). Not that it mattered much when push came to shove in September 2008.

In 1971 Merrill Lynch became a publicly traded corporation. And in 1978 it acquired the small but prestigious investment bank White Weld & Company to expand its underwriting activities and take advantage of the ability of its huge retail brokerage arm to place new common stock issues with investors directly rather than through syndicates composed of other firms.

But by 2000 Merrill (like Lehman and Bear Stearns) was becoming increasingly dependent on its collateralized mortgage obligations business to grow profits. By goosing this growth by more than doubling its 2003 leverage ratio of nineteen to one to thirty-nine to one in 2007, Merrill was able to provide its common stockholders with a 13 percent increase in investment returns during this period.

By 2006 Merrill had leaped to the top spot in the nation's collateralized mortgage obligations business, underwriting $35 billion in these securities, 40 percent of which were backed by subprime mortgages. To help secure its position, Merrill spent $1.3 billion to acquire First Franklin, one of the nation's largest originators of subprime residential mortgages. This gave it a major in-house mortgage originator and reduced its dependence on buying mortgages from numerous banks and home loan firms to back new underwritings of collateralized mortgage obligations.

Concerns about Merrill's viability increased during the summer of 2007, when two Bear Stearns hedge funds defaulted. As a short-term lender to these funds, Merrill seized $800 million of Bear's mortgage assets and proceeded to auction them off in the secondary markets. But the auctions failed to generate reasonable bids for the subprime mortgages and highlighted Merrill's exposure to these "toxic waste securities." For the last quarter of 2007 and the first three quarters of 2008 combined, Merrill wrote down more than $46 billion to bad bets on real estate and other mortgage-related instruments.

These write-downs had severe consequences for Merrill: The firm's stock price fell significantly, Moody's Investors Service placed Merrill's long-term debt "on review for a possible downgrade," traders in other firms lost confidence in the firm's ability to meet its trading obligations, and the firm had to increase its equity capital by selling off assets such as its 20 percent stake in Bloomberg for a much-needed $4.4 billion.

Additionally, between May 2007 and September 2008, Merrill laid off over 7 percent of its employees. Its board ousted CEO Stan O'Neal in October 2007, though he retained $30 million in retirement benefits and $129 million in stocks and options.

Merrill's continued write-downs of toxic mortgage assets, increasing operating losses, and difficulty refinancing its short-term borrowings made it clear that its days as an independent firm were numbered. On September 14, 2008, Merrill agreed to sell itself to the Bank of America.

Financial markets are prone to instability. But when paired with excessive financial leverage, the result can be severe economic pain.

## Stakeholder Capitalism—Really?
9/21/2019

A recent announcement by nearly two hundred CEOs that corporations should serve more than the bottom line may be great public relations, but don't hold your breath waiting for big changes in the way corporate America operates.

For four decades the popular conception is that a corporation exists to maximize returns to shareholders. This conceit is the work of economists. Milton Friedman, who was awarded the Nobel Prize in Economics in 1976, made the case in a famous 1970 *New York Times Magazine* article that the social responsibility of business is to increase profits. It laid the intellectual foundations for the shareholder value revolution of the 1980s.

As he put it, "[T]here is one and only one social responsibility of business—to use its resources and engage in activities designed to increase its profits." His former students popular-ized the idea that the great challenge of corporate governance is getting executives (agents) to act in the interest of the share-holders (principals).

This view caught on and became conventional wisdom, as universally accepted as the idea that the sun revolves around the earth once was. Over time the US stock market has focused strongly on corporations' quarterly earnings to the point that a penny up or down from expected earnings per share can cause the stock price to fluctuate.

This has created a number of potential problems. For starters the short-term focus of the stock market dictates a short-term approach by management, at the expense of long-term share-holder value. For example, management might decide to shower cash on shareholders and not invest in research and development on projects that would only pay off down the road. Also, market pressures could tempt managers to cheat or manage earnings to meet investor expectations, especially since the compensation of CEOs and other executives is linked to stock performance.

This August, nearly two hundred chief executives of ma-jor American corporations, including Apple, Amazon, General Motors, and Walmart—all members of the powerful US Business Roundtable—announced that corporations should no longer just maximize profits for shareholders but also benefit other stake-holders, including employees, customers, and citizens.

Is this all just rosy rhetoric or a real change in mission? Will these corporations who are people, really nice people, now use house money to support expansive social goals that are irrel-evant to maximizing shareholder returns? This rhetoric about the purpose of a corporation won't even rise to the level of the inconsequential unless executives address basic questions.

Will they argue for changes in how they are paid, how corporations are taxed and regulated, and instead focus on the long-term health of their companies? What metrics will these executives use to measure stakeholder returns? How will corporations pivot away from the needs of activist short-term investors? How will they balance the needs of multiple stakeholders to create value for all these shared interests? How will executives resolve stakeholder conflicts? What trade-offs have to be made? There are more unasked and unanswered questions than positions in the *Kama Sutra*.

*New York Times* columnist Farhad Manjoo believes the new mission statement is all foam and no beer. He cynically says these CEOs want you to know how much they care, but they will continue to eat your lunch while virtue signaling. Many others are quite skeptical that corporations will change the way they behave.

Former General Electric CEO Jack Welch said in a 2009 interview with the *Financial Times*, "On the face of it, shareholder value is the dumbest idea in the world." This comment may be the height of irony given that when he ran General Electric, the firm consistently met or beat analysts' quarterly earnings forecasts.

One thing is certain: The time is long overdue to shift the focus of corporations away from maximizing shareholder value and stock-based executive compensation. But don't hold your breath. This is like asking business executives to perform surgery on themselves.

## In Praise of Negative Interest Rates?
10/8/2019

Negative interest rates are widely discussed these days as a monetary policy tool to support economic growth. Pres. Donald Trump is a huge fan of low or negative rates and has been browbeating Federal Reserve Chair Jerome Powell, whom he appointed in 2017, to cut interest rates to zero or even lower. Powell and his colleagues should think long and hard before capitulating.

The apparent goal is to keep the economy percolating until after next year's presidential election. The Fed appeased the president last month, making a modest quarter-point cut. Egged on by Trump, they seem poised to lower rates further this year.

Negative interest rates have become commonplace in Europe and Japan. Central banks in Denmark, Switzerland, Sweden, Japan, and the European Central Bank have slashed rates below zero to shore up weak economies or strengthen their currencies. The notion is that weakening a country's currency makes it a less attractive investment than other currencies, giving the country's exports a competitive advantage. Worldwide, there is more than $17 trillion in debt with negative yields, almost half of it in euros. The majority of the balance is in Japanese yen. Almost all of it is sovereign debt.

Central banks usually pay commercial banks interest on the reserves they keep at the central bank. Under a negative rate policy, the commercial institutions are required to pay interest on any surplus cash beyond what regulators say banks must keep on hand. This penalty is designed to incentivize commercial banks to lend more money. The view is that low or negative interest rates encourage businesses to invest and consumers to spend rather than pay a fee to keep their money safe. Loans put money into circulation and generate economic activity.

Lower or negative interest rates present both costs and benefits for consumers.

Imagine if you go to the bank for a loan and are told the bank will pay you for taking it. Who in their right mind rejects such an offer? Conversely, if you make a deposit, under a negative interest rate scenario, you are actually paying the bank to hold your money.

A big concern, which has yet to be explained, is the impact of negative interest rates on money market funds, which are a foundational investment for many households. Negative interest rates reward borrowers at the expense of lenders or savers. The goal is to bring future consumption into the present.

One potential danger of this approach is the liquidity trap that occurs when interest rates are so low that they reduce the flow of money to the Main Street economy. Instead it goes into investments that don't generate economic activity, such as the stock market, as people desperately chase higher yields and push up stock prices.

Interest rate cuts tend to stimulate the stock market by making real returns on bonds less competitive. The president seems to think that makes for good economic policy. Negative interest rates might actually lead to lower interest costs on government debt. Debt service is one of the fastest-growing drivers of federal spending.

Low interest rates are old hat. Even during the Obama administration, when the economy rarely topped 2 percent annual growth, business did not pick up when money was cheap. For the last decade, the low-interest-rate scenario has been a secret tax on savers, who are not generally speculators in the stock market.

Millions of Americans are either behind in the race to save for retirement or living off their interest income. They may spend less in a negative interest rate environment, which would reduce economic activity.

How using this unconventional monetary policy will work in the United States is a mystery. It could leave the Fed without any ammunition when an actual recession hits and could increase the likelihood that the president is reelected. One can only hope that Powell and company make the right economic call.

## Politicians' Contempt for the Truth
10/19/2019

Russell Baker, the Pulitzer Prize–winning American journalist, said in his memoir that covering Washington was just a matter of sitting in grand marble halls waiting for someone ever more important to come out and lie to you. One could easily make the case that this happens with considerable regularity in statehouses and city halls throughout America.

If people think politicians can get ahead without untruths, they're lying to themselves. Politicians have always had a distant relationship with the truth. They have always lied, are constantly lying, and will always lie. It no longer matters if statements have any basis in reality. Get over it.

Some political lies can lead to unnecessary war. Still others conceal illegal behavior. What matters is firing up your supporters and getting reelected. They promise heaven on earth, and when they can't deliver, they spin, evade, manipulate the numbers, and knowingly engage in falsehoods.

President Trump's self-serving whoppers are overwhelming and are memorably labeled as bs. The president's body of falsehoods is singular in its multiplicity. He may be an outlier, but he is hardly unique in deliberately saying something untrue. The truth about lies is that politicians have always told them. Of course, the exception being America's first president, George Washington. He could not tell a lie, unlike most politicians who cannot tell the truth.

Trump is not the only one lying. Recall a number of prominent presidential lies. Some are as egregious, such as when President Obama told the American public over and over that "if you like your health care plan, you can keep it." Better still, the many falsehoods Pres. George W. Bush told in the run-up to the Iraq War, which were very damaging to the United States. Or when President Clinton shamelessly said in 1998, "I did not have sexual relations with that woman, Miss Lewinsky."

Then there was Pres. George H. W. Bush's "Read my lips, no new taxes." And of course, "People have got to know whether or not their President's a crook. Well, I'm not a crook," by Pres. Richard Nixon. Truth tellers in politics are an endangered species. Polling data shows politicians among the least trusted actors in society.

But do the American people care about the veracity of what politicians say? Or do they simply want to hear "their truth"? People have a tendency to view information familiar to them as the truth and search for other information that reinforces their beliefs. Daniel Kahneman, psychologist and winner of the Nobel Memorial Prize in Economics, calls it "cognitive bias"—we tend to avoid those facts that force our brains to work more.

People live in their own social network bubble in the digital world. They go on the internet to search for information that confirms their convictions. They know more but understand less, dividing into hostile tribes. They see the world as a battle between left and right, each living in separate worlds.

They fish in different information streams. Politicized media outlets and online social networks put out completely different representations of the truth. Extreme partisanship is not a new problem. George Washington warned about the dangers of it in his farewell address in September 1796.

With social media, lies have the capacity to spread faster than ever before. It is a cheap and easy way to disrupt political discourse. After all, birds of a feather flock together. These days anybody with a Twitter account can throw spaghetti at the wall and see if it sticks and for how long.

You would be right to conclude that Machiavelli would, with a few exceptions, have a lot to learn from public figures in the age of post-truth politics. The country is beset with tribalism, having forgotten the American forefathers' motto "E pluribus unum," which is imprinted on every coin in hopes of avoiding the United States becoming a nation of immigrants divided into tribes.

## Poker and Risk Management
11/2/2019

Gambling—the willingness to take actions whose outcomes cannot be known for certain—is a basic human instinct. The riskier you perceive a particular action to be, the higher its potential payoff should be to justify your taking the action.

As it happens, the risk inherent in many actions can be roughly quantified. You can rank actions by their estimated riskiness, compare them with each other and with their potential payoffs, and make intelligent judgments about which (if any) actions to take.

This is known as managing risk. And the widespread failure to manage risk sensibly was a major reason why the financial industry melted down so catastrophically in the fall of 2008. To their peril, Wall Street firms relied on oversimplified models for managing their risk.

Many people insist that financial markets are simply a large collection of gambling casinos that offer investors a variety of "games" to bet on. This is almost right—but the almost is significant.

When you walk into a casino, you face an immediate choice. Are you going to play slot machines and table games such as roulette and craps or seek out the poker rooms?

If you choose slots or table games, you are likely to lose because you are playing against the house. The payoffs of these games are structured (with the blessings of state gaming commissions) to give the house an edge that ensures you will lose in the long run. This is unlike the situation in the financial industry.

But if you choose the poker rooms, you have a chance of winning because you are playing against other gamblers like yourself. The house simply hosts the games (i.e., provides the space, tables, chairs, decks of cards, professional dealers, and so on) and takes a modest cut of the pot for doing so. This is a lot more like the situation in the financial industry.

You can sit down at a table and become a "player" (which is like being a "professional investor" in the financial industry). But you have another option.

You can engage in side betting. People who visit poker rooms simply to watch the games can place side bets among themselves about the winner of the next hand. But since they're unable to influence the hand's outcome, their betting decisions simply reflect their estimates of the raw probabilities. These bettors are spectators with no influence over who wins the next hand.

But there are ways to refine your initial assumption about the win/lose probabilities.

One way is to simply watch a half a dozen or so hands and see which player or two seem to be dominating, then make a subjective judgment about the player's probability of winning. Another is to look at the chip stacks in front of each player. If one player's stack is twice as large as anybody else's, it may be evidence of that player's superior poker skills.

But suppose you recognize at the outset that one of the players is Jennifer Harman or some other highly regarded poker maven who tends to win a significant percentage of the hands they play. You reflect this by assigning them a higher win probability. You place most of your bets on the maven winning, possibly adjusting the size of each bet based on how well the maven is doing as the game progresses and what kind of payoff odds you're getting from the other spectators.

An important point stands out about this poker example: You have a relatively large number of variables to keep track of, and their interrelationships and relative impacts are constantly changing.

This is especially true in financial markets. During the years leading up to the beginning of 2008, many firms bowed to the temptation to oversimplify their models. Many of them turned out to be less than worthless when the proverbial expletive hit the fan and blew up the world or at least lit the fuse.

## China: America's Greatest Threat
11/21/2019

The United States has gotten China wrong for the better part of four decades. Politicians, policymakers, academics, businessmen, and others naively assumed that China's communist totalitarian system would evolve toward democracy and freedom. These elites did not understand that engaging with the ninety-four-million-member Chinese Communist Party (CCP) is like having unprotected sex.

It is only recently that those who control the commanding heights in the United States have given due regard to the reality that CCP-controlled China, which regard democracy as an existential threat, is a menace to American's security and prosperity. The reasons are apparent from China's activities in the South China Sea.

If there is to be a great power military conflict in the future, it will most likely involve a rising China challenging a predominant America. The list of China's strategic initiatives is lengthy—everything from becoming a world leader in science and technology to economics and business to military might. The United States now faces a rising power, a confident, ambitious country that wants to supplant America's role as the current global hegemon.

This goal is demonstrated by China's actions in the South China Sea, which is strategically important to China's goals and is one of the battlefields on which the competition between China and the United States will play out.

The South China Sea is a part of the western Pacific Ocean and borders southern China, Taiwan, Vietnam, the Philippines, Malaysia, Indonesia, and Brunei. More than $5 trillion in trade flows through it, roughly 30 percent of all global maritime trade. A major shipping route, the sea also accounts for about 10 percent of the world's fisheries and a potentially significant amount of oil and natural gas deposits.

As the region's link between the Indian and Pacific Oceans, the South China Sea is a vital trading and military route for the countries that surround it, as well as for larger Asian economic powers, including Japan and South Korea. The country that controls the South China Sea has a strategic advantage in the region and a huge influence over global seaborne trade.

Xi Jinping, general secretary of the CCP, claims all of the South China Sea—lock, stock, and oil barrel—as sovereign territory. He backs up his claims by building aggressive military installations on existing islands, dredging new islands out of the sea itself, and building airfields, "missile defense systems," and harbors that are essentially naval bases.

China bases its claims to the South China Sea on historical records from the Xia and Han dynasties that are thousands of years old. It is unlikely that Japan, Vietnam, and South Korea will stand by while China exploits them. The United States, as an ally of Japan, South Korea, and the Philippines, could be drawn into disputes surrounding these claims. It is worth noting that actions by China's maritime forces aimed at the Japanese-administered Senkaku Islands in the East China Sea are another area of concern.

After an appeal by the Philippines that China's actions violated the United Nations Convention on the Law of the Sea, the Permanent Court of Arbitration ruled in 2016 that there was no legal basis for China to claim historic rights, while also finding that there had been several violations of the obligations set out in the convention.

China refused to accept the court's ruling and has continued militarization of the artificial islands with impunity. This is an expression of China's newfound military and political power and its "might makes right" approach to international affairs. China's expansion in the South China Sea is equivalent to Russia's annexation of the Crimea in 2014.

America should not try to contain China unilaterally but rather assemble a broad coalition with nations, including India, South Korea, Japan, and the Philippines, to confront, resist, and sanction China in the same way as it partnered with NATO and others.

# The Debt Dilemma

12/28/2019

The US debt is more than $23 trillion, by far the largest in the world. During the fiscal year that ended on September 30, 2019, Uncle Sam laid out nearly $4.4 trillion while taking in just $3.5 trillion in revenue, which adds up to a $984 billion deficit, 26 percent higher than the year before and equal to 4.6 percent of the country's gross domestic product. In the first two months of the current fiscal year (October and November), the feds ran a $343 billion deficit.

If not corrected, the fallout from exploding debt will be felt for generations.

Most of the federal budget goes toward entitlement programs such as Social Security, Medicare, and Medicaid, which account for about 47 percent of all spending. Those costs are expected to increase because of the aging population and the resulting rise in health-care spending.

Unlike discretionary spending, which Congress must appropriate each year, entitlement spending occurs automatically unless Congress alters the underlying legislation. In the past fiscal year, only 31 percent of federal spending went toward discretionary programs, with defense spending taking up roughly half of that.

The nation is looking at trillion-dollar deficits. According to the Congressional Budget Office, federal budget deficits are projected to average $1.2 trillion annually for the next decade, thanks to recent tax cuts and spending increases, along with continued growth in entitlement programs.

Federal Reserve Chair Jerome Powell recently testified that the country's current fiscal situation is unsustainable, noting that high and rising debt threatens to slow economic growth and increase federal interest payments, leaving the country vulnerable when the next recession occurs and putting an undue burden on future generations. The national debt is growing faster than the economy, and its rapid growth threatens the nation's economic health.

So far none of the leading presidential candidates, including the incumbent, have interrogated the debt issue. Stoned on their own virtues, invincible in the belief they are right, the candidates make incandescent, seductive promises, promises, and more promises to the laity who are looking for a free lunch and shortcuts to economic growth. These promises, such as Medicare for All, are to be financed by cooking up a raiding party on the 1 percent, on corporate America, and on an Amazon forest of magical money trees, postponing the day you have to square the ledger.

The reason the debt issue and its attendant risks are studiously avoided is obvious enough: Politics trumps (if we can use that word) economics. There is no incentive to put principle before career ambitions. Better to live in the eternal present and just spend, spend, spend. The public is okay with that. The fault, with apologies to Shakespeare, is in ourselves.

There are a number of risks attendant to the rising debt. For example, if interest rates rise, servicing the federal debt will consume resources that could be spent on infrastructure, education, and research. As Chairman Powell noted, increased federal interest payments could leave the country less prepared for the next recession and put undue burdens on future generations.

Correcting the debt trajectory will require politically difficult decisions. Basic economics suggest three options for balancing the books: cut benefits, raise taxes, or do both. There are no easy answers. Whether you seek to increase taxes or cut spending, you are likely to face headwinds. Benefits once given are hard to cut, much less freeze.

The path of least resistance is just to print money. Simply monetize the debt, make asset prices rise, and ignore the consequences of currency depreciation. Sound familiar?

One thing is certain: The country needs to get debt under control before the fiscal house of cards collapses and we find ourselves in another financial crisis. It would be wise to recall what Herbert Stein, an economist and member of the Council of Economic Advisers under Presidents Nixon, Ford, and Reagan, wrote: "If something cannot go on forever, it will stop."

# 4

# 2020 Columns

## The Platform Economy
*1/18/2020*

As the third decade of the twenty-first century begins, the power of digital platforms to disrupt industries is impressive. But the time may have come for tech companies to take more responsibility for the content on their platforms.

For the uninitiated a platform is essentially a marketplace that connects goods and services with people who want to buy them, bringing together producers and consumers in high-value exchanges that disrupt traditional industries and incumbent players. Companies such as Facebook, Google's YouTube, Twitter, Amazon, Uber, and Airbnb have all been built around this concept.

These online platforms play an important role in the economy and have insinuated themselves into people's everyday lives, often serving as gateways for how goods, services, information, and even people access each other. They deploy bespoke software systems to connect content creators with viewers, sellers with buyers, riders with drivers, and hosts with travelers. But the companies claim no responsibility for the products or services on their platforms.

Economists use the term "network effects" to refer to the way the value of a product or service increases in tandem with the number of people who use it. The idea is that you benefit from aligning your behavior with that of others. The argument goes that the value of a platform largely depends on the number of users on either side of the exchange. The more users a platform has, the more attractive it becomes, creating a virtuous circle.

Once a platform reaches a certain size, the thinking goes, it begins to dominate the market, dislodge incumbents, and create a formidable barrier to entry. Network effects handcuff customers to the largest player.

For example, it is much harder to switch to a different smartphone if doing so means you have to give up all your apps. Online two-sided platforms or marketplaces are among the fastest-growing internet start-ups in existence. Among notable two-sided platforms that quickly reached millions of customers were Airbnb, eBay, and Uber.

Instagram is another example. The social media application allows you to follow people of interest and share posts to those who follow you. Having more people on the service means more accounts of interest to follow and more people to interact with your posts.

Social networking sites emulate the network effects strategy used by another brand that has long held a dominant position in the tech industry. When a customer buys one of Apple's iPhones, one consideration is the number and types of apps that are available on the platform. The company has created a beautiful ecosystem, a bit like the Hotel California: Once you check in, you may never leave.

There is a dark side to these platforms. The dominance of tech companies such as Amazon, Google, and Facebook benefits customers with low prices and access to more data-driven services, but they have also become powerful monopolies, preventing new market entrants. Also, firms such as Amazon, with its considerable market power, throw their weight around by requiring some sellers to provide them with the best prices they can bestow on any online channel.

The dominance of the leading online platforms has invited bipartisan support and scrutiny from lawmakers and regulators in the United States and Europe for not doing enough to police platform content. Many lawmakers and regulators have criticized social media platforms such as Facebook and Twitter for the flood of misinformation during the 2016 presidential election.

The US Department of Justice and state attorneys general have initiated a review of market-dominating online platforms in response to concerns about lack of choice, privacy, transparency, and public safety. Of course, you can expect the leading firms to fight back and defy demands to police content and resist the heavy hand of regulation on their online digital platforms.

As always, they want to regulate their own businesses. You all know how that generally turns out.

## Big Business Dominates the American Landscape
2/15/2020

As demonstrated by the current presidential campaign, Americans live in an age of hostility toward economic power being concentrated in a few big firms. The breakup of big tech, big pharma, big banks, and firms in other industries such as airlines, beer, and hospitals may get a lot of media coverage, but the public shouldn't bet on seeing much real change.

Candidates on the left sermonize that it is time to take a fresh look at antitrust laws that have gotten little attention for the last forty years, with the exception of the Microsoft case in the late 1990s. They want to smack down companies that have gotten too big and too powerful and make it harder for entrepreneurs to build the next Google or Facebook. The candidates argue that the US economy has grown more concentrated since the early 1990s, with the spoils going to a select few in each industry.

They're right. Beyond all the left-wing piety, American industry is increasingly dominated by a shrinking handful of giant companies.

For example, the top four domestic airlines collected 41 percent of the industry's revenue ten years ago; today they collect 65 percent. It's the same story in the beer industry, where four firms control nearly 90 percent of the market despite the proliferation of craft brewers. Even in the poultry industry, Tyson, Pilgrim's Pride, and Perdue all but control US production. And three major drugstore chains—Walgreens, CVS Health, and Rite Aid—dominate that industry.

Facebook has acquired sixty-seven firms and Amazon ninety-one firms—some of which were rising, young competitors—without being challenged by regulators. And the number of companies listed on the New York Stock Exchange fell by half between 1996 and 2016. The dominant players believe that if they are to succeed, they must shore up economies of scale and erect high barriers to entry to scare off potential competitors and lock up new markets.

A handful of politicians, policy advisers, and economists contend that unrestricted concentration in certain industries is a threat to a functioning democracy. This is a fancy way of saying that the United States has massive income inequality, with the top 1 percent earning 23.8 percent of the national income and controlling 38.6 percent of national wealth. For political candidates on the left, this intensifies their meliorism and arguments that a structural dismantling of this concentrated power is necessary.

In general Washington politicians have failed to take steps to make markets more competitive, allowing superstar companies to become even more powerful. Sure, retirement accounts do okay, but wages and the economy suffer as a result of decreasing competition.

None of this is new; it's just been forgotten. Regulating market concentration has been a leitmotif in American history, starting with the passage of the nation's first antitrust law, the Sherman Act of 1890. Later, Pres. Theodore Roosevelt led the effort to break up the Standard Oil Company's monopoly, and up through the 1960s, many mergers were routinely challenged.

Fast-forward to the 1970s, when University of Chicago scholars argued that the Sherman Act was to protect consumers from high prices, not preserve competition by protecting small businesses from big ones. They claimed that large companies contribute to economic efficiency and innovation, and the government should cut back on antitrust enforcement. In effect get the government off the back of American industry.

They won the day. Other than Microsoft, antitrust enforcement on big companies has been essentially dormant for the last forty years.

It may be time to take a fresh look at the enforcement of antitrust law—especially big tech companies. But don't hold your breath. Big corporations spend tens of millions of dollars every year to push their objectives. According to the Center for

Responsive Politics, Facebook spent $12,120,000 on lobbying in 2018, and Amazon spent $14,400,000.

Former California political power broker Jesse M. Unruh was indeed right when he said, "Money is the mother's milk of politics."

## Afghanistan: Another Mission Failure
3/14/2020

More than eighteen years since Pres. George W. Bush ordered bombing in response to the 9/11 attacks, America's "forever war" in Afghanistan may finally be nearing an end. The United States signed a dicey deal with the Taliban on February 29 amid upbeat rhetoric to end the war and lead to the withdrawal of American forces.

The peace is fragile. To make it work, the Taliban and the Afghan government negotiate the political terms for ending the war and sharing power.

Afghanistan is but one of a string of dicey foreign entanglements that have marked US policy since the end of the Cold War. America's longest war came at a tremendous cost in blood and treasure. By the numbers it claimed the lives of more than 2,300 American soldiers, and 20,000 more have been injured. Tens of thousands of Afghans have been killed. It has cost US taxpayers $2 trillion, according to Brown University's Costs of War Project.

Since the disappearance of the existential threat of a nuclear-armed Soviet Union in 1991, the United States has indulged a missionary calling to remake the world in its image. It has ranged far and wide to export American values: Somalia, Haiti, Bosnia, Afghanistan, Iraq, Libya, Yemen, Syria, and the beat goes on.

In the decades before the Cold War ended, the United States used its military and economic power to defend American interests at home and abroad. America's desire to remake the world in its image was held in check by the existence of a powerful geopolitical rival: the Soviet Union.

When the fall of the Berlin Wall ended the Cold War, the American political establishment believed it had prevailed in a cosmic struggle against communism. The United States could bask in its new role as the world's sole superpower. It was perched at the pinnacle of power.

History had validated American-style liberal democratic capitalism. Political scientist Francis Fukuyama argued that humanity had reached its final stage: liberal capitalist democracy. The world was witnessing the end of history. He predicted that unipolar American influence would bring lasting world peace. The United States had no major existential threats, and everything seemed possible. The future looked bright.

This was a seismic event, yet there was no debate about America's role in world affairs. Instead the United States under three presidents chose to pursue a policy of promoting American values as universal values, what some have described as "missionary work" or, alternatively, "nation building"—using American power to reshape domestic institutions in foreign lands, regardless of whether American interests were at stake.

This foreign policy shift was embraced by both political parties. The post–Cold War presidencies of Bill Clinton, George W. Bush, and Barack Obama wandered into well-intentioned but clueless adventures in nation building, most of which have turned out badly. Elites had their heads up their hindquarters.

But it was in Afghanistan and Iraq that the notion of nation building became the ultimate policy objective. The Bush crowd, with extravagant hubris and ignorant of local conditions, thought that such transformations were feasible with limited resources. The United States failed to achieve a decisive victory in either war.

It is ironic that because the United States is so powerful and intrinsically secure, it has the freedom to wander around the world, intruding in various places. The outcomes don't have a decisive impact on American security, even if things go as badly as in the Vietnam debacle.

But the emergence of China as a global superpower and the reemergence of Russia have put an end to that post–Cold War world. Truth be told the United States no longer has the power to make unilateral changes in other political cultures.

On the other hand, Americans can take comfort in the German statesman Otto von Bismarck's reputed comment: "There appears to be a special providence that protects idiots, drunkards, children and the United States of America." Hopefully that is true.

## Selling America's Security to China
3/21/2020

Earlier this year the World Health Organization (WHO) declared the outbreak of the novel coronavirus, or COVID-19, a public health emergency of global concern. The outbreak should also prompt US leaders to ask some hard questions about pharmaceutical companies' practice of outsourcing their manufacturing to China.

Coronaviruses infect animal cells. They circulate among animals, and some are known to infect humans. This one was first detected in the city of Wuhan in the People's Republic of China.

It has since spread around the world. The long-term effects of the outbreak are unknown, but it has already brought devastating consequences for individuals, families, communities, and businesses far beyond China.

In addition to the immeasurable social and health impact, the spread of the virus has already affected business and economic activity, global financial markets, and supply chains. A global recession is imminent.

The Chinese government has leverage over America's economy and public health, as it has captured critical portions of global supply chains, including pharmaceutical drugs and medical equipment, without firing a shot.

According to the WHO, the Chinese knew of the "Wuhan virus" as early as December 8, 2019. Yet disclosure to the WHO did not take place until around January 11, 2020. This is typical when dealing with the Chinese government.

In 2002 a coronavirus had emerged in a similar wet market—where live animals are slaughtered and sold for human consumption—in southern China. When the severe acute respiratory syndrome outbreak hit in 2003, the Communist Party again concealed it from the Chinese people and the world until it was a full-blown epidemic.

The Wuhan market is also a wet market. These wild animals are believed to have tonic properties and are used for bodybuilding, sexual enhancement, and fighting disease.

The United States depends on China for pharmaceutical products. A Department of Commerce study found that over 90 percent of all antibiotics in the United States come from China.

While depending on China for thousands of ingredients and raw materials for medicine is a security issue, Americans should also be concerned about the safety and efficacy of Chinese-made pharmaceuticals. As recently as the summer of 2018, one of China's domestic vaccine makers sold at least 250,000 substandard doses for diphtheria, tetanus, and whooping cough. This instance was just the latest in a slew of scandals caused by low-quality Chinese drug products.

The time is long past to press pharmaceutical companies to bring manufacturing back to the United States. A nation's first priority is to protect itself. Public health is as essential as military preparedness and economic health. The government must intervene to protect industries that are deemed vital to national security, such as telecommunications, aerospace, and yes, pharmaceuticals. Health care is a nondiscretionary good.

The Chinese virus epidemic is a wake-up call that should make Americans ask some hard questions. How is national security defined? Does it only apply to military security, or does it encompass industries that produce the technologies needed to ensure that the country remains economically competitive? Does domestic ownership make a difference in a world where national borders are receding in importance?

And when it comes to pharmaceuticals, can the United States survive without a safe, reliable supply? Does it make sense to depend on foreign governments and companies to supply these products? What if China decides to stop exporting drugs to America?

Is the US government really powerless to stop pharmaceutical companies from outsourcing drug manufacturing to save money and increase profits? The cold reality is that the government is loath to confront China because multinational corporations and Wall Street are the winners in a global system that has seen America hand China its industrial base—good jobs, intellectual property, and global standing in exchange for alleged market access and cheap labor.

Failure to address these questions makes the ordinary American wonder if our current crop of political leaders could run a bath.

## COVID-19 Is Another Gift from the Chinese Communist Party

3/28/2020

Many of the world's recent pandemics have been traced to China: the Asian flu in 1956, the Hong Kong flu in 1968, severe acute respiratory syndrome in 2002, and the swine flu in 2009. Now COVID-19 is another gift from the Chinese Communist Party (CCP).

COVID-19 is believed to have originated at a wet market in Wuhan, China. Wet markets are a cross between a zoo and a slaughterhouse. They put people in constant contact with both live and dead animals, including illegal wildlife. That makes it easy for diseases to be transmitted to humans.

According to a study published by the University of Southampton in England, if CCP authorities had disclosed the outbreak of the COVID-19 virus three weeks earlier, the number of coronavirus cases could have been reduced by up to 95 percent, thereby mitigating the global public health crisis.

A timeline of the early weeks of the outbreak developed by the American news website Axios shows a cover-up by CCP officials. This allowed the virus to spread unchecked in Wuhan for weeks, including among the five million city residents who left going to all points of the compass without being screened, leading to a national epidemic and inevitably to its global spread.

That should come as no surprise. CCP officials prioritize stability—even if it means suppressing information the public needs to know and threatening public health.

CCP leadership covered up the severe acute respiratory syndrome outbreak for over a month after it emerged in 2002. Even as the virus spread, CCP officials continued to undercount cases and delayed reporting information. They did not alert the World Health Organization until February 2003.

United States National Security Adviser Robert O'Brien said China's cover-up "probably cost the world community two months to respond," exacerbating the pandemic. As the current outbreak has shown, an infectious disease that starts in one part of the world can spread to others in virtually no time.

So it came as no surprise that on March 17, the CCP said it would expel journalists from *The Wall Street Journal*, *The Washington Post*, and *The New York Times*. China's Ministry of Foreign Affairs said the three American outlets, as well as Voice of America and *Time* magazine, would be designated as "foreign missions" and must report information about their staff, finance, operations, and real estate in China.

The CCP's aggressive and highly centralized propaganda machine continues to sow doubt about COVID-19's origin. Zhao Lijian, a spokesman for China's Ministry of Foreign Affairs, said, "It might be the US Army who brought the epidemic to Wuhan."

Chinese President Xi Jinping and Chinese diplomats are pushing the narrative that China's response bought precious time for and made important contributions to other countries' epidemic prevention and control. They claim China is ready to share its experience and research with countries where the disease is spreading, as well as to export face masks, pharmaceutical products, and other medical supplies for which it is the dominant global supplier.

If China decided to ban such exports to the United States, the state-run news agency Xinhua noted, the United States would be "plunged into a mighty sea of coronavirus." Last year prominent Chinese economist Li Daokui suggested curtailing active pharmaceutical ingredient exports to the United States as a countermeasure in the trade war. His comments validated those made by Gary Cohn, former chief economic adviser to President Trump: "If you're the Chinese and you want to...destroy us, just stop sending us antibiotics."

Having made much of the developed world dependent on China, and because of the country's economic and military power, the CCP will likely avoid censure or sanctions for its role in the pandemic.

Perhaps it is time to get Greta Thunberg on the case to call out the CCP, hold them responsible for COVID-19, and raise the issue of decoupling the West from China.

## The Chinese Communist Party Propaganda Campaign

4/4/2020

The deadly virus that is eating the world is postmarked "Chinese Communist Party" (CCP), and it has already caused more disruption than the financial crisis of 2008 and the ensuing Great Recession.

The CCP virus is threatening lives and economies all over the globe. Social distancing and sheltering in place are necessary to slow the spread of the novel pathogen, but they also make a sharp slowdown in economic activity inevitable.

As the global economy craters, the gap between the haves and have-nots is accentuated, as the well-heeled pack their bags and escape to safer locations such as the Hamptons and Palm Beach. The limitless resources of the 1 percent ensure they will never go hungry or lack for medical care, even in a pandemic.

In the meantime ordinary people are panic buying, standing in long lines to stock up on toilet paper, facing financial instability, and trying to make ends meet while being told we are all in this together. Mostly they remain sequestered at home, apart from the occasional pilgrimage to the grocery store, pharmacy, or package store. The CCP virus has crushed the economy and shut down much of American life.

March 19 was the first day on which the CCP reported no new locally transmitted cases of the pathogen since the outbreak of the virus in Wuhan. The CCP congratulates itself on its extraordinary containment measures, limiting the movement of millions of people, and rapid medical response. Will wonders never cease?

The CCP is working hard to scrub its own culpability and turn this crisis into an opportunity. Its leader, Xi Jinping, now acts as the charitable godfather, dishing out money, medical supplies, and equipment to convince the world they are not responsible for the global public health crisis and economic chaos.

The CCP is painting China as a success story and as a friend in a time of dire need. This was after the CCP spread disinformation about the virus, claiming that American soldiers brought the virus to Wuhan last October when they attended the Military World Games. There is no evidence to support this accusation. The CCP is engaged in a massive propaganda campaign to convince the world they are a model global citizen worthy of trust and respect.

As they say in the Wuhan wet market, famous for its bat soup, this doesn't smell right.

In the past few weeks, while the rest of the world was busy battling the pandemic, the CCP erected new military bases on reefs in the West Philippine Sea, which are claimed by the Philippines, according to *Esquire* magazine. In 2016 the Permanent Court of Arbitration, an intergovernmental organization located at The Hague in the Netherlands, ruled unanimously that the CCP's reclamation activities in the West Philippine Sea were illegal. The court recognized the Philippines' sovereign rights to the contested areas. China ignored the ruling, continues aggressive actions, and stands by its sweeping claim to almost the entire South China Sea.

The CCP plays by its own rules and does so with impunity. A March 20 report by China's Xinhua news website says the Chinese Academy of Sciences has successfully established two new "research facilities" on the Kagitingan Reef and the Zamora Reef. According to the Xinhua report, these "research facilities" are to study coral reef ecosystems, vegetation ecology, and freshwater conservation.

Of course, these reclaimed islands are equipped with military facilities, including missile systems, naval harbors, and runways to accommodate fighter jets and other aircraft. The CCP is hoping the world will overlook the military angle as it focuses on the global public health crisis.

While the short-term focus is the battle against the coronavirus, the international community should not ignore the existential threat presented by the CCP. This global crisis will last a long time but not forever. Democratic governments must fundamentally rethink their relationship with the CCP and stop treating them with kid gloves.

# The United States Should Rethink Its Relationship with the CCP

4/11/2020

America is in crisis. In the midst of a pandemic, society is locked down, the economy is stalled, and the death count mounts. As of March 30, three-quarters of Americans were living under stay-at-home mandates or advisories in the fight against the spread of the Chinese Communist Party (CCP) virus.

Americans are buying all the food and supplies they can find and downloading Zoom, everyone's new favorite hangout. One of the ironies of the moment is that staying home and doing nothing with freshly sanitized hands can actually save lives. Americans are told to work together to flatten the curve and to practice social distancing, altering the rhythms and texture of everyday life.

A sense of anxiety and fragility is everywhere.

The economic fallout has been swift and dramatic. The unemployment rate climbed to 4.4 percent in March from 3.5 percent in February, the largest one month increase since January 1975. The economy lost 701,000 jobs in March, but the numbers only begin to capture the beginning of a job market collapse. Weekly initial jobless claims reports reveal nearly ten million new unemployment insurance claims in just the last two weeks of March.

These numbers are a coming attraction for what is to come, thanks to our pals in the CCP and the business, political, and academic grandees who encouraged offshoring American jobs to China. The increased reliance on worldwide production and long supply chains has undermined America's national security.

This crowd traded American industrial strength and technology for access to China's huge market and cheap consumer goods. The price they were willing to pay was teaching China how to manufacture their products and sharing their cutting-edge intellectual property, which helped China join the superpower club. The CCP has been brilliant in exploiting the imprudent greed, myopia, and corporate vanity of Western business leaders who kowtow before the CCP regime.

It is not certain whether Vladimir Ilyich Ulyanov, better known as Lenin, actually said, "The capitalists will sell us the rope with which we will hang them." But if he didn't, he certainly thought it, and if he were still around, he would likely claim the prophecy as his own. The ruling class in Washington, Wall Street, and the academy sent the CCP the money to buy the rope.

At a time when the United States should be reconsidering its relationship with the CCP, America continues to help it. A recent example of embracing the globalist agenda is that the Federal Retirement Thrift Investment Board is considering allocating retirement assets to an index fund that includes shady Chinese companies.

The board oversees the nearly $600 billion Thrift Savings Plan, a retirement savings plan similar to a 401(k), for 5.6 million federal employees and members of the military. The index fund includes companies involved in the Chinese government's military activities and companies being sanctioned by the US government. To cite one specific example, the index includes China's state-owned Aviation Industry Corporation. This firm is the sole supplier of military aircraft to the Chinese People's Liberation Army. Federal employee money is being used to support an adversary, undermining the country's national security and fueling China's economic growth.

A group of lawmakers introduced bipartisan, bicameral legislation to ban the investment of Thrift Savings Plan funds in securities listed on mainland China exchanges. Pushing back, the board's general counsel said that the 1986 legislation that created the plan shows the accounts are private, not federal property.

"The employees owns it and it cannot be tampered with by any entity including Congress," the general counsel went on to say, neglecting to mention the fund consists of taxpayer money, not private capital.

This decision is another egregious example of an organization facing no consequences for refusing to act in the best interests of the United States and never having to say you are sorry. It's bad for the United States and good for a strategic foreign adversary.

## China Is a Global Threat to Human Rights
4/15/2020

The outbreak of the Chinese Communist Party (CCP) virus has accelerated the need for the United States and others to reset the relationship with this autocratic crowd that rules by repression rather than consent. For too long America and others have become economically dependent on the CCP's totalitarian regime. Governments, corporations, and even academic institutions that are ostensibly committed to human rights have been all too happy to do business with the CCP.

China is a global threat to human rights. Consider its terrible repression and systematic abuse of the Uighur Muslims, Christians, Falun Gong, Tibetan Buddhists, and the protesters in Hong Kong. The CCP has carried out arbitrary detention and torture and imposed pervasive controls on daily life.

The CCP has constructed an Orwellian high-tech surveillance state to monitor and suppress criticism and free speech over China. It engages in these practices with total disregard of the world's view of these abuses and uses its economic clout to silence critics. Economic clout translates into political influence.

Indeed the CCP's campaign to aggressively silence criticism extends beyond its borders. Last year the party responded to a simple tweet by the general manager of the Houston Rockets supporting the Hong Kong protesters by demanding he be fired and by canceling broadcasts of NBA games. After a series of obsequious apologies, the NBA stood firm.

Also last year the CCP demanded that foreign airlines remove references to Taiwan from their websites because it regards Taiwan as a renegade province. The four American airlines affected by the order—American, Delta, Hawaiian, and United—complied with the order. Clearly, they were ignorant of Churchill's definition of appeasement: "An appeaser is one who feeds a crocodile, hoping it will eat him last."

In 2017 the CCP pressured the Cambridge University Press to remove more than three hundred articles from its *China Quarterly* journal. The censored articles covered topics the CCP considered incriminating, such as the Tiananmen Square massacre, a subject that remains taboo in China.

In April and May 1989, thousands of students and civilians protested in Tiananmen Square in the heart of Beijing, calling for a more democratic government. The CCP prohibited foreign newscasts of the protests.

On June 3 and 4, Chinese troops entered the square and fired on the protestors, ending the demonstrations. Estimates of the death toll range from several hundred to thousands. It has been estimated that ten thousand people were arrested during and after the protests. If the protestors had hoped the United States and other countries that had rhetorically championed the universal human right to freedom would support them, they were sorely disappointed.

Though Pres. George H. W. Bush initially criticized the crackdown and announced some sanctions, nothing else happened. The Bush administration believed that as the West opened up to China and the country became more prosperous, it would also become more democratic. Is anyone surprised that they were wrong?

The authoritarian regime of the CCP is not a friend. The global pandemic could have been stopped at its source. Instead the CCP suppressed the truth, destroyed evidence, and lied to the world.

It's not surprising that the CCP lied to the world. If it is willing to lie to its own citizens about how many died from the virus, why would anyone assume that it would tell the world the truth? If they don't treat their own people with respect, why would anyone believe they would treat others differently? Put another way, if the CCP has its way, it is not just China's 1.4 billion people who won't get justice; it will be the whole world.

It is an open question whether the international community and the United States will make common cause and robustly respond to the CCP's role in unleashing the coronavirus. But given the CCP's dishonesty and duplicity, now is the time to recall President Reagan's famous formula when dealing with the Soviet Union: "Trust but verify."

## Lessons from the Coronavirus
4/23/2020

The United States is in the thick of the Chinese Communist Party (CCP) virus crisis. It leads the world in the number of deaths, with reported cases in all fifty states, assuming you believe the numbers coming out of the CCP. Nearly twenty-six million Americans have filed for unemployment benefits, which means millions of people have lost their employer-provided health insurance.

Working-class Americans feel like they are living through Daniel Defoe's *A Journal of the Plague Year*. They are learning to live with uncertainty, constantly practicing hand hygiene and prioritizing needs from wants. The economy has come to a sudden stop, induced into a coma to deal with the public health crisis.

They are living through a disaster movie. It was business as usual until less than two months ago; now it's business as unusual with virus precautions engulfing nearly every aspect of American life. Their lives now depend on staying home and doing nothing. A lot of thought is put into doing nothing. Even comedy is becoming tiresome—there is nothing to joke about. They are cooped up with no end in sight. It's difficult not to be paranoid when the sky is falling and the walls of their daily existence are caving in on them and their families.

Of course, the wealthy are in a twist, grappling with the traumas of canceled golf games and visible roots. While health-care employees are working fourteen-hour days risking everything, Ellen DeGeneres is comparing living in her sprawling mansion with being stuck in jail.

Americans are searching for elected officials willing and able to work together and put aside their partisan bickering in the face of a national crisis. They want authority figures who do not engage in self-aggrandizement and can draw upon their experience to assuage the fears of an anxious country.

There is much Americans don't know, and much that they think they know is probably wrong, thanks to the CCP's dissembling. It's payback time for the globe's fatal attraction to the CCP and dependency on foreign sources of medical supplies. It may well be that the ordinary working American will be thankful that the peak of globalization will be behind them when the country emerges from this crisis.

A key question is why the country was so utterly unprepared for this crisis. Leave it to history and to a national commission to interrogate this question. But a book published by Barbara W. Tuchman in 1984, *The March of Folly: From Troy to Vietnam*, may be a good place to start to answer this question. Tuchman explains how smart people in power can do stupid things. The book illustrates how governments act against their own best interests, making policy mistakes and strategic blunders. A fundamental lesson is that humanity seems unable to learn the lessons of history. In other words why do countries keep shooting themselves in the foot?

As for history repeating itself, there was a 2019 Pandemic Flu exercise called "Crimson Contagion" run by the US Department of Health and Human Services from January to August 2019. The purpose of the exercise was to simulate the spread of a respiratory virus from China to the United States and killing nearly 586,000 Americans. The results of the exercise were defined by "confusion" and "bureaucratic chaos," with friction emerging between the state and federal governments on issues ranging from equipment shortages to guidelines for social distancing. Sound familiar?

There's more. Among the most tangible results of "Crimson Contagion" was an "inability to quickly replenish certain medical supplies, given that much of the product comes from overseas." The United States is paying a high price for being caught so flat-footed, and the government is now playing catch-up.

Best to recall the words attributed to Winston Churchill: "Americans can always be counted on to do the right thing after they have exhausted all other possibilities."

## What Went Wrong in China?
5/1/2020

The news today is totally dominated by talk of the coronavirus pandemic, with occasional relief provided by the weather report. Little effort is made to review how we got here or what to do about it.

For decades Western academics, policymakers, captains of industry, and politicians assumed that China's embrace of capitalist economic policies would set the stage for democratic reform. George Orwell was right when he said, "Some ideas are so stupid that only intellectuals believe them, for no ordinary man could be such a fool."

Put in simple terms, the theory was that economic freedom would cause the Chinese people to begin to demand political freedom, resulting in a democracy. That has not happened in China, where the Chinese Communist Party (CCP) remains firmly in power.

China has been ruled by the CCP since 1949. The regime doesn't tolerate political competitors. It is authoritarian, an all-or-nothing proposition. Its goal is to control all aspects of public and private life. It controls the army, the courts, the police, the media, and the economy.

The Chinese people are merely the state's subjects. Just consider the CCP's version of Soviet gulags, called reeducation centers, where up to a million Muslims have been incarcerated. Student-led prodemocracy demonstrations in Hong Kong show that millions of Chinese people want to be free of the party's yoke.

Calling out the CCP and its role in the COVID-19 pandemic is not racist. It began in China and could have been stopped at its source. But the CCP lied about this deadly virus, which cost the rest of the world many weeks of preparation, countless lives, and forced shutdowns of the American and other world economies.

No year in recent history has brought such devastation. As of April 26, there are over 202,000 deaths around the world and over 55,000 in the United States from COVID-19, according to numbers compiled by the Johns Hopkins University. People worldwide are struggling to get comfortable with the uncomfortable realities of a new normal.

The United States and other countries face a Sophie's choice: They cannot directly attack the CCP over the pandemic and its role in triggering an unparalleled global economic and public health crisis or hold it accountable for the COVID-19 outbreak when the world depends on the CCP for medical supplies and protective equipment. Name-calling and demands for reparations come out of Washington, but the harsh reality is that payback is not in the cards. The CCP's list of transgressions may be long and shameful, but the United States is dependent on them for lifesaving exports.

The economic downturn is a completely artificial event, and any economic rebound will depend on when the public health containment policy ends and a safe and scalable vaccine is developed. The longer pandemic containment lasts, the more parts of the economy deteriorate. Truth is, the economic pain will continue into the foreseeable future.

Congress and the White House may put together another economic relief package that they will characterize as a stimulus package similar to the CARES legislation. This is a misnomer, for much of the $2.2 trillion CARES Act simply made up for lost wages; it won't generate additional spending. Politicians in Washington will be out campaigning this summer rather than engaging in serious discussions about how to decouple essential supplies coming from China.

A modest start would be to slap "buy American" provisions on government agencies and provide tax incentives for American companies to bring back their supply chain to the United States or American allies. Notions about introducing legislation to allow Americans to sue China in domestic courts to "recover damages for death, injury, and economic harm caused" by the CCP's reckless response to the COVID-19 outbreak will simply result in the party giving the middle finger to any adverse judgments, just as they do to other international institutions.

The CCP plays by its own rules.

## A Strategy for Dealing with China
5/9/2020

On February 22, 1946, George Kennan, US chief of mission in Moscow, sent the State Department a long telegram explaining the behavior of the Soviet Union and how best to deal with it. The gist of the telegram was that the Soviets, pressed by economic failure and bound by Marxist–Leninist ideology, found a perfect enemy in the United States and were uninterested in compromise.

This being the case, the best way for the United States to deal with the Soviet Union was to build up the still-free countries of Western Europe and do all it could to contain Soviet expansion. This policy became known as "containment," and its immediate result was the massive aid program to postwar Western Europe known as the Marshall Plan.

A year later in, writing under the byline "X" in *Foreign Affairs*, Kennan expanded on these views. He was a realist who believed international relations ought to be "guided strictly by consideration of national interest," not treaties and alliances. While often revised, Kennan's containment strategy would largely define US policy toward the Soviet Union until the end of the Cold War.

Now, more than seventy years later, the United States and its allies again face a communist rival that views the United States as an adversary, seeks global influence, and wants to supplant America as the world's dominant power. The challenge of the Chinese Communist Party (CCP) is generational and cuts across economic, military, political, and social spheres.

The United States is at war. Don't be deceived because soldiers of the People's Liberation Army, a branch of the CCP, aren't running down the street.

While America and the world are in the grip of the COVID-19 pandemic that originated in China, the CCP has launched a global disinformation campaign reminiscent of the Cold War, blaming others for the spread of the virus. Equally important it is moving at warp speed as the first major world economy to end lockdowns and start up its economy. The CCP is acting to shape the pandemic narrative and geopolitical shifts in the post–COVID-19 world.

Ever since President Nixon's opening to China in 1972, the United States has largely sought constructive engagement, which would supposedly help democratize China and integrate it into the American-led international economic order. As a "responsible stakeholder" in the international system, China would be highly motivated to maintain peaceful relations with other countries.

The integration strategy has not worked, nor has the bipartisan support for China's admission into the World Trade Organization. Recent events confirm that China is challenging the existing international order with impunity.

Look no further than its land reclamation efforts, claiming some 80 percent of the South China Sea as its sovereign territory, challenging Japan's administrative control of the Senkaku Islands, the "One Belt One Road" New Silk Road Eurasian integration plan, and more.

While the United States has wasted decades in its dealings with the CCP, it is still not too late, and George Kennan's notion of containment remains relevant. The United States strategy should be to preserve and deepen relationships with Asian countries fearful of China's power and aggressiveness.

China has few allies in the region. The United States should be working closely with India, Vietnam, Japan, the Philippines, Australia, Taiwan, and others to contain China and in the process advance America's economic, political, and security interests in the Asia Pacific region. Closely related, the United States should be forging relationships with developing nations across the globe to counter China's Belt and Road Initiative.

Today George Kennan's prescription that "the main element of any United States policy toward the Soviet Union must be that of a long-term, patient but firm and vigilant containment of Russian expansive tendencies" offers the best hope of containing China's ambitions. The challenge is that Americans seek instant gratification, while China plays the long game. One thing is certain: Everyone will be feeling their age before this contest is played out.

# Humility and Effective Leadership
5/19/2020

It has been a busy year for death in the United States. In the last two months, the coronavirus killed more Americans than were killed in the Vietnam War. The world has been disrupted, and the collateral damage is omnipresent. Catastrophic events such as COVID-19 are hard to predict. They expose weaknesses in society and reveal the consequences of earlier bad decisions, such as failing to diversify supply chains.

The pandemic has placed extraordinary demands on business and government leaders. Its scale and attendant uncertainty, unpredictability, and ambiguity make it challenging to navigate the crisis.

Crises also demonstrate that recovery is most likely under effective leaders who lead with humility, make tough decisions, tell the truth, and are able to identify and deploy resources with dispatch. Leadership matters, and character is foundational to good leadership. Character refers to the distinctive qualities of an individual, and as Aristotle said, character is revealed through action.

There are scores of books, articles, and studies about leadership. They often include a checklist of the characteristics that cumulatively constitute effective leadership, including vision, accountability, courage, drive, collaboration, integrity, and many more.

One quality that receives insufficient attention is humility. If leadership has a secret sauce, that may well be it, and humility seems to be in short supply today. Humility has nothing to do with being weak or indecisive. Put simply, a humble leader understands the things they don't know, so they listen. It improves their hearing and helps them get smart on issues.

Successful leaders rely on the opinions and decisions of other people in times of crisis, especially when the cause of the crisis is outside their area of expertise. Effective leaders project self-confidence and authenticity when they check their egos at the door and acknowledge their failures and weaknesses. They understand the world is just too complicated for them to have all the answers.

Leaders with a taste for humility routinely credit others, deflecting discussion about their own contribution. When results are poor, they blame themselves. They readily admit mistakes, acknowledge their weaknesses, and ask for feedback on their blind spots. They never let ego get in the way of getting the job done.

Humility and ambition are not always at odds. Consider, for example, the case of Abraham Lincoln, who never let ego get in the way of his ambition to create an enduring union.

In contrast consider leaders who don't want people who say no. They are suspicious of any plan that doesn't originate with them. You can argue with them, but you must be careful how and when. You are better to give way on every possible point until the vital point, to position yourself as in need of guidance rather than appearing to believe that you know better than they do. Remember, these types of leaders want more than to be advised of their power; they want to be told they are always right. Other people commit errors or deceive them with false information. They are insecure in their insecurities.

These self-absorbed leaders who tell the truth less than half the time can't be trusted to keep their promises, often pass off blame to others, and are especially bad at understanding and caring for people; they lack empathy. Leaders who do not have the humility to recognize their own errors and omissions will not make necessary course corrections to ensure success. Such leaders don't catch the joke that if you think you are the smartest person in the room, you are in the wrong room and the only one who is incapable of learning.

Humility is a mindset for leaders who want to do big things in a world filled with uncertainty and ambiguity. These leaders motivate and empower those around them and listen well. As C. S. Lewis said, "Humility is not thinking less of yourself, it's thinking of yourself less."

## The Death of Hong Kong?
5/27/2020

Hong Kong's reputation as an international business city may be finished. The Chinese Communist Party (CCP) is fixing to impose a sweeping national security law that bypasses Hong Kong's own legislative process. The law would erode the city's high degree of autonomy guaranteed under the "one country, two systems" formula.

The law would ban secession, foreign interference, terrorism, and all seditious activities aimed at toppling the central government. Additionally it is designed to "prevent, stop and punish" activities that endanger China's national security. It also reveals plans to establish new national security agencies for the first time in Hong Kong. In sum Hong Kong loses the rule of law, and it is replaced by rule by law, with the courts, police, and prosecutors controlled by the CCP.

The smart money knew this legislation was coming. To deal with last year's protests in Hong Kong, Pres. Xi Jinping, the most authoritarian Chinese leader since Mao Zedong, has to show he is boss by reasserting dominance over a piece of Chinese territory.

The CCP doesn't play softball. While the international community is facing down the COVID-19 pandemic, dealing with its economic fallout, litigating the past, and reminiscing about the future, they made their move with all the finesse of German brown shirts in the 1930s. The CCP gives less than a tinker's damn what other countries think.

This is the latest in a series of aggressive foreign policy moves by the CCP since the outbreak of the COVID-19 pandemic, including upping its presence in contested areas of the South China Sea. The CCP is intent on China becoming the regional hegemon in Asia, just as United States has been in the Western Hemisphere since the late nineteenth century.

The CCP is going to do what it wants in Hong Kong without fear of the consequences. Quite apart from reigniting the prodemocracy movement, they know full well that no one in the international community is going to war over Hong Kong. Political figures around the world have decried the new national security law for Hong Kong. They argue that the new law is a "flagrant breach" of the Sino-British Joint Declaration, which returned Hong Kong to China in 1997 with the understanding that Hong Kong residents would enjoy basic freedoms until 2047.

Under the agreement Hong Kong was to be governed under the "one country, two systems" principle, which was meant to guarantee a high degree of autonomy for Hong Kong for fifty years. But the international community will not stand up to China or boycott Chinese goods. With the exception of the United States, the reaction will continue to be all rhetoric and no action. It is wishful thinking to expect Saint George to come to the rescue and slay the dragon in the guise of the CCP.

Legislation has been introduced in the United States Senate that would sanction CCP officials enforcing the national security laws in Hong Kong. It would also penalize banks that do business with any entity enforcing the law. Secretary of State Mike Pompeo has threatened to revoke certain economic and trade privileges Hong Kong enjoys with the United States that do not extend to China as a whole. Such an action might result in the city losing its status as a major hub for global finance.

For the other Asian countries, this move is the canary in the coal mine. They will have to fall in line and recognize China as the dominant power in the region while the rest of the international community is kept off-balance about their next move. For certain, Taiwan is in the CCP's line of sight.

The passage of the National Security Law will be a game changer. With the passage of this law, Hong Kong will become just another Chinese city. Undercutting Hong Kong's political autonomy and civil liberties will undermine the city's attractiveness as an international business and economic center.

## President's Proposal for a Payroll Tax Holiday
6/6/2020

President Trump has proposed to eliminate payroll taxes that fund Social Security and Medicare through the end of the year to provide the economy with a shot of adrenaline. The idea is to put after-tax take-home pay in the hands of people who are likely to spend it right away to help staunch the economic pain caused by the COVID-19 pandemic, but in practice it wouldn't make much sense.

Payroll taxes include the Social Security tax, which is 12.4 percent of earned income up to a maximum of $137,700 for 2020.

Employers and employees each pay half. The Medicare tax, also evenly split between employers and employees, is 2.9 percent of earned income with no maximum. Married couples filing jointly who make $250,000 or more and individuals who make over $200,000 pay an additional 0.9 percent.

The payroll tax cut idea is not new. In 2011 and 2012, the Congress and President Obama reduced the employee share of the tax from 6.2 percent to 4.2 percent and filled the resulting gap in the Social Security Trust Fund with general revenues.

While Trump has fixed his sights on getting the payroll tax holiday into the next coronavirus stimulus bill, it is unclear whether he can get Republicans, much less Democrats, to go along with such a proposal. Democrats argue instead for expanded unemployment insurance and aid to state and local governments.

Congressional Republicans have also been slow to endorse the payroll tax rollback, claiming it is too early to argue what should go into the next stimulus bill. They are also concerned with adding to a budget deficit that is forecast to balloon to $3.7 trillion this fiscal year.

Cutting payroll taxes does not make sense because it would do little for the more than forty million Americans who have applied for unemployment in the last three months, especially lower-income people in industries such as tourism and hospitality. If you don't have a job, a payroll tax cut does you no good at all. Even among those who are working, such a tax cut would be highly regressive. High-income people would get far more than low-wage workers.

Cutting payroll taxes would not help business cash flow since the CARES Act already allows many firms to defer paying payroll taxes until 2021 and 2022. Many economists say a payroll tax holiday alone isn't enough to bolster consumer spending, a prime driver of the economy, and spur companies to begin hiring.

Supporters of Social Security and Medicare also oppose the president's proposal. They claim any payroll tax cuts that reduce revenue flowing into the trust funds would threaten Social Security's ability to continue paying benefits to sixty-four million Americans who depend on them for their economic survival. Seniors directly affected by taking their money from the trust fund will not see a dime of relief since most of them are not working.

There are alternatives to the payroll tax cut that would provide more direct economic stimulus. One way to keep workers on payrolls and help businesses stay afloat would to be expand the existing employee retention tax credit that was part of the CARES Act. This provision provides eligible employers a tax credit against employment taxes equal to half of qualified wages. There is bipartisan support to increase the credit from 50 percent to 80 percent of wages and benefits. It would be raised to cover $45,000 of wages and benefits instead of the $10,000 currently offered.

Other proposals that merit consideration include an infrastructure package, a tax credit to incentivize domestic manufacturing, and another round of stimulus checks to directly address the pandemic-induced economic downturn.

Hopefully the parties will overcome their ideological differences and compromise on additional injections of public resources. The downside is that acting in a fiscally responsible way may significantly affect each party's presidential candidate. Now is not the time to prioritize election prospects over staring down a depression.

# The Battle of Anacostia Flats
6/12/2020

History is a foreign country to many students and to far too many Americans as well. The call for using the military to quell protests in Washington, DC, is not without historical parallel. The story of the bonus march on Washington has been ignored or forgotten by contemporary pundits.

In 1924 Congress rewarded veterans of the First World War with bonuses of a bit more than $1,000 per soldier, but they were not scheduled for full payment until 1945.

Unemployed veterans petitioned for immediate payment to alleviate the economic hardships of former servicemen who had lost their jobs in the early days of the Great Depression. In 1930, over President Hoover's veto, the Democratic Congress voted to pay the veterans a little more than half of the amount promised. More than twenty thousand veterans of the World War Expeditionary Force with their wives and children from all over the country descended on Washington in the spring and summer of 1932 and promised to stay until Congress approved legislation to pay the balance of the bonuses.

By June the veterans who styled themselves as the Bonus Expeditionary Force were camping in shacks and tents across the river from the capital and occupying vacant buildings in the city. In mid-June the House of Representatives passed a bill that authorized the immediate payout of the bonus, but the Senate rejected the bill. President Hoover, concerned about balancing the budget, continued to oppose the veterans' request. Most of the veterans returned home, but an estimated two to ten thousand had nowhere to go and remained with their families to engage in protests.

Many in the Hoover administration saw the bonus marchers as a threat to national security. In mid-July President Hoover ordered the police to clear the bonus marchers out of several abandoned federal buildings that they were occupying.

When the evictions began, several marchers threw rocks at the police, who then opened fire. Two veterans were killed, and an ugly riot followed. The local authorities appealed to President Hoover for help. The violence provided him with the excuse he had been seeking to use force, and he ordered the United States Army to help police clear out the buildings.

Late in the afternoon of July 28, Gen. Douglas MacArthur, the army chief of staff, undertook the assignment with the assistance of his aide, Dwight D. Eisenhower. He led the Third Cavalry under the command of George S. Patton, along with two infantry regiments with fixed bayonets, a machine-gun detachment, and six tanks, which, for the first time in American history, drove down Pennsylvania Avenue in pursuit of the marchers. The troops used tear gas to drive the veterans out of the buildings and then through the crowded streets of the capital.

As the marchers retreated, General MacArthur exceeded his orders, just as he would do in Korea two decades later, to secure the building and contain the marchers at their camp. He pursued them to their Shantytown across the Anacostia River and ordered his troops to burn the tent city where the former servicemen and their families camped. Reportedly, 55 veterans were injured and 135 arrested.

When General MacArthur met with the press later, he said, "That mob down there was a bad-looking mob. It was animated by the essence of revolution." He sought to justify his actions by arguing that the bonus marchers were attempting to overthrow the government.

The Battle of Anacostia Flats outraged many Americans and marked the low point of President Hoover's tenure. The bonus march contributed to his defeat to Franklin Roosevelt three months later and was a catalyst for social change.

In 1936 Congress finally passed, over President Roosevelt's veto, a bill to disburse about $2 billion in bonuses. The march laid the foundation for the G. I. Bill of Rights in 1944, which provided Second World War veterans with funds for college, housing, and other benefits.

## Strategy and the COVID-19 Pandemic
6/20/2020

Residents and workers at US nursing homes and long-term care facilities have accounted for a staggering proportion of COVID-19 deaths. The prognosis is particularly poor for elderly individuals who contract the virus. Around 80 percent of US COVID-19 deaths have been among people sixty-five and older, according to the Centers for Disease Control and Prevention. These numbers highlight the failure of government officials to think strategically.

The disease is particularly lethal to older adults with underlying health conditions and can spread easily through facilities where many people live in a confined environment and workers move from room to room. Because of residents' proximity, these places are like petri dishes for the coronavirus. At least fifty thousand residents and workers have died from the virus at US nursing homes and other long-term care facilities for older adults.

This figure may be understated because states differ in how they report deaths of residents in long-term care facilities. For example, some do not include incidents of a resident dying in a hospital.

The lack of a national strategy to ramp up COVID-19 testing in congregate care facilities and to provide protective equipment to staff made it easier for the virus to spread in these densely populated settings. State decisions to transfer recently recovered COVID-19 patients back into long-term care facilities also increased the risk to this population. New York State, for example, mandated that nursing home facilities admit actively ill COVID-19 patients.

Despite early warnings based on fatality rates in China and Italy that people over sixty-five were the most vulnerable to the novel coronavirus, the national and various state strategies for dealing with the pandemic had major shortcomings.

Successful businesspeople understand that strategy is about making choices, such as who is the target customer they wish to serve. Additionally they understand that a firm's resources represent the critical building blocks of a successful strategy. They determine not what an enterprise wants to do but what it can do.

Equally important they recognize that resources are finite. Resources don't spring full blown out of Zeus's forehead. Put simply, a key responsibility of leadership is to identify, build, and deploy resources in pursuit of business goals to provide value to the target customer and adjust as market conditions change.

Brand-obsessed leaders at every level of government have to be honest about clearly defining at-risk populations and allocating scarce resources to protect those people. In the case of COVID-19, that means the elderly and those with underlying conditions. For example, knowing that nursing home and long-term care residents and workers are most at risk, a targeted strategy would have allocated finite resources such as testing, protective equipment, and other medical supplies to this vulnerable population.

Strategy is about making hard choices with imperfect information. Anyone running a successful enterprise understands that trade-offs matter. Leaders have to make choices about what they will do and what they will not do based on facts and the reality of limited resources. This requires them to choose carefully among available resources and sensibly allocate them to the problem at hand.

Another challenge when it comes to developing a successful strategy in a competitive environment is not to confuse means with ends. You can't have everything at once, so your goals should be realistic and feasible, not pipe dreams. Words to live by.

You would be right to conclude that US political leaders could have done a better job of protecting seniors, who are most vulnerable to the coronavirus. They were left exposed by the failure to develop an intelligent strategy. Americans can only hope those leaders have developed a realistic strategy to protect seniors if a second wave of the virus comes in the fall. It's better to go too far than not far enough when it comes to protecting the most vulnerable in society.

## The Economy and COVID-19: Part 2
7/4/2020

Americans are struggling to adjust to a pandemic whose future progression is uncertain. They have not seen an economic downturn of quite such scale or scope, and people are unsure about how the United States can pull out of the crisis.

Righting the economic ship will require a delicate balance of managing debt and encouraging growth. A large infrastructure investment program that includes private contributions is a feasible way to achieve that goal.

Governments are struggling to prop up economies while confronting the serious and immediate public health challenges of COVID-19, resulting in unprecedented emergency spending and huge budget deficits throughout the world. In the United States, Congress has passed huge spending bills to help businesses and households that have swollen the national debt by about $2.4 trillion. The Congressional Budget Office numbers for its Doctor Doom scenario recently projected a budget deficit of more than $3.7 trillion for the current fiscal year.

Outstanding national debt now exceeds $25 trillion. Additional outlays in response to a second wave of COVID-19 outbreaks could further increase the debt and add to sovereign risk. Even in a low-interest-rate environment, higher debt service costs will crowd out other government spending. Trying to explain to the average politician that debt is a drag on future growth is a waste of time. Spending today and making a suitcase of promises is what helps them get reelected tomorrow. The future is someone else's concern.

The Federal Reserve Bank has taken emergency measures to make credit easier to obtain with a bigger money supply and lower interest rates. Additionally the Fed is lending more than $2 trillion to businesses and state and local governments. There is concern that the Fed's actions risk future price inflation, which would decrease the purchasing power of the dollar. The era of the dollar as the world's primary reserve currency may also come to an end. In that case the United States would no longer benefit from the typical safe-haven demand from foreign investors as the value of the dollar collapses.

Policymakers note that these concerns must take a back seat to addressing the immediate crisis. The present commands their attention, but they may insufficiently appreciate that the future may be more of the present.

The United States will have to manage the debt, deficits, and debt service payments, as well as find ways to support economic recovery to grow its way out of all this debt. While fiscal consolidation—raising taxes, cutting spending, or both—is the tried-and-true method for tackling debt challenges, it is likely to encounter some major tactical problems.

Raising taxes is politically difficult given the perception among many in Congress that voting for tax increases is tantamount to announcing your retirement from elective politics. Similarly, cutting high-dollar payment programs such as Social Security and Medicare is bound to be strongly opposed by legions of elderly voters.

Another approach is to focus and allocate resources to areas that create the most jobs. The time is long overdue for a bipartisan infrastructure investment package that rebuilds America's crumbling roads and bridges, invests in future industries, and promotes increased productivity while immediately employing people whose income would give the American economy a shot in the arm. There is a broad consensus among mainstream economists that infrastructure investment has a large multiplier effect through the economy.

The problem is where the actual dollars can come from to fund such an ambitious program. One solution is to recruit private firms to help start, fund, and run as many of these infrastructure projects as possible. If properly structured, such public-private partnerships could tap into the billions of dollars in private capital hungering for low-risk investment opportunities able to offer decent rates of return.

COVID-19 has introduced a host of new economic challenges. A robust infrastructure program that includes private participation would be an effective way to begin to address them.

## The Threat of Stagflation
7/18/2020

Turn on the TV, radio, social media, news sites, and podcasts and the COVID-19 virus story is topic number one through one hundred, with only the weather report offering relief. The pandemic has both disrupted and ended people's lives.

The federal government is facing the momentous task of reversing the effects of the resulting recession with a combination of expansionary fiscal and monetary policy. On the fiscal side, rescue spending, financed with gobs of new debt, prevented further deterioration of the economy. On the monetary side, the Federal Reserve has pursued both traditional and unconventional policies.

The public debt of the United States has risen quickly over the last several months. From February 20, 2020, through June 20, 2020, the government's total public debt has increased by about $3.068 trillion, from $23,409 trillion to $26,477 trillion. While the federal government has gone on a borrowing binge and approved huge relief spending, the Federal Reserve is creating huge amounts of dollars that end up paying for the debt.

Lurking behind the easing of monetary policy is the fear that too much money chasing too few goods will lead to inflation, thereby decreasing the purchasing power of the dollar. Once the crisis is over, there is the prospect of prices and inflation accelerating simultaneously, or what people of a certain age will remember as stagflation.

In other words one potential economic consequence of deficit-financed public spending and the Federal Reserve's emergency lending programs and interest rate cuts is the threat of inflation in a post–COVID-19 economy. Among other things, inflation eats away at the purchasing power of people's paychecks.

It also disrupts people's behavior, causing demand-pull inflation. Suppose a rise in prices sets off rumors that prices will increase still more. This is common during inflationary times, when the increasing prices of goods lead people to expect that prices will be even higher tomorrow. People rush in, causing prices to go higher still. People buy more of a product when inflation is rampant, anticipating that the price will only rise more.

Meanwhile firms selling the products see prices go up and decide not to take advantage of good times by increasing their offerings; instead they hold back, waiting for tomorrow. Thus demand goes up, and supply goes down.

At its worst the entire economy goes out of control, as happened in the 1970s. After several decades of unprecedented growth, signs of a slowdown emerged amid events such as sudden oil price spikes in 1973 and 1979, and increased global competition precipitated important economic changes. In the hope of inflating the economy out of unemployment, the government printed tons of money.

The economy was stuck between a rock and a hard place. Economists called the twin phenomenon of stagnating growth and double-digit inflation "stagflation." In 1979 Pres. Jimmy Carter appointed Paul Volcker to chair the Federal Reserve Board. He pursued tight monetary policies, pushing interest rates over 20 percent, with the desired consequence of a steep and prolonged business recession breaking the back of runaway inflation. By 1986 inflation almost disappeared entirely.

The legendary philosopher-king of baseball, Yogi Berra, allegedly once said, "It's tough to make predictions, especially about the future." Still, many financial mavens are fretting and speculating about the danger of price inflation resulting from money being printed at a frenetic pace in the United States. They fear that the country may be entering an era of double-digit inflation similar to the 1970s and that stagflation may return to the daily lexicon.

As John Maynard Keynes wrote, "Lenin is said to have declared that the best way to destroy the capitalist system was to debauch the currency. By a continuing process of inflation, governments can confiscate, secretly and unobserved, an important part of the wealth of their citizens."

Americans can only hope that Lenin was wrong or misquoted, and they will not experience the return of stagflation. Time will tell if the inflation mongers are right.

## Models Aren't Crystal Balls
8/1/2020

Every day, while folks are stuck at home, politicians, public health officials, and slick talking heads point to charts showing the latest statistics on the coronavirus pandemic as they attempt to predict what might happen next in your neck of the woods. Underlying these graphics are various forecasting models, which you should approach with a healthy dose of skepticism.

It is tempting to view the models as oracles that will help predict how the disease will spread, tell you what to do, and when to do it. But these models are simplified versions of realty. Reality is reality. Models should be read with the greatest care.

They are not a substitute for controlled scientific experiments that generate relevant data.

Models certainly provide information that can create a framework for understanding a situation. But models, including those used to predict COVID-19's trajectory, aren't crystal balls. A model is simply a tool. It consists of raw data, along with assumptions based on our best guesses at the time, which together shape an overall forecast.

A model is only as good as its underlying data, which is in short supply. For example, there is still plenty of uncertainty about how many COVID-19 deaths may occur over the next six months under various social-distancing and mask-wearing scenarios. Also, a model's accuracy is constrained by uncertainty about how many people are or have been infected.

Assumptions aren't facts. Put another way, models are constrained by what is known and what is assumed. Understanding these underlying assumptions helps explain why some forecasts have a sunny disposition, while others can't be pessimistic enough.

There are also economic models. Financial mavens develop them to take stock of how the pandemic has affected the economy and where they see it and markets heading. With so many countries experiencing sharp declines in gross domestic product, there is a lot of forecasting about what shape the recovery will take. Will there be a quick V-shaped recovery, or will it be U-shaped? Or maybe a little bit of both?

These models also have their limitations. Recall how Long-Term Capital Management, an industry-leading hedge fund run by a renowned team of mathematical experts that included two Nobel Prize winners, developed complex quantitative models to analyze markets and placed huge bets on the assumption, among others, that Russia would never default on its bonds. They did a lousy job of stress testing their assumptions, and they bet wrong. In September 1998 the firm had to be bailed out by a consortium of Wall Street banks to prevent the bottom dropping out of the financial system.

This episode was a coming attraction for the harrowing financial crisis a decade later in September 2008, which was perhaps the biggest event of the twenty-first century until COVID-19. Before the 2008 crisis, a key assumption in many models was that housing prices would always go up. Indeed one cause of the meltdown was the quant movement: the proliferation of quantitative models for designing and analyzing financial products and for risk management. Many finance professionals mistakenly believed that quantitative tools had allowed them to conquer risk. Products such as derivatives, subprime mortgage-backed securities, and activities that relied heavily on quantitative models were at the heart of how financial firms expanded their activities to take more and greater risks.

And of course, with the presidential election just months away, Americans still remember how 2016 election models forecast Hilary Clinton waltzing into the White House. Between now and November 3, many people will take election forecasts with an extra grain of salt or three.

Given the events of the last several months, people should keep a simple fact in mind: Models should not be asked to carry any more than they can bear. So when you hear about models, put on your hmmm face.

# Closing the Carried Interest Tax Preference
8/15/2020

Those who can often be found at the very top of the earnings scale—people who manage private investment funds such as hedge funds or private equity and venture funds—enjoy a tax loophole that allows the money they make by investing money for others (their "carried interest") to be taxed as capital gains rather than earned income, even though they earn the money from work, not as a return on investing their own money.

In plain terms they reap a benefit, even though they don't put their own capital at risk. It's a loophole that allows the rich to get richer, and its demise is long overdue. That is why some of the wealthiest Americans pay lower tax rates than their secretaries. Proponents argue that taxing those who run these funds at the same rate that everyone else pays on their earned income would drive away trillions of investment dollars.

These are the same folks, the one-percenters, who can enjoy indulging in any of the forty items on the Forbes Cost of Living Extremely Well Index (CLEWI). The list, which should not be shared with progressive friends, includes such items as a Learjet, forty-five minutes with a shrink on the Upper East Side of Manhattan, Russian sable fur coats, a Har-Tru crushed-stone tennis court, and more. Forbes says the CLEWI is to the very rich what the CPI is to "ordinary people."

The term "carried interest" goes back to medieval merchants in Genoa, Pisa, Florence, and Venice. These traders carried cargo on their ships belonging to other people and earned 20 percent of the ultimate profits on the "carried product."

Today those who manage investments in private equity funds are typically compensated in two ways: with a 2 percent fee on funds under management and a 20 percent cut of the gains they produce for investors. The 20 percent in profits these managers pocket, known as carried interest, is currently treated as a long-term capital gain and taxed at 23.8 percent—the capital gains rate of 20 percent plus the Obamacare surcharge of 3.8 percent on their income. The 2 percent management fee is taxed at the higher ordinary income tax rate.

Presumptive Democratic presidential nominee Joe Biden has put forward an economic policy platform under which he would repeal many of the tax cuts that went into effect on January 1, 2018. The proposals include increasing the federal corporate tax rate from 21 percent to 28 percent and restoring the top individual tax rate to 39.6 percent for taxable incomes above $400,000, up from the current 37 percent. They also include taxing capital gains as ordinary income for individuals and couples with over $1 million in annual income and increasing the Social Security earnings cap by applying the payroll tax of 12.4 percent to earnings above $400,000.

While these sweeping tax proposals do not specifically address carried interest, it might be reasonably inferred that carried interest would be taxed as ordinary income rates. In the past Biden has said he'd like to eliminate the carried interest giveaway. Both Presidents Obama and Trump campaigned on closing the carried interest dodge, yet it's still there. Their proposals to abolish the carried interest preference were met with pregnant and deadening silence in Congress.

Eliminating the carried interest provision that allows fund managers to get away with bargain basement tax rates should be low-hanging fruit given the inequality of wealth and income in the United States. Yet despite its unpopularity, this is the tax break that just won't die. Well-connected lobbyists and trade groups for private equity, hedge funds, and others have mobilized their resources and fought successfully to keep carried interest as is. The nine lives of carried interest are more evidence, if any more evidence is needed, that big money gets its way in Congress. Here's hoping that the conceit of closing the carried interest loophole will gain traction, but for sure it's a long shot.

## Executive Compensation and Economic Inequality
8/29/2020

Oceans of ink have been consumed writing about the subject of widening economic inequality, declining social mobility, and a shrinking middle class in the United States over the last forty years. More recently the subject has emerged as a social and political flash point.

The most commonly cited reasons for this phenomenon are globalization and technology adoption. Improvements in technology, such as more powerful computers and industrial robots, increase the incentive to substitute capital for labor. Increased trade competition from imports made in low-cost countries and the threat of exporting jobs to those countries put pressure on wages and employment. Others point to excessive monopoly power, market consolidation, and the hollowing out of labor unions.

For the ordinary working-class American, there is plenty to be mad about. While wage growth has remained relatively stagnant for decades, an Economic Policy Institute study reports that extravagant chief executive officer (CEO) pay is a major contributor to rising inequality, contributing to the growth of top 1 percent and top 0.1 percent incomes.

The report found that the CEOs of the top 350 US companies by sales raked in an average of $21.3 million last year, an increase from about $18.7 million in 2018. This means that the average CEO made 320 times as much as the average worker earns in wages and benefits. CEO pay went crazy in the 1990s. In 1976 it was 36 times what an average worker earned, 61 times in 1989, and 131 times in 1993.

The authors of the report argue that this "growing earning power at the top has been driving the growth of inequality in our country." The report attributes the increase to the rapid growth in vested stock awards and exercised stock options tied to stock market growth. Stock-based compensation accounted for about three-fourths of the median CEO's compensation.

The rise of executive compensation practices linked to stock prices has been the mantra of America, Inc. over the past several decades. In 1982 the Securities and Exchange Commission adopted Rule 10b-18, allowing companies to buy back their own stock without being charged with stock manipulation. Starting in the 1990s, many companies introduced stock option grants as a major component of executive compensation. The idea was to better align management interests with those of shareholders. A small circle of highly influential pay consultants, academics, and activist shareholders argued that American firms must pay top dollar for top candidates because they compete in a global market for talent.

While beneficial in some ways, this new form of compensation also created problems quite apart from resentment and lower morale among rank-and-file workers. For example, the incentive for executives to manage earnings through any means, fair or foul, and focus on the short-term earnings game become strong. Making matters worse, a favorite corporate America trick is to use stock buybacks to manipulate their companies' stock prices. By increasing demand for a company's shares, open-market buybacks lift the stock price and help the company hit quarterly earnings targets. It makes sense. Stock buybacks enrich investors, including company executives who receive most of their compensation in company stock.

There are many ideas to solve the policy of extravagant executive compensation, ranging from higher marginal income tax rates for those at the top to banning stock buybacks to allowing greater use of "say on pay," which allows a firm's shareholders to express dissatisfaction with excessive pay.

While ideas have influence, they are rarely implemented just because of their singular force. Instead there has to be a confluence between the ideas themselves, the zeitgeist of the times, and the interests of "the great and the good" who find the ideas congenial. The pandemic may serve as a wake-up call for boards of directors and institutional investors to circumcise executive pay.

## Financialization of the Economy
9/12/2020

Financialization refers to the increase in size and importance of the financial sector relative to the overall US economy. Simply put, it is the wonky term used to describe the growing scale, profitability, and influence of the financial sector over the rest of the economy. Combine it with deregulation, less antitrust enforcement, and easy monetary policy from the 1980s onward and you get financial institutions that were too big and too speculative in the years leading up to the financial crisis in 2008.

Today Wall Street buccaneers don't just exert great influence over the economy; they are also a major influence in politics and government policy. The financial industry spends millions annually in Washington promoting the Panglossian view that the financial markets promote economic growth and contribute to economic well-being. It would be more accurate to say they contribute to economic inequality and the decline of US manufacturing.

According to data from the Center for Responsive Politics, seven banks spent over $13 million on campaign contributions in the 2018 election cycle and over $38 million on lobbying during the 2017–2018 Congress. Not surprisingly the top five campaign donors were Bank of America, Goldman Sachs, Morgan Stanley, JPMorgan Chase, and Citigroup.

Any wonder why the Washington crowd favors Wall Street over Main Street? Only the health-care industry spends more.

For many Americans the stock market acts as a barometer for the economy. US financial markets are the largest and most liquid in the world. In 2018 the finance and insurance industries (excluding real estate) represented 7.4 percent or $1.5 trillion of the US gross domestic product. In 1970 the finance and insurance industries accounted for 4.2 percent of GDP, up from 2.8 percent of GDP in 1950. In contrast manufacturing fell from 30 percent of GDP in 1950 to 11 percent in 2019.

Before COVID-19, finance and insurance industry profits were equal to a quarter of the profits of all other sectors combined, even though it accounted for just 4 percent of jobs. These data are evidence of the industry's growing weight within the American economy.

The figures do not reflect the extent to which nonfinancial firms derive revenues from financial activities, as opposed to productive investments in real assets. For instance, before the

2008 market crash and meltdown, GE Capital generated about half of General Electric's total earnings. GE became an example of the financialization of American business. In the years leading up to the financial crisis, it became one of the world's largest nonbank financial services companies, meaning it avoided the level of regulatory scrutiny official players such as Wall Street banks face. After it crashed and burned in 2008, GE Capital got a whopping $139 billion taxpayer bailout.

Another example of corporate America moving to the rhythm of Wall Street is the case of Boeing's 787 Dreamliner aircraft, which famously encountered delays and massive cost overruns because of its incredibly complex supply chain, which involved outsourcing 70 percent of the airplane's component parts to multiple tiers of suppliers scattered around the world. The Dreamline supply chain reflects the pressure to maximize return on net assets and was consistent with Wall Street's approach.

Return on net assets is a key measure that financial analysts use to evaluate how effectively management is deploying assets. The goal is to make the most money with the fewest possible assets. In the end the Dreamliner became an embarrassing failure that cost billions more than it should have. In such instances financialization reduces the dependence of corporate America on domestic workforces, which leads to offshoring manufacturing jobs.

The financial sector has amassed great power since the 1980s and contributed to the decline of US manufacturing, as well as income and wealth inequality. As Supreme Court Justice Louis Brandeis allegedly said in 1941 with great foresight, "We can have democracy in this country, or we can have great wealth concentrated in the hands of a few, but we can't have both."

# The Debt Bomb
9/26/2020

This year the federal debt is on track to exceed the size of the entire US economy.

The United States' debt-to-GDP ratio rose sharply during the Great Recession of 2008–2009 and has continued to rise, reaching 106 percent in 2019. Last year the GDP was $21.4 trillion, but it is expected to shrink this year. US debt is projected to exceed about $20 trillion and is growing like kudzu.

While the subject of debt and deficits may be dishwater dull to the average American living unemployment check to unemployment check, consider that the Congressional Budget Office (CBO) has warned that the Social Security Trust Fund will run out of money by 2031. Closely related, Medicare's hospital insurance trust fund is now on track to run out of money in 2024.

The debt-to-GDP ratio compares a country's public debt with its gross domestic product. By comparing what a country owes with what it produces, the ratio indicates that country's ability to pay back its debts.

Debt is eating away at the American economy like a swarm of termites invisibly consuming a house. The fiscal follies continue, with the only certainty being that the accumulated debt will be passed on to future generations and jeopardize their chance to live a prosperous life.

It may be time for Washington to consider a new financing instrument to address America's debt bomb so future generations have a chance to enjoy greater prosperity once the pandemic is behind us. The issuance of one-hundred-year Treasury bonds to fund ballooning deficits, with the interest income indexed to the CPI as a hedge against inflation, may be an idea whose time has come. It would give the next generation, which has to pay down the debt, a break by locking in rock-bottom interest rates. These bonds may appeal to long-term investors, such as pension funds and insurers, and be used to fund infrastructure projects.

Long-term bonds are not unusual. Disney issued one-hundred-year bonds in 1993, Norfolk Southern did so in 2010, and Coca-Cola, IBM, Ford, and other companies have done the same. Oxford University, Ohio State, Yale, and other universities have done the same. Fourteen Organisation for Economic Co-Operation and Development countries have issued debt with maturities ranging from forty to one hundred years. Austria, Belgium, and Ireland have all issued century bonds within the last two years.

With COVID-19 and the economic contraction, the CBO and Organisation for Economic Co-Operation and Development estimated that the deficit for fiscal year 2020, which ends this month, will exceed $3 trillion. According to the Committee for a Responsible Budget, this amounts to around 18 percent of GDP for the year. As things stand, the federal debt is expected to reach 108 percent of GDP by next year.

To put these figures into perspective, the United States' highest debt-to-GDP ratio was 112 percent at the end of World War II. The war was financed with a combination of roughly 40 percent taxes and 60 percent debt.

If the great and the good in Washington don't address how to reduce the deficit-to-GDP ratio and find a fiscally sustainable path after COVID-19, large debt burdens can slow economic growth, raise interest rates, and lead interest on the debt to consume an ever-larger proportion of the federal budget, crowding out spending on other priorities. But there is a trust deficit when it comes to the faith sentient Americans have in Washington's ability to deal with the issue intelligently.

The only approach politicians can agree on to manage the debt and deficits is to steal from future generations by passing on to them the accumulated debt burden. So much for intergenerational fairness. As Adm. Mike Mullen, the former chairman of the Joint Chiefs of Staff, said, "Our national debt is our biggest national security threat."

Extraordinary situations call for extraordinary measures, and the issuance of one-hundred-year bonds might be one way to deal with intergenerational equity.

## The Rise of the New Left
10/10/2020

When 2020 began, seemingly a century ago, Americans could not have anticipated the year to come: a tenacious pandemic that has killed over two hundred thousand people, a faltering economy, heightened social divisions, and violent street battles.

Much has been said and written about our divided society, in which there appears to be more tension than ever. The nation is angry, and America's polarized discourse leaves many Americans rightfully fearing for the future.

Some claim the contemporary ideology underlying this division derives from cultural Marxism, a contentious term that refers to the strategy propounded by new left-wing theorists in the last century to use the institutions of a society's culture to bring about revolution.

Cultural Marxism had its roots in the political philosophy propounded by far-left thinkers known as the Frankfurt School. Founded in Germany in 1923, the "Institute for Social Research" was the official name for a group of intellectuals who would play an important role in Europe and the United States. Among their ideas was to dismantle and undermine the totality of a capitalist society.

Fleeing Hitler in the 1930s, these German academics first set up shop at Columbia University in New York City and then, beginning in 1940, in California. They identified popular culture as wielding a pervasive influence that conditioned the masses into acceptance of capitalist society.

From the 1960s onward, the strategy was to infiltrate and eventually dominate social and cultural institutions and thereby achieve cultural hegemony. Rather than the class warfare and the plight of workers, which was the focus of classical Marxist thinkers, they concentrated on areas such as racial, ethnic, and gender warfare, as well as identity politics.

The Frankfurt School's new-left intellectuals realized that a Soviet-style revolution was not attractive to democratic Western societies and was unlikely to succeed. Conditions for the working class were improving because of trade union representation and an expanding franchise, among other things. Communism held little appeal to the industrial working class in whose name it had been invented.

Rather than expecting workers to seize control of the levers of political and economic life, they believed the way to bring about revolutionary change was to seed radical ideas within core institutions of society, such as the media, the arts, and universities.

They understood that culture mass-produces consent for the West's political system, and political revolution would be impossible without a cultural revolution. A successful revolution requires not just seizing political and economic power but also conquest of the culture, broadly defined as everything from art and entertainment to social and sexual norms. The 1960s radical left-wing German student leader Rudi Dutschke described the strategy of capturing society's commanding heights as the "long march through the institutions"—a cultural revolution to be achieved by using existing institutions, not overthrowing them.

One of the Frankfurt School's leading luminaries, Herbert Marcuse, who moved to America and became a darling of the 1960s new left, was featured in the Coen Brothers' masterpiece *Hail, Caesar!*, a satire of the 1950s film industry. The movie's subplot was about a gaggle of communist screenwriters who worship the Soviet Union trying to influence popular culture, namely Hollywood movies. In a 1967 essay, Professor Marcuse argued, "Liberating tolerance would mean intolerance against movements from the Right and toleration of movements on the Left." Suppressing the public expression of those who step out of line was a marginal perspective back then but is now quite mainstream.

The outcome of the culture war, like all wars, is wholly uncertain. But what is certain is that the late great Sen. Daniel Patrick Moynihan was right when he said, "The central conservative truth is that it is culture, not politics, that determines the success of a society. The central liberal truth is that politics can change a culture and save it from itself."

In plain terms, if you capture culture, politics will surely follow.

## Anti-Catholic Bigotry
10/27/2020

When President Trump nominated Seventh Circuit Judge Amy Coney Barrett to the Supreme Court last month, some media outlets and politicians suggested she would bring her Catholic faith onto the bench when deciding matters of law.

The roughly fifty-one million Catholic adults in the United States are racially and ethnically diverse. Politically, registered Catholic voters are evenly split between those who lean toward the Democratic Party (47 percent) and those who favor the Republicans (46 percent).

For a long time, many Americans have seen Catholics as taking their cues from Rome and not the US Constitution. In the mid-nineteenth century, nativist groups combined to form the Supreme Order of the Star Spangled Banner, which was obsessed with a hatred of Catholics. Ultimately members of the movement were labeled the "Know-Nothings." Among their demands were to ban Catholics from holding public office, along with fears that the growing Irish population was making the church a force in American government.

For years American politics remained plagued by widespread anti-Catholic sentiment, especially in the South. The Irish bore the brunt of tensions that sometimes erupted into violence between Catholics and the Protestant majority. It was another instance of where white privilege was not equally distributed.

Today Catholics are fully assimilated into society. They inhabit an increasingly secular world in which theological dictates from the church carry far less weight than in earlier generations. Catholics, like members of any faith, pick and choose which teachings to follow. For instance, many US Catholics want the church to allow priests to marry, allow women to become priests, and come down hard on child abuse by priests and the church's shameful cover-up of it.

The nomination of then-Professor Amy Coney Barrett to the Seventh Circuit Court of Appeals in 2017 stirred up an awakening of anti-Catholicism. California Senator Dianne Feinstein, who had the kind of voice that made you wish you had a remote control, tried to undermine the candidate's legitimacy because she was a Catholic. Feinstein, the top Democrat on the Senate Judiciary Committee, told Professor Barrett, "When you read your speeches, the conclusion one draws is that the dogma lives loudly within you. And that's of concern."

The senator's anti-Catholic remarks revealed her ignorance of the constitution. Article VI states that "no religious test shall ever be required as a qualification to any office or public trust under the United States." Feinstein's overt expression of anti-Catholic bigotry sparked a bipartisan backlash, contributing to Barrett's rise as a conservative judicial star.

Senator Feinstein's brand of bigotry was less like old-fashioned anti-Catholicism and more about the failure of Catholicism to distinguish between public and private moral duties, such as when the Little Sisters of the Poor fought the Affordable Care Act's contraception mandate all the way to the Supreme Court and won or the church's opposition to capital punishment. Of course, there was no mention of how some governors and mayors are keeping houses of worship closed because of the coronavirus while opening schools, businesses, and even athletic events. Hypocrisy is alive and well.

Ironically, it was because of the questioning of Judge Barrett during her previous confirmation hearing three years ago and the subsequent blowback that Senate Judiciary Committee members avoided obsessive and nauseating spritzing about Judge Barrett's Catholicism. Republican senators were smart to repackage questions about the judge's religious beliefs into bigotry, hoping the Democrats would alienate Catholic voters just before the November 3 election.

Democrats avoided the trap. While arguing that a Justice Barrett would jeopardize *Roe v. Wade* and the Affordable Care

Act, they bent over backward to make clear that they did not oppose the nomination because of her Catholicism. Other senators asked probing questions such as, Do you support white supremacy? Have you ever committed a sexual assault? Who does the laundry in the Barrett household? And do you play a musical instrument?

The rest, as they say, is pure commentary.

## Revisiting the Tragedy of the Commons
11/9/2020

During the 1990s the term "paradigm" became increasingly fashionable as an intellectually upscale replacement for the traditional and somewhat shopworn term model. But decanting this old wine into new bottles can still leave a bad taste in our mouths if we define a paradigm in too simplistic a manner.

Dictionaries define "paradigm" as a model or intellectual framework that seeks to explain some phenomenon in a clear and simple manner. A relevant example for our times is Garrett Hardin's essay, "Tragedy of the Commons." In this paradigm there is a common pasture in which local farmers can freely graze their cattle. Needless to say each farmer will want to graze as many cattle as they can on the common because each cow they add will provide them with a marginal economic benefit at no additional cost. So all the farmers continue adding more cows.

This works only so long as the total number of grazing cows remains within the carrying capacity of the commons. Once that limit is exceeded, the viability of the commons for grazing begins to break down as the grass wears out and provides less nourishment per cow.

So each farmer finds that their herd of cattle is producing less milk for them to sell. Under the circumstances their only rational response is to increase the size of the herd, which means adding still more cows to the overutilized commons. When all the local farmers keep doing this, the result can only be an increasingly dysfunctional commons.

In Hardin's words, "Each man is locked into a system that compels him to increase his herd without limit—in a world that is limited. Ruin is the destination towards which all men rush, each pursing his own best interest in a society that believes in the freedom of the commons."

By way of a solution, some people may propose expanding the commons if it is no longer large enough to support existing herds and to pay for it out of tax revenues so users of the commons can continue to obtain its benefits without directly paying for them. Such people believe that the purpose of the commons is to serve the community's economy and that its size should be tailored to the demands of that economy as it grows.

Others insist that the real problem is not too little grass but too much demand. They argue that the time has come to "think green" about the future of public commons in the context of the overall environment. People should begin shifting to more sustainable ways of managing their communities so they can phase down grazing and turn the commons into public parks.

Then there are those enamored of the stained glass verities of undergraduate microeconomic theory. They suggest that the time has come to start charging farmers user fees—so much per hour of grazing time for each cow. In this way each user will pay for the benefits received from the public facility in accordance with how much they use it.

By using a sensible pricing system to ration the use of these scare resources, each farmer will be motivated to make the most efficient use of it. Meanwhile the revenue from user fees can cover the cost of expanding the public commons when necessary rather than the government taxing everyone to pay for this.

Hardin's grazing pasture paradigm appears to go a long way toward answering socioeconomic questions about the inevitable tendency toward overuse of public goods when they are perceived to be "free." It explains why this tendency leads to a condition where supply can never really catch up with demand. It describes how the widespread availability of free public goods can significantly influence the underlying economics of many private activities. And it demonstrates the ease with which an entire society can become locked into behavioral patterns that may turn out to be "antisocial" in the long run.

It's your call. After all Rorschach tests are not graded.

## Powell Addresses Economic System under Attack
11/28/2020

History often has a hidden beginning. Since the 1970s people who are already well-off have enjoyed a rising percentage of income and wealth. Meanwhile ordinary Americans face declining social mobility, a shrinking middle class, widening income inequality, and crumbling infrastructure. There is plenty to be mad about and plenty of blame to go around.

The economic struggles of the American working class since the late 1970s were not just the result of globalization and technology changes. A long series of public policy changes favored the wealthy. Some argue that these changes were the result of sophisticated efforts by the corporate and financial sectors to change government policy—from tax laws to deregulation—to favor the wealthy.

In August 1971, less than two months before he was nominated to serve as an associate justice of the Supreme Court, Lewis F. Powell Jr. sent a confidential memorandum to his neighbor and friend Eugene B. Sydnor Jr., chair of the Education Committee of the US Chamber of Commerce. Powell was a leading Virginia corporate lawyer, a former president of the American Bar Association, and served on eleven corporate boards.

The thirty-four-page memo was titled "Attack on the American Free Enterprise System." It presented a bold strategy for how business should counter the "broad attack" from "disquieting voices." The memo, also known as the Powell manifesto, did not become available to the public until after he was confirmed.

He began the memo this way: "No thoughtful person can question that the American economic system is under broad attack." He went on to write that the assault was coming from "perfectly respectable elements of society: the college campus, the pulpit, the media, the intellectual and literary journals, the arts and sciences, and from politicians." American business believed that it was facing a hostile political environment during the late 1960s and that it was under attack with the growth of government authority under the Great Society and an increase in regulations ranging from the environment to occupational safety to consumer protection.

The memo outlined a bold strategy and blueprint for corporations to take a much more aggressive and direct role in politics. Powell was following the Milton Friedman argument that it was time for big business to focus on the bottom line; it was time to fight for capitalism. Powell proposed waging the war on four fronts: academia, the media, the legal system, and politics.

The memo influenced, for example, the creation of new think tanks such as the Heritage Foundation, the Manhattan Institute, and other powerful organizations. As Jane Mayer wrote, the Powell Memo "electrified the Right, prompting a new breed of wealthy ultraconservatives to weaponize their philanthropic giving in order to fight a multifront war of influence over American political thought."

The venerable National Association of Manufacturers moved its offices from New York City to Washington. Its CEO noted, "The relationship of business with business is no longer so important as the interrelationship of business with government." The number of corporations with public offices in Washington grew from 100 in 1968 to over 500 in 1978. In 1971 only 175 firms had registered lobbyists in Washington; by 1982 nearly 2,500 did.

When it comes to lobbying, money is the weapon of choice. It looms over the political landscape like the Matterhorn. The number of corporate political action committees (PACs) increased from under 300 in 1971 to over 1,400 by the middle of 1980. The money they spread around gave lobbyists the clout they needed. The growth of super PACs and lobbyists ensured that any piece of relevant regulation would be watered down, first in Congress and then during implementation.

The Powell Memo galvanized corporate America and enlarged the influence of big business over the political landscape. It encouraged business to play a more active role in American politics. Corporate America and the one-percenters got the memo.

# 5

## 2021 Columns

### The Downside of Low Interest Rates
1/2/2021

The Federal Reserve loves low interest rates. With rates stuck at low levels since the 2008 financial crisis, they have become the rule rather than the exception.

When the coronavirus pandemic plunged the economy into a sudden freeze, the Fed lowered its benchmark borrowing rate to near zero and purchased corporate and government securities like there is no tomorrow to curb unemployment and to stimulate the economy.

The funds rate defines the cost of lending from bank to bank through the Fed and serves as the benchmark interest rate for the economy. While low interest rates may be great for driving up sales of homes and automobiles, artificially low interest rates punish savers. Money market and certificate of deposit rates head to near zero when the Fed sets the federal funds rate at near zero.

This action disproportionately hurts senior citizens, retirees, savers, and those folks who prefer less risk. In accepting the lower yield, those people get less income, less ability to consume, and a lower quality of life, as well as take on more risk in the stock market for which they are not prepared. Nasty choices.

Low interest rates force savers to pursue more risky investments in the hunt for yield. Ten-year Treasury bonds offer a laughable less than 1 percent, making stocks look attractive. Thank the Fed for the stock market's run. The rise in stocks benefits the wealthiest 1 percent or 10 percent or wherever you want to draw the line, who own more than $11 trillion of stock and mutual fund shares.

The Fed's fundamental imperative is to strong-arm ordinary Americans to spend, spend, spend or to invest. The notion is that if, for example, a savings account provides an interest rate that rounds to zero percent, savings makes no sense—especially when inflation is rising faster than the interest earned on a savings account. Low-risk investments don't keep up with inflation, and your money doesn't have as much purchasing power.

The situation for savers isn't likely to get better soon. The Fed chair has said rates would remain near zero at least through 2023, though the Fed insists it won't take interest rates negative. The reality is that when inflation is factored in, people are already experiencing negative interest rates.

When more people spend and invest, the economy expands. Of course, every dollar consumers spend instead of saving amounts to several dollars that would have been available in the future had it been earning interest instead. As low rates discourage people from saving, they must become more and more reliant on government entitlements in old age.

To put the worst construction on it, a policy of constant low interest rates is an idea that deserves to be put on a stretcher and carried back to the leisure of the theory class where it was born. You don't have to be Philip Marlowe to know these policymakers have more than they can say grace over and are permanently out of the financial wars.

Low interest rates add to the Iliad of woes faced by ordinary Americans. The working class was in chronic crisis, alliteration aside, even before the pandemic. They work hard to make ends meet and stay out of the grasp of poverty, play by the rules, and do everything asked of them but kick extra points.

What is the right interest rate? Here's a crazy idea: the free-market interest rate. Cut out the middleman. This is the rate you get when the Fed does not interfere in financial markets.

Don't bet on it; the Fed wants to preserve the status quo—preserve, in other words, the wealth of the 1 percent and all that.

But not to worry, money isn't everything—as long as you have enough of it.

## The Fed and Inflation
1/16/2021

Life has changed substantially for ordinary working-class Americans in the first two decades of the twenty-first century. The deification of technology, the growth of globalization, the harrowing financial events of 2008 followed by the Great Recession, and the COVID-19 pandemic have left them struggling psychologically, physically, socially, and economically.

Growing income and wealth inequality were on the radar screen long before the coronavirus pandemic, but the pandemic has made the problem more obvious and urgent. The actions of the Federal Reserve have widened the gap. Quite apart from persistently low interest rates, there is the issue of inflation.

Last August, Fed Chair Jerome Powell introduced a policy that not only allows but welcomes an inflation level above 2 percent.

The Fed assumes it will be able to just snap their fingers and stop inflation at the point they like, which is the pinnacle of hubris.

Inflation matters. It tends to redistribute income and wealth toward groups that are better able to hedge against inflation by sheltering their assets in ways that earn decent returns.

But for the ordinary American, prices that rise faster than wages mean a decline in real income, less purchasing power, and lower living standards. Inflation, coupled with wage stagnation, is eating away at the working class.

While the cost of many discretionary goods has fallen during the pandemic, basic necessities such as housing, health care, education, and food are absorbing an ever-larger portion of the incomes of ordinary Americans.

The cost of groceries has been rising at the fastest pace in decades since the pandemic seized the economy. It's as if working-class Americans are involuntarily observing Lent all year round. They experience life at the sharp end.

In the United States, the consumer price index (CPI), which reflects retail prices of goods and services, including housing costs, transportation, and health care, is the most widely followed indicator of inflation. Food inflation is a major part of the CPI.

But the Fed generally focuses on "core inflation" or "core CPI." This excludes nondiscretionary items such as food and energy prices and can give a misleading picture of inflation trends. In the real world, people can't exclude food from their weekly budget.

According to the latest inflation data published by the US Labor Department's Bureau of Labor Statistics, another light—or as they now say, lite—read, food prices have increased by nearly 4 percent in the last year, higher than at any point since the 1970s.

The increases are even more dramatic for some food items, with beef and veal prices up 25 percent year over year, egg prices up 12 percent, potatoes up 13 percent, and tomato prices up 8 percent.

The report is broken into price changes for "food away from home" and "food at home." In November the categories registered year-over-year increases of 3.8 percent and 3.6 percent, respectively.

Rising food prices affect everybody, but they are always top of mind for ordinary working Americans. Even more affected are the poor and the unemployed because they are unable to afford basic necessities. Cutting back on food budgets is one of the first things people do to make ends meet.

Central bankers suffer from a Copernican complex—the belief that the sun and planets revolve around them. Real-world experience and history demonstrate that inflation can't be controlled like a thermostat. But one thing you can be certain of is that inflation has a painful effect on working-class Americans.

As the COVID-19 pandemic recedes, the national goal should be to Make America's Working Class Great Again. If you believe the intellectual gratin and shekel dispensers in DC will internalize that notion, perhaps you would be interested in some prime real estate—something deep in the Everglades.

## Leadership Lessons from the 1948 Movie *Command Decision*
1/30/2021

COVID-19 has turned the world upside down, and it is clear that things will not return to the status quo ante anytime soon. The pandemic has provided a test for societies and for their leaders.

One dimension of leadership always in short supply is the ability to tell people the truth, even if the message is unwelcome, such as that things will get worse before they get better.

In the current climate of fear and uncertainty, the United States needs leaders who can make strategic decisions independent of politics and do the right thing. This dimension of leadership is captured in the excellent 1948 movie about strategic bombing in World War II, *Command Decision*.

The film deals with strategy, leadership, and corporate politics and is probably the most sophisticated American war film ever made. It dramatizes a fundamental strategic conflict between two Army Air Force generals. Both are West Point graduates who committed themselves early on to Billy Mitchell's schtick of airpower as a "war-winner in its own right."

The younger general commands the Eighth Air Force's strategic bombing units in England during 1943. He's learned that the Luftwaffe has begun production of a whizbang new jet fighter at three plants deep inside Germany. He believes these factories must be bombed into oblivion as soon as possible, no matter what the cost in bomber and air-crew losses, to prevent the jet fighter program from creating a defensive shield over Germany, which will make strategic bombing impossible and threaten the planned 1944 invasion of France.

But his older and more politically savvy boss is convinced that the ultimate success of strategic bombing depends on the size of the bomber force Washington allocates to the Eighth Air Force. This will be determined by how effective they are at producing acceptable bombing results without high loss rates, which rules out the go-for-broke raids the younger general wants to mount against the three jet fighter factories.

The younger general insists that they must take advantage of a period of clear weather to complete the destruction of the factories if strategic bombing of Germany is to have any future. The older general believes the future of strategic bombing depends on the Eighth Air Force getting enough bombers. This will be determined at an allocation meeting in Washington, where heavy bomber losses certainly won't help their case.

In other words the younger general fights the Germans in Europe, while the older general has to fight the US Navy, which wants bombers for the Pacific theater, and army ground forces, which wants to recycle bomber pilots now in training as company commanders.

These dramatic debates between the two generals are breathtaking—two dedicated pros with very different perspectives about the strategic issue at hand pour out their arguments, hopes, fears, and differing career expectations.

The movie's sympathies lie with the younger general and show that he was right. At the time the movie was made, there was widespread public acceptance of air force propaganda that its strategic bombing concept had been successful. It turned out, in retrospect, that the prewar strategic bombing advocates grossly underestimated the resources needed for this concept to succeed, so the older general was actually right.

The problem the two generals confront is similar to the COVID-19 crisis. You can impose a protracted lockdown and harm the economy to the point where recovery will take decades or forgo lockdowns and get the economy moving but with a significant increase in illness and death.

Few people like to hear bad news, but telling the public what it needs to hear and facing problems is an important test of leadership. The role of a leader is to do the right thing in addressing a wicked problem that may have no clear solution—only an array of possible approaches, each with deleterious consequences.

## Leadership Lessons from *Twelve O'Clock High*
2/13/2021

The two best examples of crisis leadership for contemporary students of management and leadership are World War I and World War II. The former, a gold mine of information illustrating virtually every conceivable way of doing things wrong and the latter, a nice balance between doing things wrong and doing things right.

World War II was actually three separate wars that took place at the same time: United States versus Japan in the Pacific, the United States and the United Kingdom versus Germany in Western and Southern Europe, and the Soviet Union versus Germany in Eastern Europe.

Germany and Japan started World War II having great successes by doing things right. Then they lost their way and ended up doing everything wrong.

In contrast the Allies (US, UK, and the Soviet Union) started off doing many things wrong, mainly out of ignorance and false illusions, including the misuse of airpower. But they managed to get their respective acts together and wound up doing most things right. They won the war and, in so doing, reshaped the world.

Running a business has a great many parallels with running a war. To succeed in either, you must set realistic goals, identify and deploy the relevant resources necessary for achieving these goals, and then skillfully implement the options you select. After that you have to roll with the punches that inevitably whack you from unexpected events and adjust your strategy with dispatch.

Two fine Hollywood movies made in the late 1940s effectively dramatize "war situations" that are also common in business.

*Command Decision* is one of the movies with themes that translate to business. It deals with strategic decision-making at the command level. The other is *Twelve O'Clock High*, which is about a manager taking over a failing bomber group and whipping it into shape through a program of stern discipline.

It is the harrowing story of the first B-17 bombers in England in World War II and the terrible losses they took before long-range fighters were available to escort them on combat missions over Europe. The movie was adopted from a popular novel that was, in turn, based on a real event that affected the Eighth Air Force in England during 1942 and 1943.

The head of Bomber Command in England decides that the current group commander of the bomber group has allowed discipline to erode and is too emotionally involved with the crews. He relieves the popular group commander, replacing him with a young general.

The new leader immediately incurs the hatred of aircrews when he comes down hard on the lack of discipline. He deals harshly with slackers, segregating the worst misfits into a crew known as "the Leper Colony." He openly criticizes mistakes, insists on a high level of professionalism, and is a straight talker who appreciates straight talk in return.

Resentful of the new management style, all the pilots ask to be transferred out of the unit. But the new commander sticks to his principles. As the bomber group develops combat effectiveness, the group's performance improves, and the loss of life decreases, the pilots change their minds and support the new commander and his leadership style.

This story dramatizes the steps the leader took to restore the morale of people who had come to regard themselves as "hard-luck failures" who had accumulated the highest loss rate and the worst bombing effectiveness record and motivated them to become a winning team.

The film highlights timeless leadership lessons such as creating a strategy, setting clear expectations, creating performance standards, giving clear directions, putting the right people in the right jobs, communicating the why, restoring accountability, and pushing, pushing, and pushing until the job is done.

Whether commanding a bomber group or managing employees toward making their numbers, these leadership qualities are essential and universal, especially in situations of extreme emergency and crisis.

## The Forgotten Tribe: America's Working Class
2/27/2021

Countless working-class Americans of all races and ethnicities, who work hard and play by the rules, are fed up with the extreme partisanship that permeates the country and with meaningless acts of violence, including the storming of the capitol. These people are the forgotten tribe in America.

In general working-class people are those with a high school diploma but less than a four-year college degree who live in households with annual incomes roughly between $30,000 and $70,000 for two adults and one child. They are somewhere between the poor and the middle class.

Americans, by some measures, are more deeply divided politically and culturally than ever before. We live in a period of competing moral certitudes, of people who are sure they are right and prepared to engage in violence to make their point.

For the last many years, political correctness; cancel culture; social justice; multiculturalism; the all-pervasive claim to victimhood; judging people on their ethnicity, gender, and race rather than the merits of their work; and the politicization of just about everything has generated more heat and fumes than light. For all their rosy rhetoric on the subject, the ruling elites have less experience with ethnic and racial diversity than the working class.

These factors, and probably dozens of others, are contributing to the breakdown in the American genius for reaching compromises that meet the real social and economic needs of the working class.

Both the extreme right and the extreme left are corroded by ideology. Extremists on the right label their counterparts on the left socialists, and the left calls the right fascists. Each faction takes the law into their own hands while politicians see which way the wind is blowing and refuse to intervene. The growing divisions help explain why the nation's political center is shrinking.

At the same time, the media, both traditional and social media, have accelerated the fragmentation of cultural and political identities. Conservative and liberal TV networks only highlight information that confirms their audiences' biases, creating ideological echo chambers.

The worst of the fallout from this polarization will be felt by the forgotten tribe. These issues have done little to help them make ends meet and keep their families safe from COVID-19. Is it any wonder when they walk past a statue of that schnorrer Thomas Jefferson they don't experience any trauma? Working people, after all, have to work.

America's working class doesn't have the luxury of engaging in ideological pursuits; they have to take care of their families, paying for groceries and medical bills and making mortgage or rent payments. The pampered and self-consciously fortunate regard the working class as "deplorables," half of whom believe Elvis is still alive. Their understanding is the comic book version of diversity. They live in white neighborhoods, send their kids to private schools, and spend summer in the Hamptons.

These ruling elites don't have to live with the unintended consequences of their decisions. The working class are the ones who have to work. As long as they do, it hardly matters what color their skin is or what accent they have. All the while, the economic system directs food, shelter, and energy away from those who need them most and toward those who need them least.

The causes of the forgotten tribe's problems have been well documented: the rate and speed of technological changes, growing monopoly power and concentration, and globalization. Is it any wonder why the working class is losing hope in a better future (get real, they are not Bill Clinton)? They are an endangered species, living paycheck to paycheck.

Despite copious amounts of cash provided to families and unemployed workers, COVID-19 rescue plans don't provide long-term solutions for making work pay, giving the working class the education and skills needed to get better work, or strengthening families and communities to support work. These omissions only exacerbate the fraying cohesion of America's society and political fabric.

# Demystifying the Rule of Law

3/13/2021

America's constitutional order is under great stress, and foundational principles such as free speech and the rule of law are under attack. The breakdown in respect for American institutions has helped instigate a season of violence and unrest.

The rule of law (ROL) is an expression most Americans are familiar with. It is a popular but vague term often used in political and economic contexts. Americans routinely hear politicians, judges, legislators, and prosecutors mention the ROL right up there with freedom and democracy.

Few have paused to say what they actually mean by it. The concept is defined in many ways. For starters the ROL is an ideal, something to look at as a standard, a criterion. It is another way of saying that laws as written are applied equally to everyone. The ROL, in its most basic form, is captured in the popular quote "no one is above the law."

It also means that laws should govern a nation and its citizens, as opposed to power resting with a few individuals. In theory the law of the land is owned by all, made and enforced by representatives of the people.

The notion of the ROL comes with a host of concepts, such as the law should be clear, known, and enforced; people are presumed innocent until proven otherwise; and the police cannot arbitrarily arrest or detain people without good reason. Laws are interpreted by an independent judiciary, which ensures the peaceful settlement of disputes.

The ROL requires that the law be enforced equally. The most marginalized people in our society are entitled to be treated exactly the same way as anyone else. It also requires that laws should not discriminate against people for no good reason, such as the color of their skin, nationality, or gender.

The concept of the ROL dates back thousands of years. For example, the ancient Greeks started democratic law courts back in the fourth and fifth century BC with juries that had hundreds of members. At Runnymede in 1215, English leaders signed the *Magna Carta* (Latin for "Great Charter").

One might argue that the exalted *Magna Carta* was the beginning point of English-speaking peoples' understanding of the ROL. It was a document in which, for the first time, monarchs and government leaders agreed to subject themselves to the law and recognized that people were entitled to equality before the law and had a right to a jury trial. The immediate practical consequence of *Magna Carta* was the establishment of an elected assembly to hold the monarchy to its side of the bargain. These were momentous new concepts.

In the United States, the most visible symbol of the ROL is the Constitution, which was drafted by a special convention in Philadelphia in 1787. It is the framework for effective and limited government and the supreme law of the land. A congressman once delivered one of the truest statements of American political theory: "There is a straight road which runs from Runnymede to Philadelphia."

The American effort to make good on the promise of the ROL has been difficult and sometimes bloody. There is no getting around it—America has struggled to create a legal system that is fair to all its people.

The most glaring example is that the US Constitution did not address the problem of slavery, despite the words in the Declaration of Independence that "all men are created equal." This was the great flaw in American constitutional history.

America and other countries subscribing to the notion of the rule of law have considerable hard work to do to negotiate the distance between the ideal and the reality on the ground.

## Threat of Rising Inflation Could Burst Any Number of Asset Bubbles

3/27/2021

Identifying an asset bubble is not easy. They are only obvious after the bubble has burst—time alone gives definition. Americans may soon get another lesson in asset bubbles. The threat of rising inflation could burst any number of them.

One working definition of a bubble is when an asset's market price far exceeds its fundamental value and is not justified by estimated price earnings, resulting in artificially high asset valuations that are based on misconceptions that distort reality.

There is certainly disagreement about what the correct measure of price earnings is, and one can only estimate fundamental value. Even if the diagnosis is correct, you don't know when the bubble will burst.

Put simply, bubbles are booms that went bust, followed by a crash—a rapid decline in market prices. After all that is what bubbles are supposed to do.

Bubbles make for interesting stories. Charles Mackay's classic book, *Memoirs of Extraordinary Popular* Delusions and the Madness of Crowds," was first published in 1841 and is still in print. Fabled asset bubbles are the Dutch tulip bubble of the 1630s, the South Sea and Mississippi bubbles of 1720, the run-up in American stock prices in the 1920s, the dot-com bubble of the late 1990s, and the housing bubble of the mid-2000s, when US housing prices were 50 percent above their long-term trend.

Today there may be asset bubbles in specific markets, such as housing, cryptocurrencies, and stocks. US housing prices rose more than 10 percent last year. The housing market is booming for one key reason: low interest rates. Prices for cryptocurrencies, an asset that doesn't produce cash flows, rose more than 500 percent in the last year. This surge in the price of unregulated cryptocurrencies such as Bitcoin and Dogecoin has attracted the attention of many investors.

Then there is the incredible explosion in special-purpose acquisition companies (SPACs). This is a company that is formed strictly to raise capital through an initial public offering for the purpose of acquiring an existing company. Also known as "blank check companies," SPACs have been around for decades. But new issuance of SPACs has skyrocketed over the past year. Over $75 billion was issued in 2020. Less than three months into this year, they have raised more than $78 billion.

The US stock market ended 2020, another year that will live in infamy, at record highs. After bottoming out during the initial COVID-19 lockdown in March, the S&P 500 rose 68 percent in 2020, finishing the year up more than 16 percent, shattering all-time records along the way. The Dow Jones Industrial Average and the tech-heavy Nasdaq gained 7.25 percent and 43.6 percent, respectively, despite the public health and economic crises.

One condition that typically accompanies asset bubbles is easy credit that turbocharges speculation and benefits borrowers.

Federal Reserve Chair Jerome Powell is continuing the massive expansion of money and credit. Americans hope these policies don't make a monkey out of Darwin.

Powell recently said the Fed won't raise rates until they see a 3.5 percent unemployment rate and inflation averaging better than 2 percent. Inflation is not high on the Fed's list of worries.

Their top concern is mending the labor market. Both the Fed and the Biden administration are focused on getting the ten million unemployed back on payrolls.

The bond market appears skeptical about letting inflation rise as ten-year bond rates are increasing—a signal from investors that they expect higher inflation. The bond market is apparently concerned that inflation would cut into buying power and force the Fed into rate hikes that could pop some of these asset bubbles that inflated, thanks to rock-bottom interest rates, creating big risks to the economy.

To strike an optimistic note, if faintly, the accelerating rollout of COVID-19 vaccines has set the stage for rapid economic recovery in the second half of this year, hopefully with limited inflation. So place your bets accordingly.

## Managing the Demographic Risk of an Aging Population

4/10/2021

One trend that has been largely overlooked by the movers and shakers is our aging population. It is one of the forces that will shape society and the global economy over the next decades, and governments need to adjust their policies accordingly.

Around the world, workforces are steadily aging. Among the key drivers of a rapidly aging population are declining fertility rates, increased longevity, and the decline in mortality rates. For example, retiring baby boomers in the United States will live longer, but there will not be enough new births to offset the surge in the ranks of the elderly.

The world's fertility rate fell from 5 children per woman in 1950 to roughly 2.5 today and is projected to drop to 2 by 2050.

This decline has been the result of such factors as the rising social status of women and their increased participation in the workforce, widespread availability of birth control, and the increasing costs of raising children.

On the other hand, global life expectancy has increased from 50.09 years in 1960 to 72.6 years in 2019 and is expected to rise to 75 years by 2050. In the United States, life expectancy is projected to increase by about six years from 79.7 in 2017 to 85.6 in 2060. By 2035 there will be more people in the United States aged 65 and over than there will be children under 18, according to the Gerontology Institute at the McCormack School of Policy and Global Studies at UMass Boston.

The reasons for increased longevity include advances in health care, increased emphasis on personal and social hygiene, and increased government programs for the elderly.

In the developed world, the ratio of dependents to workers is rising sharply as baby boomers retire. Retirees are not only living longer but are increasingly prone to dementia at older ages. As the CEO of Dana-Farber/Harvard Cancer Center said, 1 out of 3 people who reach 85 will have Alzheimer's. This is a group largely dependent on others to help with daily living. As the need for caregivers intensifies, there will be fewer workers available for other work.

A rising dependency ratio is inflationary because dependents consume but do not produce. The growth in retirees may trigger a vicious cycle of slower economic growth and higher taxes. Policymakers should consider a progressive decline in the size of the labor force.

With fewer people producing goods and services and significantly more nonworking people consuming them, global supply will tend to lag demand. Combined with a greater bargaining power of the workforce in wage negotiations, this may increase inflation.

Meanwhile workers are likely to consume more as a labor shortage pushes up wages. Investment will rise in advanced countries as companies substitute capital for more expensive labor. Rising wages may improve the galloping inequality gap.

Despite these facts, many business leaders and policymakers lack a good grasp of the realities of an aging population and the economic challenge it will pose. Aging populations increase the financial burden on governments, creating a pension time bomb and increasing demands on health care and elderly care systems.

But these outcomes are not inevitable. Greater longevity presents individuals, employers, and policymakers with opportunities to help the elderly live more purposeful lives. Policymakers should take steps to harness the productive potential of older people. For example, by promoting an education policy that includes a strategy for supporting lifetime skill formation.

The famous maxim that "demography is destiny" may or may not be attributable to Auguste Comte, the nineteenth-century French sociologist. But it was certainly true that it was Comte who first wrote about how population trends could determine the future of a country.

What is not true is that destiny is not susceptible to change. Just as societies must adjust their lifestyles to adapt to climate change, societies with aging populations must adjust their policies to promote economic growth.

## Electric Cars Among Several Disruptions That Will Steer Auto Industry

4/24/2021

Electric vehicles, driverless cars, ride-sharing, changing patterns of vehicle ownership and use, and the recognition that climate change poses an existential threat are just a few of the major disruptions that may force automakers to modify their current business models.

Climate scientists contend that electric vehicles are one of the best ways to reduce greenhouse gas emissions, most of which come from cars and trucks. In the United States, the transportation sector is the largest source of emissions, and the automobile industry is under great pressure to meet regulatory emissions targets and do its bit for the planet. Automobile firms, their suppliers, and other mobility players must adapt to an emerging future that threatens their existing business models.

For example, car sharing may undermine the pattern of single-family ownership that has been fundamental to automobile firms' business model for over a century. If a ride-sharing company such as Lyft or Uber is able to send a fully self-driving vehicle to customers' doors and take them wherever they want to go on command, those customers may be most closely connected to that service, not the automaker.

Electric vehicles will also affect the traditional business model. For starters, there is a dramatic increase in new entrants into the market, and sales and distribution channels are moving from physical dealerships to online stores. Service requirements for electric vehicles are less than for the gas-powered internal combustion engine because of their simplicity, and gross margins may shrink because of much higher competition and lower pricing for electric vehicles over time. In addition, policymakers in Washington will continue to promote and support faster electric vehicle adoption to deal with climate change.

Increasing electric vehicle ownership is at the heart of the Biden administration's $2.3 trillion infrastructure package. It would provide $174 billion to spur the development and adoption of electric vehicles, including incentives to buy them and to get more EV charging stations installed across the country—500,000 of them by 2030—so people will feel confident they won't run out of juice. There are currently about 41,000 charging stations in the United States, compared with more than 136,000 gas stations.

Surveys indicate that while consumers' appetite for electric vehicles has grown significantly, they remain concerned about the price of battery-powered cars, which can cost up to $10,000 more than conventional vehicles. But total operating costs for electric vehicles may well be less than for conventional ones. Fewer maintenance and charging costs may offset the higher upfront price over time. Electric vehicles also have fewer moving parts, and they don't require oil changes.

The hope is that federal largesse will push the growth of electric vehicles, which currently make up just 2 percent of the new car market and 1 percent of all cars, sport utility vehicles, vans, and pickup trucks on the road, according to the Department of Energy.

Autonomous or fully self-driving vehicles represent perhaps even greater disruption for the automotive industry, although there remains considerable uncertainty around fully self-driving vehicles, despite considerable investment in them. It is difficult for potential customers to imagine what a community in which these are a viable transportation option would look like.

Even once fully self-driving cars are available, it is extremely difficult to predict their rate of proliferation. It remains unclear whether they are five, ten, or fifteen years away. In any case they may lead to declining traditional car sales.

All these factors are significantly altering the auto manufacturing landscape. Incumbents will be forced to change their business model, leading to wholesale modifications in their manufacturing base, the closure of current facilities, adjustments to their dealership network, and fundamental changes to their overall cost structure. This kind of disruption does not come easy to large, mature companies.

One thing is certain: How people move from one location to another affects numerous aspects of daily life, along with hundreds of related industries, and it will be changing in the near future.

## The First Amendment and Free Speech
5/8/2021

While many national constitutions come and go every few decades, the US Constitution has served the purpose for which it was intended for more than two centuries. The United States is proud of its tradition of freedom of speech, which was established in the First Amendment to the Constitution.

It allows for public criticism of the government. Without it, such behavior could land you in prison—just ask Russian opposition leader Alexei Navalny. Still, there were many times in American history when this principle was traduced.

For example, some of the same people who ratified the Bill of Rights voted in Congress in 1798, during the presidency of John Adams, to pass the Alien and Sedition Acts that made it a crime to utter "false, scandalous, or malicious" speech against the government or the president.

The first ten amendments to the Constitution are known as the Bill of Rights. They were proposed by Congress in September 1789 and ratified by the states in December 1791.

Freedom of speech isn't the only freedom protected by the First Amendment. It reads, "Congress shall make no law respecting an establishment of religion, or prohibiting the free exercise thereof, or abridging the freedom of speech, or of the press; or the right of the people peaceable to assemble, and to petition the Government for a redress of grievances."

Freedom of speech is considered a fundamental bedrock of liberty, allowing citizens to express their ideas and bring about changes that reflect the needs of its people. It gives voice to conflicting or dissenting opinions. promoting healthy debate that moves society closer to realizing America's founding ideals.

The civil rights movement is a perfect example of free speech in action. During the 1950s and '60s, activists such as Dr. Martin Luther King Jr. used free speech as a tool to force change in society. Exercising their voice, these activists were able to outlaw racial discrimination that plagued the country.

But freedom of speech is not an unlimited right. The First Amendment only protects individuals' speech from US governmental oppression, control, and censorship; it does not extend to private entities. Companies have significant leeway to set their own standards and policies regarding employee conduct.

There is nothing illegal about a private firm censoring people on its platform. For example, Facebook banning former President Trump indefinitely from its platform and Twitter permanently banning him were within the companies' legal rights in the aftermath of the Capitol incursion on January 6.

The nation has long grappled with which types of speech should be protected and which should not. Interpreting the broad guarantees of free speech in the First Amendment has not been an easy task. Over time the Supreme Court has spilled barrels of ink defining the freedom of speech. It has upheld people's right to critique the government and hold political protests but hasn't extended protection to those who incite action that might cause harm.

But what constitutes harm is still a matter of debate. For some, it is limited to physical harm, as in the case of falsely shouting "fire" in a crowded movie theater. For others, harm encompassed a compromise to the dignity of others, as in the case of hate speech. Another recent argument is that free speech should be curtailed if it causes offense and the speaker makes you feel disrespected. This argument may be setting a lower bar for limiting free speech. But that is a story for another day.

In today's politically charged climate, some people believe the government should restrict certain speech. But thankfully, the First Amendment protects everything, from car commercials to fiery protests.

While it may be unfashionable to quote America's first president, it merits recalling what he said about free speech: "If freedom of speech is taken away, then dumb and silent we may be led, like sheep to the slaughter."

Naturally, everyone has their own interpretation of those comments.

# The United States, China, and Taiwan
5/22/2021

There is no getting around the fact that the United States' primary strategic competitor for global leadership is the People's Republic of China, which continues to extend its diplomatic, economic, and military influence internationally. Quite apart from China becoming the world's second-largest economy and its leading trading nation, policymakers increasingly describe its military buildup as a threat to US and allied interests in the Indo-Pacific.

Put simply, the Pentagon considers China its most serious competition. Taiwan may be the issue with the greatest potential to turn competition into direct confrontation. Many military analysts note that after two decades of counterinsurgency wars, the United States can no longer be certain of its ability to uphold a favorable balance of power in the Indo-Pacific.

By contrast China has the military strength and, in particular, the long-range missile capability, to overwhelm the United States in the Indo-Pacific region, according to the United States Studies Centre at the University of Sydney. China is now an adversary that is also a military peer. It is in the enviable position of being able to use limited force to achieve a fait accompli victory over Taiwan before the United States could respond.

This is not unthinkable since the Chinese Communist Party regards Taiwan as an inalienable part of China. The United States needs to defend Taiwan effectively against a Chinese invasion or blockade because it is important to frustrating China's strategy to achieve regional hegemony. For many countries in the region, it is the canary in the coal mine—a strong indicator of how far the United States would go to defend them against China.

The two-million-strong People's Liberation Army (PLA) is the primary concern of US defense experts. According to a 2020 Department of Defense report, the PLA has "already achieved parity with—or even exceeded—the U.S." in several areas in which it has focused its military modernization efforts in the Indo-Pacific region, where China certainly has the home court advantage.

The PLA's modernization program has been supported by China's rapidly growing economy and augmented by the purchase and alleged theft of militarily useful technologies. In 1996 China was deeply embarrassed and humiliated in the Taiwan Strait Crisis when the United States responded to Chinese missile threats meant to intimidate Taiwan with a massive show of force.

Two US aircraft carrier groups emerged in the strait and exposed the weakness of the PLA's Navy compared with the US Fleet. In response China's defense budget rose by about 900 percent between 1996 and 2018 and is now the world's second-largest behind the United States.

For context it should be acknowledged that the threats along China's vast frontier should not be discounted. With a 13,743-mile land border, it counts fourteen sovereign states as neighbors. It also shares maritime borders with Brunei, Indonesia, Japan, South Korea, Malaysia, the Philippines, and Taiwan.

It should come as no surprise that among China's grand ambitions is to extend its influence along its frontiers through means such as building and militarizing islands to gain exclusive control over the South China Sea, through which about three $3 trillion of trade, or a third of the world's cargo transport, flows each year.

Failure to respond to the growing threat that China poses to its Indo-Pacific neighbors would raise questions about the Unites States' willingness and capacity to act as a security guarantor in the region. Essentially, the United States needs support from allies and partners in the region to deter Chinese adventurism, including a potential attack on Taiwan.

The stakes could not be higher in this contest. As historian Niall Ferguson recently wrote, "Perhaps Taiwan will turn out to be to the American empire what Suez was to the British Empire in 1956: the moment when the imperial lion is exposed as a paper tiger." Losing Taiwan would be seen all over Asia as the end of American predominance.

## Is the United States Heading Toward Another Great Inflation Postpandemic?

6/5/2021

Capital markets are signaling increasing concerns about inflation as the economy recovers from the great virus crisis. Many experts are concerned that further cost-of-living increases will result as consumer demand outstrips supply.

On the other hand, the Federal Reserve believes inflation pressures caused from a near-term imbalance between demand and supply is transitory. But history teaches that inflation fears must be addressed early to avoid serious economic pain.

As the economy reopens, the danger is that the United States will experience a classic case of too much money chasing too few goods. There has been rampant money printing, and money that has been sitting in people's bank accounts can now finally be spent.

Supply has been restricted by furloughs, mask wearing, social distancing, and other policies to contain the pandemic. The Fed's position is that recent increases in the prices of food, construction materials, used cars, and gasoline, along with scattered labor shortages and surging home prices, will quickly fade postpandemic.

But the Fed flooding the economy with massive amounts of liquidity may set the stage for a possible surge in price levels, stoking inflation. These fears are grounded in the 1970s, when the United States underwent a period of double-digit inflation that led to painful memories for Americans who experienced the so-called Great Inflation.

During that time inflation soared from a negligible 1.6 percent in 1965 to 13.5 percent in 1980. Stable prices provide people with a sense of security. They are like safe streets and clean drinking water. During the Great Inflation, people couldn't predict whether their wages would keep pace with large price increases that had become the norm.

Inflation was blamed on such factors as President Nixon suspending the convertibility of the dollar into gold, which caused the value of the dollar to drop and triggered higher import prices; two oil price shocks; the massive cost of the Vietnam War; monetary policy mistakes; and the breakup of the Beatles.

People began to expect continuous price increases, so they bought more goods. Increased demand pushed up prices, leading to demands for higher wages, which triggered even higher prices, leading to a continuing upward spiral.

For example, labor contracts increasingly included automatic cost-of-living clauses that contributed to the inflationary wage-price spiral, and the government began to peg some payments, such as Social Security, to the consumer price index, the best-known gauge of inflation. While these practices may have helped workers and retirees cope with inflation, they also perpetuated it.

The government's ever-rising need for revenue increased the federal budget deficit and led to more government borrowing, which, in turn, pushed up interest rates and further increased costs for businesses and consumers. With energy costs and interest rates high, business investment languished, and unemployment exceeded 10 percent. The simultaneous inflation and recession that followed wrecked many businesses and hurt countless Americans.

The Fed took drastic steps in the late 1970s and early 1980s, tightening monetary policy under legendary Chairman Paul Volcker to promote price stability and combat the persistent surge in inflation. Consequently, the federal funds rate soared from 10 percent at the start of 1979 to 19 percent by the middle of 1981. The unemployment rate peaked at 10.8 percent in late 1982.

During this severe recession, thousands of businesses failed because they did not have access to capital, and credit-dependent sectors of the economy, such as home and car sales, suffered dramatically. Volcker's tight money policy was a tough pill to swallow, but it eventually had the desired effect. By the mid-1980s, inflation dipped below 5 percent.

The history of the Great Inflation holds important lessons for the future. One is that rising prices should be nipped in the bud because there is no quick and painless fix for rampant inflation. The longer you wait to deal with it, the harder it becomes.

As the economist and philosopher Friedrich Hayek put it, "Taming inflation is like catching a tiger by the tail."

# The Fed's Latest Challenge with Inflation on the Rise

6/21/2021

Bad news on the inflation front: Over the past twelve months, the Labor Department said that the US consumer price index (CPI) rose by 5 percent from a year earlier, the biggest increase since August 2008.

The Federal Reserve uses a different index to measure inflation—the personal consumption expenditure. This index, which ignores the often volatile categories of food and energy, jumped 3.8 percent in May from the year before, the largest increase for that reading since June 1992.

Last August, the Fed adopted a historic shift to interest rate policy that places more emphasis on boosting employment, allowing inflation to rise above their 2 percent target and keeping rates lower for a longer period. The Fed said it believed that this inflation target is most consistent over the long run with meeting its challenging goals of maximum employment and stable prices, often called the dual mandate.

Now, with inflation on the rise, the critical question is whether higher-than-expected price increases are just because of the economy reopening or if they're being caused by something more persistent.

Government policymakers and economists argue that it's the former. They claim some of the surge can be explained by a low base—prices fell dramatically last spring as consumers spent less in the face of the pandemic. Most Americans spent last May quarantined in their homes rather than shopping or taking a holiday, so the price of goods and services were quite low.

The Fed argues that the recent increase in inflation has been fueled by an unusual combination of short-term supply bottle-necks and pent-up demand from consumers finally emerging from their homes. Demand is also being driven by Americans who are flush with cash after multiple stimulus checks.

That said, it may be that the impact of COVID-19 on global supply chains and production will prove more durable than antici-pated and render inflation less transitory than the Fed expects. For example, the Federal Reserve Bank of Atlanta's sticky price index, a weighted basket of items that change price relatively slowly, increased 4.5 percent in May, the largest increase since April 2009.

Also, labor scarcity is reversing decades of wage stagnation. Thanks, in part, to some people choosing not to look for work after Congress's extension of an extra $300 a week in unemploy-ment benefits until September, demand for workers is outstrip-ping the supply, enabling workers to secure higher wages. The Fed argues that the strong labor market before the pandemic did not trigger a significant rise in inflation.

Inflation, defined as a general rise in the level of prices, is insidious. It erodes purchasing power over time if wages don't keep up. Even at an annual inflation rate of 2 percent, the pur-chasing power of $10,000 put under your mattress today is about $8,200 in ten years.

By allowing inflation to rise above 2 percent, the Fed wanted to avoid inflation's evil twin: deflation, or a sustained decline in the general price level.

Why does the Fed want to avoid falling prices? For starters, if consumers come to expect prices to decline in the future, they may delay purchases for as long as possible. Consequently, sales volume fall, corporate profits decline, unemployment rises, and the economy grows more slowly, causing prices to decline further.

There is a trade-off between price stability and maximum employment, and each scenario has winners and losers. The intellectual heavy hitters at the Fed will surely wait for additional data before deciding whether to sacrifice full employment on the altar of price stability. Of course, they might also face political pressure not to raise interest rates because, in an era of soaring debt and deficits, higher rates would increase government costs.

Such are the consequences in the Fed's high-stakes game of determining whether rising inflation is a passing phase or a more permanent problem.

## Rising Interest Rates May Affect Several Key Economic Players

7/3/2021

It's a mug's game to be forecasting inflation, but it's starting to look like the Federal Reserve may have to tighten monetary policy sooner rather than later to get it under control.

Last week the May core personal consumption expenditure price index rose 3.4 percent from a year ago, the fastest increase since April 1992. This is the key inflation indicator the Fed uses to set policy.

Though the reading could add to inflation concerns, Fed leaders, backed by an army of economists armed with models and datasets, insist the current situation will subside as economic conditions return to normal.

They continue to argue that inflation has spiked recently because of supply chain disruptions that have left manufacturers unable to keep up with the escalating demand that has accompanied economic reopening. Soaring real estate prices also have played a role, along with the natural bounce back after plummeting demand depressed prices last year.

Economist Friedrich Hayek once likened controlling inflation to trying to catch a tiger by its tail—an impossible task with unpleasant consequences for the economy and for personal finances. Judging by the most recent inflation reading, the cat may be already out of the bag.

As William McChesney Martin, the Fed chair from 1951 to 1970, said in a 1955 speech, the job of a central banker is to "take away the punch bowl" before the party gets out of control.

This metaphor referred to a central bank's action to stop flooding the country with easy money and ultralow interest rates. There is no silver bullet, magic wand, or get-out-of-jail-free card when dealing with inflation.

The federal funds rate is the most important benchmark for interest rates in the US economy, and it also influences interest rates throughout the global economy. Raising it may affect several key economic players.

Banks will be copacetic with higher interest rates. They will see an increase in their net interest margins, an important measure of banks' profitability. Net interest revenue refers to the difference between interest earned on loans and interest paid on deposits. They will charge more interest for their loans, while deposit rates increase more gradually.

Life insurance companies will also welcome higher interest rates. Most insurers earn substantial income from investing premiums and favor high-quality bonds whose yields have plummeted in recent years in the sustained low-interest-rate environment.

Rising interest rates negatively affect the stock market because higher rates make it more expensive for companies to operate and borrow money. That reduces profitability, which, in turn, hurts the value of company stock. Also, when stocks decline, investors may move into bonds to take advantage of the higher interest rates.

Bonds are particularly sensitive to interest rate changes. When the Fed increases rates, the market price of existing bonds declines. New bonds come into the market offering investors higher interest rates, which causes existing bonds with lower coupon payments to become less valuable.

While higher interest rates are bad for borrowers, they're great for folks with savings accounts, certificates of deposit, and money market mutual fund accounts who currently earn a hair above nothing on these accounts. Conversely, a hike in interest rates adversely affects consumer credit such as student, auto, and personal loans; lines of credit; and credit cards.

As for the housing market, rising mortgage rates will hurt home prices since higher interest rates may force borrowers to buy a cheaper house to maintain the same monthly payment. Higher mortgage rates may have the biggest impact on the lower end of the housing market.

Stepping back from the immediate issue of inflation or deflation, it is useful to recall that a consensus of British economists predicted that Margaret Thatcher's economic policies would be disastrous. As her first chancellor of the exchequer, Geoffrey Howe, said, "An economist is a man who knows 364 ways of making love, but doesn't know any women."

## What Will Globalization Look Like in a Post–COVID-19 World?

7/17/2021

The COVID-19 pandemic continues to wreak havoc across the globe, disrupting the globalized and interconnected world. With the vaccine rollout, some regions are finally getting a handle on both the disease and the economy.

Many world leaders believe globalization was in retreat even before the pandemic. They argue that to prepare for the post–COVID-19 era, new energy must be infused into global governance through multilateral actions.

Finding common solutions to the challenges of climate change, transitioning to clean energy, terrorism, cybersecurity, and emerging technologies will require much more global governance than the international community has been able to muster.

Governance advocates point to the July 1 agreement by 131 countries to establish a minimum tax rate of at least 15 percent for multinational corporations as a historic step in the right direction and that globalization of governance is becoming a reality.

Globalization is not a new concept. At some level, trade across national borders has been an important determinant of the wealth of individuals, companies, and countries throughout history. The search for trading opportunities and trade routes was a primary motivation for exploring much of the world.

The roots of today's globalized world were put down at the end of the Second World War. The allied nations created a rules-based system for international commerce and finance that allowed products, science, and technology to move across borders in an effort to lay the foundation for lasting peace.

In the 1990s the world entered an era of hyperglobalization, becoming more interconnected than ever before. In this era the big new player was China, which joined the World Trade Organization in 2001. Along with the United States, it grew to dominate global trade.

Many still question the benefits of globalization. They argue that interconnection and dependency between nations made economic and public health crises even worse for many countries.

While the globalization of governance may placate some, it hardly offers comfort to those who have lost good jobs and experienced the pain of economic globalization. For them, globalization is just another name for globaloney, although many support the concept with their wallets by shopping at firms that source their products from Chinese suppliers such as Walmart.

Others argue that the benefits of globalization are not distributed equitably. For example, many who oppose globalization of the US economy do so on the basis that firms make manufacturing, marketing, and other strategic choices in ways that maximize profits for shareholders, often to the detriment of a firm's other stakeholders, such as employees and the communities in which they do business.

American manufacturing has suffered severe disruption or outright collapse as a result of increased foreign competition and the outsourcing of manufacturing to countries where labor is cheaper. Globalization has become a polarizing issue in the United States, with entire industries moving overseas and the resulting economic squeeze on the middle class.

Others believe the COVID-19 pandemic has exposed developed countries' excessive dependence on Chinese manufacturing. They believe that after the pandemic, countries such as the

United States must take action to gradually reduce their dependence on China's low-cost global supply chain.

Countries will look to build some duplication and flexibility into their global supply chains to guard against putting themselves into adverse bargaining positions. Such actions may well push China–United States relations even further toward confrontation.

Even before the pandemic arrived, globalization had taken two big hits. The first was the 2008 financial crisis, when cross-border investments, trade, and supply chains all contracted.

Second, a wave of populist leaders were elected across the globe, championing economic nationalism and attacking the existing global economy. Free trade went out of fashion, and a trade war broke out between China and the United States.

While the post–COVID-19 world will not see a complete unwinding of globalization, it is likely to be more fractured and regionalized. The basic challenge will be reconciling a deglobalized world with the need for collective action to address global issues.

## With Regard to Aging Infrastructure, We Can Pay Now or Pay Later

7/31/2021

The list of America's infrastructure shortcomings is long, and deferred maintenance is near the top. A 2019 report from the nonprofit, nonpartisan Volcker Alliance warned that repairs to the nation's aging infrastructure (roads, highways, and other critical public assets) could cost more than $1 trillion, or about 5 percent of the country's gross domestic product.

Reflecting the poor condition of US infrastructure, the American Society of Civil Engineers gave it an overall grade of C-minus in 2021.

Congress is considering a $1.2 trillion, eight-year bipartisan physical infrastructure package that includes about $579 billion in new spending on roads, broadband, and other public works projects.

It is unclear how much, if any, of the new funding will be used to eliminate the backlog of deferred maintenance that plagues America's public works infrastructure. Deferred maintenance is broadly defined as maintenance and repair needed to bring current infrastructure assets up to a minimum acceptable physical condition.

Democrats hope to follow up this legislation by moving a $3.5 trillion spending package that includes funds for education, climate change, Medicaid, and other social programs. They plan to expand the social safety net without Republican support using the budget reconciliation process, which avoids the sixty-vote threshold typically needed in the Senate.

When it comes to the hard infrastructure package, it is important to remember that maintenance funding is often seen as the stepchild of infrastructure assets since it does not generate the excitement associated with new capital projects.

Given maintenance's relative invisibility (except when a system failure occurs), it is often the first expense to be deferred, a short-term stopgap that usually leads to higher costs in the long run. Another challenge is that government often sets the price for using the asset too low to cover the cost of service delivery.

Lack of maintenance leads to premature deterioration of the physical infrastructure, which results in poor service. This creates a vicious cycle, as customers are unwilling to pay more for subpar service, which makes it difficult for a government agency to raise the price.

The maintenance of existing infrastructure is not politically compelling. Short-term political incentives conflict with asset management activities that focus on the long-run sustainability of infrastructure assets. Guaranteed media coverage for ribbon cutting events and the ability to issue debt (to be paid by future taxpayers) encourage politicians to favor new public works projects, perpetuating the Build, Neglect, Rebuild model.

Ignoring or reducing ongoing maintenance funding enables politicians to move resources to more politically rewarding investments in new infrastructure. The idea of states having balanced budgets is fiction if they fail to account for the cost of infrastructure maintenance that has been deferred.

Poor asset management means infrastructure maintenance is conducted on an ad hoc basis and is reactive rather than routine and preventive. Delayed maintenance of infrastructure assets can add billions of dollars to the cost of assets and accelerate the time when they must be replaced.

Infrastructure investment has traditionally been divided into two categories: capital and operations and maintenance (O&M). A more useful breakout would include four categories: new capacity, rehabilitation, maintenance, and operations. These represent the life cycle cost of an infrastructure asset.

Sure, a rigorous breakout of spending into each category is difficult. For example, maintenance and rehabilitation, in particular, are easily confused. Maintenance focuses on short-term improvements, while rehabilitation has a long-term focus. Effective maintenance reduces rehabilitation costs.

Still further it is difficult to separate maintenance from operating activities. But an effective asset management program must account for the full life cycle costing of a public infrastructure asset.

In short, the story of maintaining infrastructure assets is pay me now or pay me many times more later. Current funding programs need to be modified to make sure maintenance is not ignored.

If government is to be a responsible steward, new infrastructure projects should not be pursued until the sponsor has demonstrated the true life cycle costs of existing assets can be paid for.

## A Look at How the Nixon Shock Changed the Global Economy
8/14/2021

If you asked scholars to name the most important happenings in the last fifty years of American history, they would likely list events ranging from the Vietnam war, the civil rights movement, the invention of the computer chip, the September 11 terrorist attacks, the Great Recession that officially lasted from 2007 to 2009, and the COVID-19 pandemic.

Missing from this list would be the so-called Nixon shock, the fiftieth anniversary of which is upon us.

In a televised address on August 15, 1971, President Nixon (America's very own Richard III) announced that he was "closing the gold window," ending the dollar's convertibility into gold. Unilaterally ending the last vestiges of the gold standard and eliminating the final link between gold and the dollar was a consequential moment in US financial history.

The Nixon shock had profound implications for the US and the global economy. The United States unleashed an era of floating exchange rates, which created a much less stable world economy, since currency values fluctuated because of the disconnect between them and something that was tangible. Many contend it was the beginning of an inflationist era of fiat money and created decades of turbulence in currency markets.

The president announced the end of the American commitment to redeem other countries' dollars for gold at $35 an ounce, a bedrock of the Bretton Woods system of mostly fixed exchange rates that had been in place since 1944 and established the dollar as the world's reserve currency.

Closing the gold window marked the end of a commodity-based monetary system and the beginning of a new world of fiat currencies backed entirely by the full faith and trust in the government that issued it. This gave the government and the Federal Reserve greater control over the economy because they can control how much money is printed.

The president's main concern in 1971 was avoiding a recession that might cost him the 1972 election. He strong-armed Federal Reserve Chair Arthur Burns into keeping interest rates low in the face of rising consumer prices. President Nixon allegedly told Burns, "We can take inflation if necessary, but we can't take unemployment," setting the stage for the birth of the Great Inflation of the 1970s, the Age of Aquarius.

In fairness to President Nixon, he inherited an economy from President Johnson that was under serious strain. Federal spending to simultaneously fight the Vietnam War and build the Great Society created budget deficits that fueled inflation along with the growing US trade deficit.

The United States had printed more dollars than it could back with gold. Inflation had started to rise in the second half of the 1960s, soaring from a mere 1.4 percent in 1960 to 13.5 percent in 1980.

Put plainly, too many dollars were abroad. By 1971 the pledge that an ounce of gold was worth $35 became void. The feds could not make it happen. So they severed the link. The value of the dollar in foreign exchange markets suddenly plummeted, which caused increases in import prices, as well as in the prices of most commodities priced in dollars.

For sure, the Nixon shock was not the only reason for the accelerating inflation of the 1970s. For example, the Organization of the Petroleum Exporting Countries announced an oil embargo against the United States during the October 1973 Yom Kippur War in Israel. Oil prices surged by 400 percent, and US economic activity instantly dropped. In 1973 the United States entered into the deepest recession since the Great Depression, but this time it was coupled with price inflation, not the deflation of the 1930s.

The Nixon shock was another painful example of the politicization of the economy. Sound familiar? A key lesson for today is that price stability is paramount for a strong and growing economy. Tolerating high inflation in an effort to stimulate the economy is a dangerous game to play.

## The Return of the Taliban—What Went Wrong in Afghanistan?
8/29/2021

Writing about recent events is always hazardous. It can be difficult to establish precisely what has happened and why. There is also a lack of clarity about the relative significance of events.

Americans don't yet know where the collapse of Afghanistan ranks among American military and foreign policy disasters, such as the debacle in Iraq, the fall of Saigon, the failed Bay of Pigs Invasion in Cuba, and the 1979 Iran hostage crisis.

But three points are surely certain: First, the shambolic exit from Afghanistan is a major setback that will undermine US credibility for years to come. As Henry Kissinger said, "It may be dangerous to be America's enemy, but to be America's friend is fatal."

Second, Afghanistan fell because America forgot the lessons of history. It does not understand the world beyond its borders, which is very different from the United States.

Finally, given how the atrocious implementation of the pullout of US troops from Afghanistan was, Joe Biden will have to wait a bit before he receives his Nobel Peace Prize. Another black eye for the United States.

There will be lots of talk in the coming days about the harsh lessons to be learned from America's retreat from Afghanistan. In April, Biden announced the United States would withdraw our military from the country without conditions on the twentieth anniversary of the 9/11 attacks. What an awful historical irony that the Taliban will once again be in control on September 11.

Looking back, there are some indisputable facts about what went wrong in Afghanistan, and responsibility is certainly divisible by more than one president.

On October 7, 2001, the first of these presidents, George W. Bush, launched Operation Enduring Freedom—the invasion of Afghanistan. The operation sought to bring the architects of 9/11 to justice and reduce the threat of terrorism. Then the Afghan mission, which often lacked strategic clarity, morphed from counterinsurgency to counter-narcotics and then into capacity building to remake Afghanistan as an award-winning liberal democracy.

The result is a painful lesson of what can happen when immense military might is put in the hands of politicians and their minions who lack the understanding to employ it properly. Equally culpable are politicized American military leaders who consistently lied about the strength of the Afghan security forces.

The result is that the Taliban, a UN-designated terrorist group, defeated the world's greatest military power—another self-inflicted blow to America's reputation that will complicate the Biden administration's goals to check China's rise by building coalitions in the Asia Pacific.

According to the Costs of War Project at Brown University, the United States has spent more than $2 trillion in Afghanistan since 9/11. That's $300 million per day for two decades.

And the human costs are even greater. There have been 2,448 service members killed and over 21,000 American soldiers injured in action, along with 3,846 contractors killed. That pales beside the estimated 66,000 Afghan national military and police and over 47,000 Afghan civilians who were killed.

And because the United States borrowed most of the money to pay for the war, generations of Americans will be burdened by the cost of paying for it. The Costs of War researchers estimate that by 2050, interest payments alone on the Afghan war debt could reach $6.5 trillion. That amounts to $20,000 for each US citizen.

You do not need to support a continued presence in that arid, stone-age country to recognize that things have gone badly. The execution of the US withdrawal has been disastrous, deadly, and humiliating, handing power back to the Taliban in a matter of days. The dramatic unravelling of the situation in Afghanistan puts President Biden's reputation for foreign policy expertise at risk.

It is worth bearing in mind what former Bush and Obama Defense Secretary Robert Gates wrote in his memoirs: Biden has "been wrong on nearly every major foreign policy and national security issue over the past four decades."

But not to worry, this is not your father's Taliban. They are smarter and tougher.

## The Ripple Effect of the Volcker Shock for the Economy

9/11/2021

Pres. Jimmy Carter nominated New York Federal Reserve Bank President Paul Volcker to chair the Federal Reserve in July 1979 to deal with the immediate issue of hyperinflation. He was confirmed by the Senate in August and served as chair until 1987.

The no-nonsense, independent-minded Volcker oversaw a program of financial austerity that left a deep imprint on the US economy and financial system. Unlike elected officials, he understood that there are times when you must incur short-term costs to achieve long-term benefits. Volcker is widely regarded as one of the best Fed chairpersons in history.

When he took the reins of the central bank, the United States was mired in a decade-long period of rapidly rising prices and weak economic growth, which had come to be known in the 1970s as "stagflation." The month Volcker took office, unemployment was 6 percent, and inflation was barreling toward 15 percent.

One advantage he enjoyed was that the nation was far less in debt than in the current environment. Unlike today, Volcker did not have to be concerned that raising interest rates to fight inflation would risk triggering a debt crisis. Conversely, if the current Fed maintains a loose monetary policy, it risks double-digit inflation.

In a moment market watchers will never forget, Volcker opted to cleave to his monetarist teaching by attempting to control interest rates by contracting the money supply rather than the fed funds rate. The Fed had historically targeted an interest rate in the short-term money market to loosen or tighten the money supply.

Then, as now, the Fed set a target for short-term interest rates, then bought and sold securities to ensure that rates actually settled at that level. Volcker concluded that the Fed needed to change strategies and start targeting the actual amount of money floating in the economy. As he said, "[I]t was time to act—to send a convincing message to markets and to the public."

So just two months after taking office in August 1979, Volcker attacked inflation by using the Fed's powers to directly target the growth in the quantity of money. He would leave interest rates alone to set themselves freely in the market.

It was shock therapy. By April 1980 interest rates had spiked above 17 percent, and in the second quarter of 1980, the gross domestic product contracted by 7.9 percent. The extreme rise in interest rates was called the Volcker shock.

The action indeed triggered what was then the deepest economic downturn since the Great Depression and drove thousands of businesses and farms to bankruptcy. Unemployment peaked at 10.8 percent.

But by the mid-1980s, Volcker's medicine was working. The reduced money supply and high cost of credit finally vanquished inflation and inflationary expectations.

Volcker's steadfast commitment to his shock therapy and willingness to take unpopular policy actions made him the target of opprobrium by politicians of all ideological stripes. He believed central bankers needed to steer the economy free of political considerations. Protesting his policies, home builders sent the Fed unused two-by-fours, auto dealers mailed keys to the cars for which there were no buyers, and farmers drove their tractors around the white marble Fed building.

But the double-digit interest rates and sharp double-dip recession that followed the tightening of credit finally slayed the inflation dragon. It plunged below 4 percent in 1983, and by 1986 it was down to around 2 percent.

Interest rates eventually followed. Once the out-of-control inflation ended, he cut rates. This restored faith in the dollar, the Coca-Cola of money, and laid the groundwork for a quarter century of low inflation, steady growth, and rare and mild recessions.

It can be said of Volcker as Hamlet said of his father: "He was a man, take him for all in all. I shall not look upon his like again."

## What Will the Taliban Do with US Military Weapons Left Behind?

9/25/2021

With the war in Afghanistan having officially ended on August 31, the world's thoughts have turned to how the Taliban will govern the country and what equipment left behind by coalition forces they now have at their disposal.

The calamity in Afghanistan raises questions not just about what the American mission was but about how much of the US military budget seems to provide little in the way of benefits. The United States dumped over $2 trillion into nation building in Afghanistan over a twenty-year period, including $85 billion in technically advanced equipment and training for Afghan security forces.

Say what you will about the decision to withdraw, it should be obvious by now that the boneheaded, hasty, and chaotic US exit from Afghanistan cost the lives of thirteen brave servicemen and women and left behind hundreds of Americans and thousands of Afghan allies the United States repeatedly promised to get out.

If that sounds like one of the less significant charges one might level against the American government, consider how, after a war that lasted twenty years, the United States has nothing to show for it but a fully equipped Taliban parading around in US Army fatigues, cradling American M16 rifles and other weapons. The Taliban staged victory parades showing off the US military hardware they have seized, replacing sandals with American military boots they could never have imagined.

A rough estimate of the total amount of equipment sent to Afghanistan during the twenty-year occupation includes up to 22,000 Humvee vehicles, nearly 1,000 armored vehicles, 64,000 machine guns, and 42,000 pickup trucks and SUVs. Other weapons included up to 358,000 assault rifles, 126,000 pistols, and 200 artillery units.

Oh, and the Taliban will likely inherit state-of-the-art military helicopters, warplanes, late-model drones, and other aircraft from the United States as well. Thanks to the largesse of the American taxpayer, the Taliban now has more Black Hawk helicopters than 85 percent of the countries in the world, according to Cong. Jim Banks, who is also a veteran.

While it is always frustrating to read about the many ways the federal government wastes taxpayer money, it pales in comparison with the appalling reality that the United States left an estimated $85 billion in taxpayer-purchased military equipment in the hands of the Taliban. This was just part of the American taxpayer money that evaporated as the Taliban marched toward Kabul. There was also the opportunity cost of what these funds could have done to improve the quality of life in the United States.

Even if the equipment is not used by the Taliban, it may end up going to the highest bidder or to hostile states that can reverse engineer the technology.

But there are other dangers as well. For example, the Taliban has seized biometric devices from the US military that might allow them to identify and capture Afghans who worked with the US and the NATO allies that were part of the Afghan enterprise. These devices have the fingerprints, eye scans, and biological information of all the Afghans who were with the coalition forces over the last twenty years.

There is no sugarcoating the American defeat in Afghanistan. But trying to get the straight skinny from the Pentagon and the White House on why all the US weaponry was abandoned is like trying to put out a bushfire.

Having closed the chapter on Afghanistan, Americans who pride themselves on having notoriously short memories will move on to other issues, such as the still-raging COVID-19 pandemic and things that affect them and their families more directly. Politicians have made careers betting on the public's historical amnesia and short memory.

And unlike the 1979 kidnapping of fifty-three Americans at the US Embassy in Tehran, the media will not report on the fiasco in Afghanistan for 444 days and nights, as they did throughout the Iranian hostage crisis.

## Federal Reserve Is Betting on Inflation Being Transitory; We'll See

10/9/2021

In a highly anticipated announcement several weeks ago, Federal Reserve Chair Jerome Powell said the Fed would start reversing its pandemic stimulus programs. Removing the training wheels from the US economy will likely begin as soon as November.

The Fed continues to believe that inflation, while painful, is transitory. This Panglossian scenario may turn out to be a pipe dream.

The Fed cut its short-term benchmark rate to near zero when the coronavirus hit in March 2020. The pandemic lockdown and subsequent recession led to ultraloose monetary policies and massive asset purchases by the central bank aimed at keeping the economy from heading over a cliff.

Powell said the process of dialing back the government's buying spree, or tapering, from buying $80 billion in Treasuries a month and $40 billion in mortgage-backed securities since June 2020 should be complete by mid-2022. He indicated that interest rates could start to rise again next year but stressed that the reduction of monthly asset purchases is not tantamount to hiking interest rates.

This move comes even though the Fed does not expect inflation, which is running at the highest rate in decades, to persist. The central bank has consistently contended that this year's surge is transitory and that inflation will soon be close to the Fed's 2 percent target. Transitory has become a byword of pandemic-era central bank policymaking.

In August overall consumer prices rose 5.3 percent compared with last year, a slightly slower pace than in June and July but high nonetheless. The Fed still sees core inflation, which excludes food and energy prices, running at 3.7 percent this year before falling to 2.3 percent in 2022 and 2.1 percent in each of the following two years.

The Fed is also cutting its economic growth projection for this year to 5.9 percent from a 7 percent growth forecast in June. It projects that unemployment will fall from the current 5.2 percent to 4.8 percent by year's end.

It merits noting that a 2 percent inflation rate is still a big deal to everyday Americans. If realized, it would result in prices rising by 22 percent over a decade with no assurance that wages would match the increase.

Closely related, inflation makes life more complicated for savers and retirees living on a fixed income since it erodes the purchasing power of every dollar, which is the equivalent of raising prices. Within living memory, the average price of a cup of coffee was fifty cents. Today it's around three dollars.

The Fed appears to believe that relatively high inflation rates are a temporary phenomenon; prices are rising because of the pandemic and the production shortages that accompany it.

Put differently, the Fed anticipates that inflationary pressures such as spiking energy prices and global supply chain bottlenecks will eventually dissipate. It does acknowledge that factors that are contributing to the recent rise in inflation may last longer than originally projected.

Of course, there is no mention that massive monetary and fiscal stimulus over the past year and a half is contributing to inflation. The Fed continues to blame the supply side for inflation without recognizing that monetary policy is pushing the demand side when there is insufficient supply.

But not to worry, the Fed could be correct as it navigates the fog of uncertainty—but it could be wrong. How long is transitory? Will inflation simply go away on its own? One could conclude from the data that the economy has long been overheating, and inflation may continue rising for the foreseeable future.

If that is the case, the Fed should snatch away the punch bowl immediately. Realistically, it will not increase interest rates to deal with inflation until Americans are angry enough to vote for the opposition party next year. Then they will have to slam on the brakes by raising interest rates aggressively, and the country may well enter a period of stagflation reminiscent of the 1970s.

## The Fight over the Federal Debt Ceiling Is Kabuki Theater

10/25/2021

The United States is once again flirting with a default crisis. The clock is ticking on a deal to raise the federal borrowing limit, or debt ceiling, and prevent a default on the national debt. After months of wrangling, Congress struck a short-term deal to temporarily avoid a first-ever default, but it sets up another showdown in a matter of weeks.

The recent legislation raised the nation's borrowing limit by $480 billion, the amount the Treasury Department said it needed to meet the country's cash needs until December 3, setting up yet another deadline for Congress to resolve the issue.

The debt ceiling, also known as the debt limit, is the maximum amount of money the feds can borrow cumulatively by issuing debt in the form of bonds to meet its obligations.

The fight over the federal debt ceiling is Kabuki theater in the city of sound and fury. Tracing its origins to the seventeenth century, Kabuki is the stylized Japanese drama in which performers wear elaborate makeup and costumes. Actions aren't literal but metaphorical, conveyed through singing, dancing, and mime.

In Washington, DC, the Kabuki theater of America's debt ceiling is a debate with overheated rhetoric and extravagant gestures, as politicians of both parties engage in the silly debt ceiling dance until the eleventh hour, when each gives ground to save face, resolves the standoff, and avoids a default just in the nick of time.

A default would be a catastrophic blow to the economic recovery from the COVID-19 pandemic. Global financial markets would be disrupted, and Americans would pay for this default for generations, as global investors would come to believe that the federal government's finances have been politicized, and they are not going to get paid what they are owed. Going forward they would demand higher interest rates on the Treasury bonds they purchase.

Congress enacted the debt ceiling in 1917 to placate antiwar lawmakers who were uncomfortable about letting the Treasury Department borrow too much money to finance World War I. Since then the limit has been raised or modified ninety-eight times, according to the Congressional Research Service. Yawn.

It's a mechanism that allows the US Treasury to borrow money for any approved spending up to a certain limit without first getting approval from Congress. Lifting the debt limit does not initiate any new spending. Rather, it simply allows the United States to finance obligations already authorized by Congress, including interest on the debt and payments to Social Security, Medicare, and Medicaid.

There have been regular congressional battles over the debt ceiling. Despite partisan disagreements, Congress and the president have never allowed the country to default on its debt. During the Obama administration in 2011, when Republicans refused to raise it without significant spending cuts, a deal was finally struck to resolve the debt ceiling issue. But coming within days of the Treasury being unable to pay out certain benefits did lead to Standard & Poor's to strip the United States of its triple-A credit rating for the first time in history.

There were also government shutdowns in 2013 and 2018, when the government closed nonessential services, such as national parks, and sent federal employees on forced leave. President Trump's demand for $5.7 billion to build a wall on the Southern border led to a thirty-five-day shutdown in 2018.

If the debt ceiling is not raised and the government can't borrow to pay the bills, it would have to suspend certain pension payments, withhold military and federal workers' pay, and delay interest payments on outstanding debt, potentially roiling financial markets and raising borrowing costs.

But not to worry, Americans have seen this movie before. The debt ceiling will be raised, and the government will not default. After all the Sturm und Drang, all will be fine after Democrats and Republicans have used it to embarrass each other and seize some electoral advantage.

## Sausage Making and the President's Build Back Better Legislation

11/4/2021

The legislative process is rarely pretty in the best of times, never mind in times like these. Many people console themselves with this reality by quoting Otto von Bismarck, the pragmatic Prussian politician who, among other things, was the first chancellor of the German Empire from 1871 to 1890.

He is often erroneously quoted as saying, "Laws are like sausages. It's better not to see them being made." There has been a lot of sausage making going on in full view at the White House and in Congress over the last several months on the president's Build Back Better legislation.

When a big bill makes its way through Congress, it highlights political divisions and can seem disconnected from the average American's life. The Biden administration's quest for a legislatively viable version of its Build Back Better agenda is an example.

Originally presented as a $3.5 trillion package on social welfare and climate change mitigation, the slimmed-down version of the legislation now stands at $1.75 trillion over ten years—a sum roughly equal to 0.6 percent of projected gross domestic product. The president said he will have more to say on the legislation when he returns from a week of summit meetings in Europe. It represents the culmination of months of tense negotiations between moderate and progressive lawmakers.

Several of the administration's promises have been abandoned in the new package, such as free community college and instituting a clean electricity standard with penalties for utilities that don't comply. Sen. Joe Manchin (D-West Virginia) kneecapped the provision to retire coal and natural gas plants.

Other programs that were initially going to be permanent will instead be set to expire in a year or two or five, such as the expanded child tax credit and expanding Medicaid in the twelve states that have not already done so. It merits noting that once entitlement programs are established, they are famously difficult to repeal.

Still, the $1.75 trillion package contains a wide-ranging set of programs, such as universal preschool for all three- and four-year-olds, subsidized child care that caps what parents pay at 7 percent of their income, expanded Medicare to cover the cost of hearing benefits, and expanded tax credits for ten years for utility and residential clean energy to reduce pollution, including electric vehicles. Also notable is that although an overwhelming majority of Americans favor government action such as Medicare negotiating with drug companies to reduce drug prices, that policy is not in the proposed legislation.

While the White House claims the legislation would not add to the deficit because of tax increases on corporations and the affluent, finding the taxes to pay for this package is proving difficult. For example, Sen. Kyrsten Sinema (D-Arizona) is opposed to increasing the corporate tax to 25 or 26 percent and raising personal income tax rates. The progressive wing of the Democratic Party is now proposing annual taxes on billionaires for unrealized capital gains on stocks that have not even been sold and received as income.

According to an analysis from the University of Pennsylvania's Wharton School of Business, the proposed new taxes and tax increases to pay for the $1.75 trillion bill would raise nearly $470 billion less than the White House claims.

With the president out of the country, Democrats are arguing among themselves over the details of the legislation. House progressives are adamant about requiring the bill to be a done deal before they will vote for the $1.2 trillion bipartisan infrastructure bill that has been passed by the Senate because they don't trust moderate Democrats to keep their word.

As the late great New York Yankee catcher Yogi Berra said, "It ain't over 'til it's over." So the public sausage making, also known as lawmaking, will continue on Capitol Hill over the president's Build Back Better legislation. As always, the devil is in the details.

## Hold Social Media Accountable for What Appears on Their Platforms

11/20/2021

Large social media platforms such as Alphabet (Google), Facebook (now Meta), and Twitter like having it both ways when it comes to taking responsibility for the content on their platforms.

On one hand they say they are merely platforms for people who post content and, as platform providers, are not responsible for what appears. On the other hand (isn't there always), they actively determine what appears on their platforms, in the same way newspapers decide what stories to run.

Can social media platforms really say with a straight face that they are not responsible for what appears on their platforms when they determine what constitutes suitable content?

Internet social media platforms are granted broad safe harbor protections against legal liability for any content users post on their platforms. The arguments these platforms make for escaping legal liability are spelled out in one sentence in Section 230 of the 1996 Communications Decency Act: "No provider of an interactive computer service shall be treated as the publisher or speaker of any information provided by another information content provider." In essence Section 230 gives websites immunity from liability for what their users post.

As Congress considers amending or repealing Section 230, perhaps one immediate step should be to give the Federal Communications Commission oversight of the platforms' content decisions.

The Communications Decency Act passed in 1996 when the internet was in its infancy and Congress was concerned that subjecting hosting platforms to the same civil liability as all other businesses would retard their growth. It was written before Facebook and Google existed.

In effect, big tech companies benefit from a federal law that specifically protects them. The same sweetheart deal is not available to traditional media companies and publishers. When you grant platforms complete immunity for the content their users post, you also reduce their incentives to remove content that causes social harm.

Congress's expectation in enacting Section 230 was at least twofold. First, it hoped protection from civil suits would provide an incentive for websites to create a family-friendly online environment that would shield children, hence the Good Samaritan title of this section. Second, Congress hoped it would promote the growth of the fledgling internet economy by giving it partial protection from federal and state regulation.

Fast-forward twenty-five years and things look a whole lot different than they did in 1996. The Section 230 protections are now desperately out of date. The largest and most powerful companies today are big tech companies that have enormous resources and advanced algorithms they use to help them moderate content. It is time to rethink and revise the protections.

There is growing consensus for updating Section 230. Both Democrats and Republicans apparently agree that these companies should not receive this government subsidy free of any responsibility and that they should moderate content in a politically neutral manner to provide "a forum for a true diversity of political discourse." During his presidential campaign, President Biden said Section 230 should be "revoked, immediately." Sen. Lindsey Graham (R-South Carolina) has said, "Section 230 as it exists today has got to give."

Before amending Section 230, Congress should make sure that changing it won't do more harm than good. While lawmakers argue about whether Section 230 should be amended or indeed repealed, one simple and immediate step toward making big tech companies more transparent would be to require them to submit to an external audit conducted by the Federal Communications Commission.

Such an approach is not perfect, of course, but it would force the network platform companies to have to prove that their algorithms and content-removal practices moderate content in a politically neutral manner, not partisan instruments, and prioritize truthfulness and accuracy over user engagement.

This would be consistent with one of Congress's findings when it enacted Section 230: "The Internet and other interactive computer services offer a forum for a true diversity of political discussion, unique opportunities for cultural development, and myriad avenues for intellectual activity."

## Another Ugly Inflation Report Worries Working Americans

12/23/2021

After yet another ugly inflation report, the United States has its highest inflation rate since 1982, an eye-popping 6.8 percent. It was an increase that surpassed anything even the most pessimistic forecasters expected.

Inflation is up almost a whole percentage point in a single month and is three times the Fed target of 2 percent. It may climb higher still before it starts to come under control.

Inflation has become impossible to ignore. Working people are struggling to meet the cost of basics such as food and housing because of skyrocketing prices. In November food prices were up 6.1 percent from the year before, with meat, poultry, fish, and eggs up 12.8 percent; cereals and bakery products up 4.6 percent; and nonalcoholic beverages up 5.3 percent. Energy prices increased 33 percent. Used trucks and vehicles went up 31.4 percent.

All these items are basic necessities. This year working Americans have had trouble affording basic needs amid soaring inflation.

Is it any wonder why the ordinary working American is anxious when they go to the grocery store or gas station? Basic necessities have become unaffordable for many middle- and low-income families whose salaries have not kept up with inflation. Ignoring these numbers is like going to the Grand Canyon and keeping your eyes shut.

The Federal Reserve, after having been caught flat-footed, is now struggling to get ahead of inflation. After nearly a year of insisting that inflation is transitory, the Fed finally acknowledged otherwise. It will cut back its stimulus program more quickly than planned, ending asset purchases by March and raising interest rates as much as seventy-five basis points by the end of 2022.

That word "transitory" has been put to pasture as the Fed gradually tightens monetary policy to put the economy on a smooth glide path back to a growth and inflation equilibrium and the promised land. Good luck with that.

The Fed's hawkish pivot comes as the economy faces the fastest inflation since the 1980s and a tight labor market. The Fed made a historic mistake that they now have to fix by slamming on the brakes without sending the economy into recession. Prices rise when goods become scarce or the money supply expands rapidly.

For sure, pandemic-induced supply chain disruptions have caused scarcity, but the Fed increased the money supply more than 40 percent in the past two years, creating excess demand that has contributed to inflation. Say what you want about inflation, and everybody does, today's version is an unusual combination of both the demand and supply side.

Stopping inflation is a slow and painful experience for ordinary working-class Americans. Inflation may become self-perpetuating through price and wage-setting behavior. American workers will demand higher wages to compensate for inflation, and firms will raise prices, creating a vicious cycle. It eats away at consumer purchasing power and has historically required crushing interest rates to bring it under control.

Anyone whose pay is not rising by at least 7 percent will, in effect, feel like their pay has been cut. Inflation is now America's public enemy number one.

It should be clear as gin that the pay hikes the country is seeing for workers traditionally at the lower end of the pay spectrum are long overdue after decades of stagnation. But higher wages are only meaningful if working Americans can afford more as a result. Next year's price surges threaten to cancel out bigger paychecks, as working people will be paying more for less.

# 6

# 2022 Columns

## Once-Powerful GE Is Making Dramatic Moves to Survive

1/15/2022

General Electric (GE), the iconic American corporation that says it brings good things to life, announced in November that it is splitting into three public companies. The firm hopes to focus and simplify its business while reducing its debt.

One of the three new companies will focus on aviation, another on health care, and the third on energy. GE plans to spin off its health-care division, which makes hospital equipment, in early 2023. The following year it intends to combine its power units and renewable energy unit, which makes turbines for power plants and wind farms, leaving only the aviation business.

The firm will then focus on making and servicing jet engines. Existing GE shareholders will get stakes in each of the new public companies.

This is certainly a dramatic move for the 129-year-old industrial conglomerate. The company started in 1892, after the company, which was, of course, founded by Thomas Edison, inventor of the light bulb, merged with its rival manufacturing company, Thomson-Houston Electric Co., to become General Electric, as it is known today. A few years later, the company became one of only twelve companies listed on the newly formed Dow Jones Industrial Average.

During the 1980s and '90s, the firm was run for twenty years by the larger-than-life Jack Welch. He transformed the manufacturer into a conglomerate, buying up companies, including RCA, owner of the NBC TV network.

At its height, under Welch, GE had expanded into the financial sector and was making everything, from refrigerators and plane engines to medical equipment and, of course, light bulbs. It became the most valuable company in the world.

But GE's problems didn't come out of the blue. There were many factors involved in its demise. One was Welch's focus on GE Capital, the firm's financial services arm. In 2000 the lion's share of GE's profitability and almost half its revenue came from GE Capital.

During Welch's tenure it became far larger and more successful than GE's other business units. At its height GE Capital was the seventh-largest US financial institution. GE Capital enabled the company to smooth over its quarterly earnings report and keep Wall Street happy.

GE Capital moved into retail banking, private-label credit cards, brokerage services, home loans, mortgage-backed securities, and insurance. It had also become the world's largest lessor of cars, equipment, and ship containers and the biggest private mortgage insurer.

In effect, GE, a household name and established global brand, was more of a financial services company than an industrial manufacturing company making stuff the economy needs. This finance arm was a major factor in GE's demise. In some ways GE Capital was the tail wagging the dog.

All hell broke loose when the financial crisis hit in 2008, and GE barely survived, as the crisis revealed it to be overstretched. Despite GE's reputation for management excellence, the firm was overly dependent on its finance business, which melted under the heat of the excessive risks it had taken during a period of low interest rates and a long bull market. With GE struggling to meet is financial commitments, Warren Buffett's Berkshire Hathaway Inc. famously stepped in and invested $3 billion.

The American taxpayer guaranteed tens of billions in debt. The US government designated GE Capital a systemically important financial institution, meaning that it had the potential to wreck the economy if it were to collapse (too big to fail).

So much for the myth that Jack Welch was the greatest manager of the twentieth century, elevating management to a kind of science, and for the belief that great management can work miracles. GE was supposedly the textbook case of a corporation creating synergy and value across various companies around the world. Soon, you will barely be able to recognize it.

## GE, J&J, and Toshiba Are Moving in a New Direction
2/5/2022

Last November three major conglomerates—General Electric, Johnson & Johnson, and Toshiba—all revealed plans to break themselves up in an effort to maximize shareholder value. They won't be the last to do it.

Conglomerates are large parent companies made up of smaller business units that operate across multiple markets in an effort to diversify the risk of being in a single market. The financial health of a conglomerate is difficult to discern, as the parent company reports results on a consolidated basis. Recall the key role GE Capital played for many years as the catalyst for growth and profitability at General Electric.

Johnson & Johnson (J&J), the biggest pharmaceutical company in the United States based on market cap of $435 billion, announced its intent to break off its consumer health division in the next eighteen to twenty-four months. J&J is the thirty-sixth largest company in the United States based on total revenue, according to the 2021 Fortune 500 list.

It will spin off its consumer business, which includes such brands as Band-Aid, Tylenol, Nicorette, and Neutrogena, into a new publicly traded company by November 2023. Its prescription drug and medical device businesses will continue to operate under its banner.

What is behind these breakups? There is an argument that these firms have become too diversified, too complicated, and too challenging to manage efficiently.

The recent history of all three has also been tumultuous. General Electric was nearly taken down during the financial meltdown in 2008. J&J is facing over twenty thousand lawsuits related to claims that its baby powder causes cancer and for its role in the opioid crisis. The firm took a hit when the Centers for Disease Control and Prevention recommended that Americans not receive its COVID-19 vaccine because of adverse side effects. Toshiba is still trying to recover from a massive 2015 accounting scandal.

At first blush it would appear that the era of the conglomerate and the notion that brilliant management can successfully run businesses in varied industries is over. While traditional industrial corporate conglomerates may be pushing up daises, the success of tech giants such as Amazon, Facebook (parent Meta), Microsoft, Apple, and Alphabet as modern-day conglomerates should be noted.

These firms are not throwbacks to the traditional conglomerate model whose main purpose was to allocate financial capital across various businesses and rebalance the portfolio through acquisitions and divestments.

Take Amazon, for example. While the company does not describe itself as a conglomerate, it operates online and brick-and-mortar retail stores, sells outsourced computing services, runs global logistics operation, produces movies, and the beat goes on.

These tech conglomerates do differ from traditional industrial conglomerates. They have created platforms that knit together and support the varied businesses. Put differently, the businesses in these companies rely on a common infrastructure to provide the unifying thread.

A platform is essentially a marketplace that connects the supply side and the demand side. Amazon links shoppers and sellers, producers and consumers in high-value exchanges. The company enables Prime members to order Whole Foods deliveries on the Amazon website.

The spectacular growth of these businesses has been explained by network effects. The value of a platform depends, in large part, on the number of users on either side of the exchange. The more users a platform has, the more attractive it becomes, leading even more people to use it. This allows business to scale up quickly and creates a competitive advantage. The tech companies are exploiting the power of platforms and the relatively low capital investment they require. These network effects are the driving force behind every successful platform.

# Debt Matters as US Deals with Highest Inflation Rate in Forty Years

2/20/2022

The United States' total public debt has ballooned to nearly $30 trillion. Split among the nation's roughly 130 million households, that is about $229,000 per household. And the bill is about to go up, as rampant inflation triggers rising interest rates.

Few in the media took notice when the nation's debt hit the $30 trillion mark. There was little, if any, reaction from the denizens of DC's political and policy establishment, busy as they are fighting over just about everything. Budget hawks are nowhere to be found.

Setting aside the intergovernmental debt that one part of the government owes to another part, such as what the federal government owes the Social Security Trust Fund, debt held by the public is about $24 trillion. That is more than GDP, a level previously seen only at the end of World War II.

Much of the national debt owed to foreign institutions is held by the Japanese and the Chinese, who definitely want to get paid. It should not be overlooked that a growing debt burden may undermine confidence in the US dollar as the world's reserve currency, making it more difficult to finance economic activity in international markets.

But why worry about debt when vast sums of money can be created out of thin air to pay the interest on all that debt, and nominal interest rates are near zero? It's a free lunch!

The federal government spends about $300 billion annually on interest payments on the national debt. This is the equivalent of nearly 9 percent of annual federal revenue and more than the federal government spends on science, space, technology, transportation, and education combined.

The cost of servicing debt from past spending reduces the money available for other spending programs. Each 1 percent rise in interest rates would increase debt servicing costs by about $225 billion at today's debt levels. This is not chopped liver.

Even in a historically low-interest-rate environment, the amount of debt we've accumulated results in daunting interest costs. It will get even more expensive when the Federal Reserve gets around to raising interest rates significantly to deal with the highest inflation in forty years.

Who would have thought trillions in stimulus spending and money being printed by the nominally independent Federal Reserve and plowed back into the economy when companies couldn't produce enough of what consumers wanted would drive prices higher? More demand plus less supply equals higher prices. The Fed ignored the inflation risks inherent in monetary financing of the government deficits. After all there is virtually no limit to money creation under a fiat monetary system.

The hard truth is that these folks were out to lunch as the cost of living for ordinary Americans was rising. Paychecks will feel tighter than usual as inflation outpaces wage increases.

Americans are then told that a key way to help relieve rising prices is to pass a $1.85 trillion collection of spending programs and tax cuts known as the Build Back Better bill, which is currently languishing in the Senate. It will deliver good economic outcomes: low inflation and low unemployment.

And now financial markets are nervous about the prospect of the steepest monetary tightening cycle since the 1990s, with markets pricing in more than five quarter-point Federal Reserve interest rate hikes in 2022.

Debt matters. Fiscal responsibility matters. The short-term pain associated with fixes that will bring long-term gains is a real challenge for politicians—especially in even-numbered years. They much prefer to kick the can down the road hoping the bill will come due on someone else's watch.

The American public is equally culpable, electing politicians who don't have the courage to advocate for solutions to the debt issue. Those who do are run out of office.

To paraphrase Hemingway's words from *The Sun Also Rises*, "How do you go bankrupt? Two ways: gradually, then suddenly."

## Trudeau Went Too Far in Dealing with Canada's "Freedom Convoy"

3/5/2022

The "Freedom Convoy" of trucks that converged in Ottawa on January 28 began in response to the Canadian government's requirement that Canadian truck drivers crossing the US border be fully vaccinated to avoid testing and quarantine requirements upon their return. Then it evolved into a protest against all public health measures aimed at fighting the COVID-19 pandemic.

Organizers said they would not end their protest until all pandemic-related public health measures were dropped.

After three weeks of protests, Prime Minister Justin Trudeau invoked the Emergency Act to deal with the blockades. It was the first time the law had ever been used, and it was invoked even though there were plenty of other laws on the books to deal with peaceful protests. It was a classic example of using a machete when a scalpel would have worked just fine.

The act gave the Canadian government broad powers to restore order, ranging from placing significant limits on peaceful assembly to prohibiting travel to requiring financial institutions to turn over personal financial information to the Canadian Security Intelligence Service and freezing the bank accounts of protestors and anyone who helped them.

The act also gave the government broad authority over businesses, such as dragooning private tow truck companies to provide services against their will. Insurance companies were required to revoke insurance on any vehicles used in blockades.

The Emergency Act is only supposed to be invoked in a genuine crisis, such as in wartime. The War Measures Act, its predecessor, was last invoked under the current prime minister's father, Pierre Trudeau, in response to the 1970 October Crisis, when a group of militant separatists who wanted to create an independent socialist Quebec engaged in numerous bombings and kidnapped and murdered a cabinet minister.

There is a very real difference between invoking a law against violent terrorists and using it to combat a largely peaceful protest by Canadian citizens tired of COVID-19 restrictions and lockdowns.

Ottawa police clad in riot gear, with provincial and federal help, towed dozens of vehicles that were blocking Ottawa's downtown streets. They retook control of the area around Parliament buildings and used pepper spray and stun grenades to remove demonstrators. Ottawa's streets are now back to normal; there is only snow and silence in the country's capital.

All this could have been done under existing law. As Alberta Premier Jason Kenney put it, "We have all the legal tools and operational resources required to maintain order." Put simply, the prime minister could have restored and maintained public order without marginalizing substantial segments of the population.

Trudeau, born and bred elite, first described the truckers as a fringe minority who held "unacceptable" racist and misogynist views. He refused to meet the protesters or negotiate with them, and he was not interested in hearing about the mandates' impact on their lives. Many of these truckers had spent the last two years keeping the supply chain running.

Instead of finding ways to defuse the situation, Mr. Trudeau issued the emergency order, which he called a "last resort." After a conservative member of Parliament and descendant of Holocaust survivors asked him tough questions about his handling of the truckers' protest, Trudeau denounced conservatives who "stand with people who wave swastikas and confederate flags." These comments came from someone who spent his youth wearing blackface.

The role of government is to maintain public order while respecting civil liberties, including the right to peaceful assembly. Many protests are disruptive and often unlawful, so it is reasonable to impose limits on the right to assemble.

But a real leader and statesperson would have gone to the protesters and said, "I'm here. What do you want to say?" Seeking out and meeting with protesters and pursuing dialogue is a far more strategic way to restore the rule of law than imposing martial law.

## Nothing Justifies Russia's Invasion of Ukraine
3/15/2022

Vladimir Putin is not crazy. He has not lost touch with reality. He is evil, a KGB thug, a murderer, and a war criminal, and he knows what he is doing. Many believe that he will stop at nothing to recreate the Russian Empire. Others believe that Putin is vehemently opposed to NATO expansion.

Whatever Putin's motives, nothing justifies Russia's horrific invasion of Ukraine. It is a flagrant violation of international law that has resulted in a humanitarian disaster. It seems strange now that anyone ever imagined that Putin might not invade Ukraine.

The West is told that Putin has made a strategic mistake in thinking his military could overwhelm Ukraine, capture Kiev within seventy-two hours, decapitate the Ukrainian government, install a pro-Moscow puppet regime, and face little popular resistance. But he knows he can achieve his objectives by behaving badly.

On August 8, 2008, Russian forces began the invasion of Georgia, marking the start of Europe's first war of the twenty-first century. The conflict itself was over within a matter of days, but the repercussions of the Russo-Georgian War continue to reverberate.

The international reaction to Russia's military campaign in Georgia was remarkably muted. It minimized Russia's bad behavior, with Moscow suffering few negative consequences. The invasion of Georgia should have been a wake-up call to the international community.

Understandably, Putin interpreted this accommodating approach as an invitation for further acts of aggression in what he perceived as Russia's traditional sphere of influence. The 2008 invasion of Georgia was a Beta test for future aggression against Russia's neighbors and a dry run for the tactics and strategies that would later be deployed in the 2014 invasion of Ukraine: launch a cyberattack, a disinformation campaign, and an all-out effort to meddle in a country's domestic politics. Six years after the Russo-Georgian War, Russia embarked on a far more comprehensive military campaign against Ukraine, which again went unchecked.

Even after the illegal annexation of Crimea in 2014 and the launch of Moscow's war in eastern Ukraine, the United States and Europe still failed to acknowledge that Russia had become a revisionist power seeking to establish its dominion over the eastern half of Europe.

One can only speculate whether firmer Western responses in 2008 and 2014 could have prevented the tragic events of 2022. Now Ukrainians are paying the ultimate price. Based on the West's behavior, Putin could only have concluded that the benefits of invading Ukraine would exceed the costs.

Europe and the United States keep learning the wrong lessons; their weakness begets weakness. Showing restraint and searching for a diplomatic solution encourages Putin, who has no retirement plans, to exploit the West's vulnerability and double down.

Putin is holding the world to ransom. Few thought he would actually invade Ukraine, but he did just that. Why would you put anything past him, including widening the war leading to a nuclear Armageddon? An economically cornered Russia coupled with continued Ukrainian resistance could cause Putin to escalate.

Putin understands that the United States and Europe will not resort to measures such as a no-fly zone that could lead to direct conflict with Russia and risk nuclear war over Ukraine, which is not a NATO member. He knows full well that nuclear brinkmanship has prevented the West from bombing his army into the ground. The result would be World War III. After all Russia has nearly 6,000 nuclear weapons, with an estimated 1,600 active and deployed.

Will all this end with a diplomatic solution in which Russia withdraws its forces in exchange for Ukraine's neutrality? Who knows? It is too early to start considering the shape of things to come. As Yogi Berra famously put it, "It's tough to make predictions, especially about the future." This is especially true when your calculations depend on the actions of an evil man.

# With Budgets Stretched, the Fed Finally Raises Interest Rates

4/2/2022

The Federal Reserve has chosen to do the bare minimum when it comes to raising its benchmark interest rate. Last month's 0.25 percentage point increase was no more than the markets had expected.

It was the first time the Fed has raised rates in more than three years and marked a reversal of a zero-interest rate policy and injecting unprecedented levels of cash into the economy. Still, real interest rates—nominal rates adjusted for inflation—remain extremely low. Taking interest rates to near zero has caused one of the greatest asset bubbles in history. The Fed has its hands full to achieve a soft landing and get inflation back to its 2 percent target over the next three years.

That may be the triumph of hope over experience. After all the Fed ignored all the warning signs, spending much of the last year telling Americans that inflation would be but a transitory problem.

The Fed feared that a larger hike would hold back the economy. On the contrary the real threat to economic growth and living standards may come from a sustained period of high inflation, not small changes in short-term interest rates.

Inflation skyrocketed to 7.9 percent over the past year, according to the February report from the Bureau of Labor Statistics (BLS), the fastest increase since January 1982 when the US economy confronted the twin threats of higher inflation and reduced economic growth. Excluding food and energy, both of which moved sharply higher during the month, core inflation still rose 6.4 percent, the highest since August 1982.

Wherever you look, prices of essential materials, products, and services are shooting up at rates unseen in a decade or more. The most recent inflation problems have also been compounded by fast-rising gas prices. In February gasoline cost 6.6 percent more than in January, which translates to a nearly 40 percent annual increase.

The White House has largely blamed the inflation problem on supply chain disruptions during the COVID-19 pandemic, corporate greed, and now Putin's war. Blaming Putin is utter nonsense. For sure oil prices have increased over the last two months, but consumer inflation rose from 2 percent to over 7 percent in the last year.

Food, housing, cars, recreation—it has all gotten more expensive. This is attributable to an unprecedented government spending blitz, coupled with persistent supply chain disruptions that have been unable to keep up with stimulus-fueled demand, particularly for goods over services.

That's putting upward pressure on wages. But although wages are increasing, inflation is rising faster, meaning that workers are falling further behind. Inflation-adjusted average hourly earnings fell 0.8 percent in February, contributing to a 2.6 percent decline over the past year, according to the BLS.

After allowing for inflation, the fed funds rate is still exceptionally low, especially in real terms. Indeed with the CPI measure now expected to top 8 percent, raising nominal interest rates by just a quarter of a point hardly even counts as monetary tightening. A larger hike would have sent a clear signal that the Fed is serious about getting inflation under control.

Inflation is something a large majority of Americans have not experienced in any meaningful way. Those who are under fifty have no memory of the high inflation rates from forty years ago, so the current price increases come as a shock.

While the consensus view is that the Fed will raise the benchmark interest rate six times this year, these passive increases may be too little and too late to get inflation under control. The longer the Fed waits to raise rates aggressively, the harder it will be to bring down inflation and the worse it will be for the American economy and the living standards of ordinary people.

## Billionaire Tax
4/11/2022

The return of inflation has changed politics. For months the Federal Reserve and the White House dismissed inflation as the dog that had not barked in over forty years. Inflation has now started to spiral out of control, and the country may be on the brink of a recession.

Inflation is one of the main reasons why Biden faces record-low poll numbers, and Democrats may lose control of both the House of Representatives and the Senate in the November midterm elections.

The president's political response has been to include a "Billionaire Minimum Income Tax" in his $5.79 trillion fiscal 2023 budget proposal. Despite the name, it would require that households with a net worth over $100 million (the top 0.001 percent of US households) pay a rate of at least 20 percent on their income, as well as unrealized gains in the value of assets such as stocks and bonds. The Biden administration refers to the name of the proposal as a "Billionaire Minimum Income Tax" despite the $100 million threshold.

Attempting to impose a minimum tax rate of 20 percent on the likes of Jeff Bezos and Elon Musk may be good politics in an era when the prevailing wisdom is that the superrich don't pay their fair share of taxes, but this proposal is highly questionable from a governing standpoint. Essentially the proposal is taxing gains from their wealth.

It is beyond debate that the gap between the richest and the poorest Americans has widened in recent decades. According to the Pew Research Center, in 1970 upper-income households had a 29 percent share of US aggregate income. By 2018 it was 48 percent. Middle-income household income was 62 percent of the total in 1970; by 2018 it was 43 percent.

It gets even worse when you look at wealth inequality. The richest 1 percent of the population owns 56 percent of all US equities. The least-wealthy 40 percent of the population owns no assets at all—nada.

Rather than waiting for a taxpayer to sell an asset and be taxed on those gains, the administration's plan would allow the federal government to start collecting revenue now. The proposal raises complicated questions about how the IRS and taxpayers would assess the value of assets that are not publicly traded. It would be more efficient to simply tax profits from the sale of stocks and other assets at the same rate as ordinary work income.

Another basic question is whether Biden's proposal would raise the $361 billion over a decade that the White House says it would. Taxes based on capital gains coming from tradable assets such as stock and bond prices are certainly more volatile than income earned by taxpayers. What are the assumptions about stock and bond prices over the next ten years that are behind the $361 billion projection, and how do you value nontradable assets?

Broad-based taxes are more likely to deliver projected revenues than those that focus on a subset of the population. But Biden promised during the campaign that he would not raise taxes on anyone making less than $400,000 a year, effectively locking out 98.2 percent of taxpayers from any proposed tax increase.

Like the COVID-19 pandemic, Russia's war in Ukraine has contributed to stagflation pressures in the United States and other advanced economies where prices are increasing beyond what many ordinary people can afford.

Global food prices set a record last month, according to the United Nations. People are on edge. The only certainty when people go food shopping these days is the price will be cheaper today than tomorrow.

Inflation is a very real problem, but Biden's political response of proposing a minimum income tax on the ultrawealthy doesn't address it. Instead it is all about political virtue signaling.

## The War in Ukraine and COVID-19 Could Spell the End of Globalization

4/30/2022

Times are changing. The global pandemic and Russia's unprovoked invasion of Ukraine have sparked debate on the future of globalization—nations trading with few barriers, focusing on the industries and services they do best.

The war in Ukraine has strained ties between countries that were already under pressure because of the coronavirus pandemic. It has exposed the risks inherent in economic interdependence among nations with different ideologies and security interests.

It may well be that globalization, as it has been known, is dead in a post–COVID-19, post–Ukraine war world.

The war has had a big impact on the global economy, especially as supply chain shocks threaten everything, from energy supplies to auto parts to exports of wheat and raw materials, and send prices skyrocketing. It has also raised concerns about food shortages because Russia and Ukraine are among the major breadbaskets of the world. Many countries have banned the export of food grains, fearing supply disruptions and higher prices due to shortages.

The CEO and chairman of BlackRock, the world's largest asset manager, said in a letter to shareholders last month, "The Russian invasion of Ukraine has put an end to the globalization we have experienced over the last three decades." He added that companies and governments will now be forced to further "reevaluate their dependencies and reanalyze their manufacturing and assembly footprints."

The pandemic dramatically demonstrated vulnerabilities in long supply chains and made countries look closer to home. While it is impossible to predict the outcome of the war, Russia's invasion of Ukraine on February 24 has upended a world order that has been in place since the end of the Cold War in the 1990s. It signals changes to globalization as the world has known it.

The combination of technology and a relatively stable geopolitical landscape promoted steady expansion of global trade over the last fifty years. In 1970 trade accounted for 25 percent of global GDP, meaning one quarter of all goods produced were traded with international partners. By 2000 global trade had doubled to 50 percent of all goods and services produced.

But the trend toward globalization recently started to run in reverse. The world trade share of GDP output peaked in 2008 at

61 percent. In 2020 global trade accounted for just 51.6 percent of worldwide GDP, the lowest since 2003.

Even before the pandemic, the 2008 financial crisis dealt a blow to globalization, as cross-border investments, trade, and supply chains all contracted. In the last decade, globalization has suffered multiple setbacks in the form of Brexit, the US–China trade war, the pandemic, and now the Russia–Ukraine war.

The conceit that economic interdependence promotes political stability has been shaken. Russia, the ninth-largest economy in the world, is being economically isolated from the West, which has responded to Russian aggression with harsh economic sanctions. Consider that the European Union is Russia's main trading partner, accounting for 38 percent of its exports. Of course, this is partially neutralized by its dependence on imports of Russian gas and oil.

Governments and corporations are recognizing the limits of having supply chains spread out in multiple locations. For instance, shortages of surgical masks and personal protective gear at the outset of the pandemic in 2020 showed the vulnerability of the world's dependence on Chinese factories for all sorts of goods.

Many countries are now moving toward strategic autonomy— reducing dependence on trade with adversaries, focusing more on like-minded partners, and moving manufacturing capacity closer to home to mitigate risks, including lockdown-induced disruptions as in China.

All this means global trade may have crossed the Rubicon and is heading toward cold war–era trade blocs, one led by the United States and the other by China.

Globalization may not fully recover from the pandemic and the war in Ukraine. A version of it based on different principles and moves away from pure efficiency to consider security, reliability, and partnerships may be in the offering.

## Do Economic Sanctions Work?
5/9/2022

When Western policymakers want to influence an outcome and military intervention is deemed too risky, economic sanctions are a favorite nonlethal tool in their bag of tricks. The war in Ukraine is the latest example of their use.

Attacking a country's economy through sanctions can be a way of hitting your enemy where it hurts—in the pocketbook. And it's a lot easier than going to war. The question is whether sanctions cause as many problems as they solve.

Economic sanctions are not a novel concept in international diplomacy. The aim of weakening the enemy through the material deprivation of its population long predates modern times. In fact it dates back to the ancient Greeks, when Athens imposed a trade embargo on its neighbor Megara in 432 BC, which helped trigger the Peloponnesian War.

Economic sanctions come in different forms depending on the desired outcome. Besides economic and trade sanctions, these measures include targeted actions such as arms embargoes, freezing assets, commodity restrictions, and travel bans on key individuals and organizations.

These sanctions can be imposed by a single country or multilaterally, by like-minded nations, or by international bodies such as the United Nations and the European Union. Sanctions can be wide ranging, banning all transactions with a specific country, while targeted or smart sanctions aim to minimize collateral damage to the general population and instead focus on specific individuals or entities believed to be responsible for offending behavior.

The economic sanctions placed on Russia after its invasion of Ukraine are the widest ranging ever placed on a major economic power. Will they work? Restrictions on Iran, Venezuela, and North Korea, for example, impoverished their populations but haven't led to political change.

To take just one example, the war in Ukraine has put pressure on European energy markets where supply and demand were already being disrupted. Will the proposed oil sanctions of the European Union (EU) on Russia weaken Putin's ability to finance the war? Fossil fuel exports provide the revenue for Russia's military buildup and brutal aggression against Ukraine.

The twenty-seven members of the EU buy a quarter of their oil and more than 40 percent of their gas from Russia, paying $450 million per day for oil and $400 million per day for gas. There is no consensus yet among EU members on stopping Russian gas imports.

The EU recently stopped Russian coal imports, and after dithering over a decision to sanction Russian oil imports, the EU Commission has committed to weaning itself off Russian oil. The president of the commission announced that oil imports from Russia will be banned after six months and refined petroleum products by the end of the year, ratcheting up its efforts to cut off a key source of funding for the Kremlin.

This was the EU's sixth package of sanctions against Moscow and its biggest and costliest step yet toward supporting Ukraine and ending its dependence on Russian fossil fuels.

Now the EU is struggling to replace that oil. It is also making a big bet that Russia will not retaliate by turning off natural gas supplies, as they have already done with Bulgaria and Poland for refusing to pay in rubles. Just as Europe hopes to find new oil suppliers, Russia is working hard to line up alternative buyers, such as India, to minimize the impact on their bottom line and to continue to take advantage of higher oil prices to compensate for lower volume.

China is a likely market. Last year a third of Russian oil exports went to China. While Russia relies on oil and gas exports for 45 percent of its revenue, according to the International Energy Agency, it may well be that the EU's oil ban won't cause large and lasting damage unless China joins the Russian oil boycott, and that is highly unlikely.

But it's very likely that the proposed ban will hurt the European economy, and Europeans are going to have to deal with higher energy prices.

## Putin's Tactics in Ukraine Rival Stalin's Engineered Famine

5/28/2022

Vladimir Putin's brazen and barbarous invasion of Ukraine is reminiscent of the artificially engineered famine Soviet dictator Joseph Stalin used in 1932–1933 in an attempt to extinguish Ukraine.

Stalin unleashed a famine referred to by Ukrainians as the Holodomor ("killing by hunger") to break Ukrainian resistance when they refused to cooperate with the Russian system of collective agriculture. Like Putin's actions today, it was an act of genocide.

Just as energy is Putin's gold, grain was Stalin's. He strove to gain control over Ukraine's fabled breadbasket to finance his ambitious industrialization and militarization plans by forcing millions of peasants onto collective farms.

When the people resisted, Stalin deployed the secret police and military to ruthlessly crush what he considered to be Ukrainian nationalism while continuing to requisition grain for export in exchange for hard currency and engaging in the widespread persecution, deportation to the Gulag, and execution of the noncompliant.

During 1932–1933 Ukraine suffered mass starvation. Nearly four million people, about 13 percent of the Ukrainian population at the time, are estimated to have died of famine in a land of unrivaled fertility. Many in the international human rights community consider the famine genocide.

Today Russian tactics in Ukraine, such as indiscriminate bombing of civilian areas, is fueling a death toll not witnessed in Europe since the days of Stalin and Hitler.

Put bluntly, after the Russian invaders were forced to withdraw from Bucha, a small town in the Kyiv region, the graphic images of mass graves, tortured and mutilated bodies, executed civilians with their hands bound behind their backs suggesting they had first been taken captive and then killed, and streets covered with corpses provided photographic evidence of Russia's open and horrific war crimes. The available evidence makes it unlikely that these people died as a result of collateral damage resulting from a military exercise.

While many Ukrainian allies expressed shock and grief, the Russian president dismissed the accusation that his army committed war crimes in Bucha, accusing Ukraine of staging the atrocities—another example of the numerous official fictions Putin monotonously propagates.

President Biden, who previously called Mr. Putin a war criminal, and Ukrainian President Volodymyr Zelensky have accused Russian forces of committing genocide in Ukraine. Zelensky said Putin was trying to "wipe out the idea" of a Ukrainian identity.

Moscow has categorically disputed the genocide claims and accused the United States of hypocrisy over its own crimes. The International Criminal Court in The Hague has opened an investigation into alleged war crimes and crimes against humanity in Bucha and elsewhere in Ukraine.

Genocide is regarded as the gravest crime against humanity and has a strict legal connotation. The 1948 United Nations Genocide Convention defines it as crimes committed "with intent to destroy in whole or in part, a national, ethnic, racial or religious group." It is exemplified by Nazi efforts to eradicate the Jewish population, during which more than six million Jews were killed.

Genocide is harder to prove than other violations of international law because it requires evidence of specific intent. While proving intent beyond reasonable doubt is difficult, genocide is recognizable. Russia has targeted and killed civilians; is reported to have forcibly deported hundreds of thousands of Ukrainians, including children, to Russia; and has bombed a maternity hospital. Given the scale of Russian violence, genocide warnings need to be taken seriously.

As evidence of Russian atrocities are revealed, one after another, the use of the term "genocide" echoes the Holodomor, the genocidal tactics favored by Stalin in the 1930s to starve the Ukrainian people.

The blame lies with Putin. He is trying to reabsorb Ukraine into Russia, push back against NATO expansion into eastern Europe, and regain Russia's position on the world stage.

Many Russians have long been suckers for greatness.

In the process Putin has turned Russia into an international pariah. Given what he has done, the thought of anyone in the West negotiating with him is difficult to stomach.

# Why China's Moves in "America's Backyard" Are Alarming

6/11/2022

The United States is losing ground to China in the battle for influence in Latin America and the Caribbean (LAC). The People's Republic of China (PRC) is strengthening its relationships in the region often called "America's backyard."

China's growing footprint in the region has raised concerns in Washington that the PRC is leveraging its economic might to further its strategic goals and displace American dominance in the region.

As Gen. Laura J. Richardson, commander of the United States Southern Command, testified before Congress in March, "The PRC continues its relentless march to expand its economic, diplomatic, technological, informational, and military influence in LAC and challenge U.S. influence in all these areas."

The region is increasingly important to China in both economic and political terms. It possesses an abundance of natural resources and raw materials, as well as a productive environment for trade and investment.

In addition to securing strategic resources, expansion in the region helps China increase its sphere of influence and achieve certain political goals in the global geopolitical chess game by challenging the United States in its own neighborhood—one the United States overlooked for years as it focused on the Middle East and elsewhere.

The PRC is now South America's top trading partner and a major source of foreign direct investment and lending in energy and infrastructure. It is also forging cultural, educational, and political ties.

For instance, in 2000 less than 2 percent of LAC exports went to China. By 2021 that number had risen to $450 billion. China is currently the second-largest trading partner for LAC after the United States, and LAC–China trade is expected to more than double by 2035.

Another Chinese objective is to use economic agreements to isolate Taiwan by persuading LAC countries to abandon diplomatic recognition of Taiwan's sovereignty. Currently, twenty-five of the thirty-three Latin American countries recognize the PRC rather than Taiwan.

The COVID-19 pandemic further elevated China's status in the region. Beijing supported Latin America early on with large shipments of masks, personal protective equipment, medical supplies such as ventilators, diagnostic test kits, and vaccines to curry favor with the various countries.

In September 2013 Beijing officially launched the trillion-dollar Belt and Road Initiative (BRI), using a name that harkens back to the famed Silk Road. It is at the center of Chinese foreign policy and includes a web of investment programs that seek to develop infrastructure and promote economic integration with partner countries. It represents a direct threat to the United States because China is seeking to use it as a connective link with the whole world on its path to becoming the global superpower.

Since 2017 twenty-one LAC countries have signed on to the BRI, and more are expected to join. In the face of China's footprint in LAC, the Monroe Doctrine seems to have been forgotten.

In response to China's impressive trajectory in LAC, President Biden, who took the lead on LAC policy during the Obama administration, and the G-7 leaders agreed in June 2021 to launch a global infrastructure initiative, Build Back Better World (B3W). This initiative is consistent with the view that China is a strategic competitor to the United States in the global superpower game that some call a new Cold War.

B3W seeks to offer an alternative to China's BRI. Its goal is to advance infrastructure development in low- and middle-income countries, including LAC. It is an international extension of the White House's domestic Build Back Better proposal. The LAC is the first region on the B3W's radar.

How the initiative will be implemented to compete successfully with China in LAC is an open question. What is clear, however, is that the superpower rivalry is good news for LAC countries.

History may show Latin America to be among the winners of the new Cold War. The United States will now pay the requisite amount of attention to the region and provide welcome resources.

## Corporate America and Income Inequality
6/18/2022

Economic inequality, the gap between the rich and poor, has always existed. This disparity has increased dramatically in the United States over the last four decades. Inequality can be measured in many ways, frequently using income.

The Gini coefficient is one of the most utilized measures of how income is distributed across the population with zero being perfectly equal (where everyone receives an equal share) and one being completely unequal (where 100 percent of income goes to only one person). The measure has been in use since its development by Italian statistician Corrado Gini in 1921.

The United States has a Gini coefficient of 0.485, the highest it has been in fifty years according to the Census Bureau, outpacing that of other advanced economies. This measurement finds that the United States is the most unequal high-income economy in the world.

The top 1 percent of earners made a little over 10 percent of the country's income in 1980. Currently they take home about 20 percent, more than the entire bottom half of earners.

Academicians and politicians argue over whether automation or overseas manufacturing is more responsible for eliminating American manufacturing jobs and keeping wages lower. The question is debatable, but the answer is surely a mosaic from globalization to automation.

One factor that catches the eye time and time again has been the role of corporate America. Sure, automation and globalization have transformed labor markets across the globe, but it is important not to overlook corporate America's role in accelerating these effects.

The late Jack Welch, the CEO of General Electric from 1981 to 2001, captured this reality when he talked of ideally having "every plant you own on a barge." He turned the firm from a manufacturing company into more of a financial services firm while offshoring American manufacturing jobs. In 1999 *Fortune* magazine named him manager of the century.

Other leading companies followed Welch's path. For example, General Motors moved production to low-wage areas such as northern Mexico starting in the 1980s. In 2017 Boeing, America's biggest exporter, opened a plant in China for its 737 planes.

From both an economic and national security perspective, the United States needs to strengthen smart manufacturing and provide good jobs for future generations through effective public policies. War and the pandemic have exposed the fragility of supply chains. Increasing domestic production of items such as energy, food, and medicine would better secure supply chains and create high-value jobs and support American workers and their families.

For example, semiconductors (chips) are foundational for many industries, as everything digital has transformed all sectors of the economy. Bear in mind that digital technologies are disrupting entire industries and blurring industry boundaries. Still, the United States is suffering from a severe shortage of semiconductors.

While the US global share of semiconductor manufacturing capacity was 37 percent in 1990, the number has fallen to an alarming 12 percent today. The United States has become an outlier in an industry that is a major engine of US economic growth and job creation.

The United States has grown dependent on other countries that provide government subsidies and incentives to make it easier and cheaper to manufacture semiconductors. The European Union is planning to provide the industry with $48 billion over ten years.

More importantly China is investing $100 billion into the sector. The Chinese government is funding the construction of more than sixty new semiconductor fabrication plants and is poised to have the single largest share of chip manufacturing by 2030.

When push comes to shove, the political class should remember that the United States must be the world leader in advanced manufacturing: "Not only the wealth but the independence and security of a country appear to be materially connected with the prosperity of manufacturers."

Who said that? The never-less-than-interesting Alexander Hamilton, of Broadway fame, in his *Report on the Subject of Manufactures* in 1791.

## The Fed Fighting Inflation
6/25/2022

Prices at the gas pump and in the grocery store are climbing at the fastest pace since 1981. As inflation spreads throughout the economy, it is proving painful for working families.

The Federal Reserve has raised interest rates three times so far this year and has signaled it plans to keep doing so in coming months. The country is in the eye of the storm; the price spiral is nowhere close to over.

The Fed is passing off these interest rate increases, in bits and bobs as the British say, as a coherent strategy organized around a defining theme: to fight inflation and put the beast back in its cage without tipping the economy into a recession.

The American public has been told with monotony by various media outlets that the central bank has a laser-like focus on cooling the economy and limiting demand for goods and services, noting that the Fed has not hiked interest rates by 0.75 percentage points in one go since 1994.

The media was so transfixed with this figure that if you had a frequent flyer mile for every time it was mentioned, you would have enough miles to circumvent the globe by now.

What is absent from this reporting is that the funds rate is now in the 1.5 to 1.75 percent range. The Fed plans on the rate reaching a relatively modest 3.4 percent by year's end.

Meanwhile inflation hit 8.6 percent in May, the fastest rise in forty years, with more pain to come. Interest rates are still way below the rate of inflation. It is crucial that the Fed take the cost of borrowing well above the inflation rate for price pressures to cool.

The reasons behind the current inflation are not hard to fathom, from the global pandemic to supply chain issues and the war in Ukraine. The expansionary monetary and fiscal policies of 2020 and 2021 surely put a fire under the economy, driving up consumer demand and putting upward pressure on prices.

While it might not quite be true that, as Milton Friedman memorably put it, "inflation is always and everywhere a monetary phenomenon," it is still a large part of the explanation. Skip overblaming Putin. To believe that is to think in political cliché. Inflation was high before the Russian invasion of Ukraine.

By any normal reckoning, the Fed and others steering the economic ship remained conspicuously in the wrong for a long time when it came to dealing with the rise in prices. By to-ing and fro-ing and insisting that inflation was transitory last year and hoping it just went away as though it didn't exist, inflation got out of hand.

For the United States to defeat inflation, it will take real leadership. To put it crassly, the Fed needs leadership like that provided by its former Chair Paul Volcker, the consummate public servant, a rarity on par with Halley's Comet.

As Volker understood it, inflation can be defeated, but it takes a willingness to make tough choices and the minerals to face down critics. He did everything except kick extra points to deal with runaway inflation, explaining to the public the tough road ahead, the sacrifices to be made, and the fact that there was no alternative.

For example, when inflation reached 15 percent in 1980, Volcker understood the need to go for inflation's jugular and ratchet up interest rates above the rate of inflation. He raised interest rates to over 20 percent to crush raging inflation.

That gives a foretaste of what the United States will experience in the coming years if the Fed does not move more aggressively and quickly to combat inflation.

While predicting the future is beyond difficult, if the Federal Reserve is to get inflation under control, it has a long way to go when it comes to raising interest rates.

## The Shrinking Labor Force
7/16/2022

The country is in a fragile state—burned out from three years of pandemic, social upheaval, the war in Europe, and an economy that is cooling under the weight of high inflation, rising interest rates, and the scarcity of labor. The United States may have reached the point where its past is more appealing than its present.

So when good news comes along, you might as well seize it. This could apply to a recent announcement by the Bureau of Labor Statistics that the economy added a seasonally adjusted 372,000 jobs in June, well above the 250,000 economists expected.

But this sliver of good news must be set against the continuing cost-of-living crisis, or "Bidenflation," as some call it, which is impoverishing working Americans. The consumer price index rose 9.1 percent in June on a year-over-year basis, the worst inflation since December 1981. It is unclear how the Federal Reserve will put the inflation genie back in the bottle without creating a whole lot of pain.

Education and health services led job creation, followed by professional and business services, and leisure and hospitality. Meanwhile the unemployment rate remained at 3.6 percent, a touch above the fifty-year low reached before the pandemic hit in early 2020. Job growth continues, although fewer people are looking for work.

The COVID-19 pandemic turned the labor market upside down, and it is currently drum tight. There were more than 11 million job openings at the end of June—up substantially from 9.3 million open jobs in April 2021 and 7 million before the pandemic.

The pandemic led many people to reevaluate what they want from a job and from life, and it prompted a wave of early retirements. Others left to start their own businesses. Still others left to care for children, elders, or themselves. Some people simply threw in the towel and decided to stay at home, courtesy of the taxpayers.

The demand for workers far exceeds the number of unemployed people looking for work. The labor participation rate—the share of adults working or looking for a job—was 62.2 percent in June, down from 63.4 percent before COVID-19.

Workers are taking advantage of the tight labor market by switching jobs for better pay, which represents a new source of inflation for many American companies.

Average hourly earnings rose 5.1 percent over the last year. Rising wages could make it harder for the Federal Reserve to tame inflation. Nearly 79 percent of American workers are in the service sector, where higher labor costs are a large burden.

In addition to a shrinking labor force driving up wages, a steady decline in birth rates is expected in the United States and many advanced economies, which will sharply reduce the growth of the labor force.

For example, life expectancy in the United States has increased from 1980 to 2019, and improvements in morbidity and mortality rates will lead to a rapid increase in the number of people who are over sixty-five and retired. As a result dependency ratios—the ratio of the number of dependents to the total working age population—are set to rise sharply.

Put simply, deteriorating dependency ratios in the United States and globally means dependents who consume but do not produce will outweigh those who are working. In effect, too few people carrying the load.

This translates to lower productivity per capita, an ever-intensifying war for talent and skills, and upward pressure on inflation.

As the supply of labor contracts, their bargaining power will increase, and wages will continue to rise. The growing leverage of labor may have beneficial effects on inequality, but it may manifest an increasing risk of structural inflation.

## Technology Is Disrupting the Transportation Industry

7/30/2022

The increasing pace of change is a defining feature of our times. This is one of the most discussed topics among consenting adults, right there with the ongoing debate about what exactly constitutes a recession. Far more than those who lived during the Renaissance or the Industrial Revolution, people today are self-consciously aware of the transcendent characteristic of this period in history.

Americans truly live in an age of innovation. Even the most conscientious technophobes find it difficult to ignore the waves of technological change that are rolling through the global economy.

One challenge to implementing technological advances is outdated regulatory structures. The pace of change far outstrips government's ability to serve the public interest by managing and regulating these new developments. Government at all levels needs to rethink the application of old-style bureaucratic tools to today's fast-changing, high-tech industries, especially when it comes to transportation.

A healthy transportation system is the lifeblood of American commerce and industry and is central to America's ability to compete with its economic competitors, particularly China. Indeed there is a robust link between the level of transportation investment and the nation's ability to increase its productivity.

Technological innovation is transforming the transportation system. In addition to the number one trend—the move to electric cars—there is autonomous driving (not just for cars but for low-cost micromobility); ride-sharing; in-vehicle connectivity; 5G wireless technology; companies such as Uber and Lyft adding to the concept of on-demand mobility; robotics, such as robo-taxis currently operating in Phoenix and San Francisco; and mobility technology, to name just a few salient trends.

Consider mobility as a service the holy grail. Ideally it would offer customers the ability to plan, book, and pay for transportation services by digitally connecting to a variety of public and private transportation options across all transportation modes.

The future of transportation is being shaped by a convergence of these trends—a huge set of disruptive forces to reckon with. While it is extremely difficult to predict when these new technologies will be ready for prime time and their rate of proliferation and adoption, it is important to understand and consider the impact they will have on mobility and the transportation system.

Such improvements could help reduce the costs of traffic congestion, which some experts believe cost the economy over $120 billion per year. Such costs include road accidents, which killed nearly forty-three thousand Americans in 2021; and air pollution, which contributes to health problems such as respiratory ailments. Improvements could enhance mobility for seniors and individuals with disabilities, and provide other societal benefits.

Underscoring the discussion about the rate of technological change is the major implications advances in mobility will have for urban centers, as they determine how to tailor new mobility approaches within each city context.

Just as the Federal Communications Commission manages the airwaves for the public good, so, for example, must cities manage their streets and public transit. Their challenge is to become mobility managers, leveraging all the new technology to provide better and safer service to their riders.

There are opportunities and threats that cities have never encountered before, presenting a daunting challenge to the current crop of public sector managers. They might not be willing to buck the status quo and reimagine the future of mobility, especially in their quixotic quest to improve mobility, particularly in cities where transportation assets are reaching the end of their expected life span after suffering from decades of benign neglect.

The challenge for providers of transportation services is to leverage current assets while wisely exploring the development and deployment of new technological innovations that indeed may cannibalize existing core assets. Just how many public sector managers and leaders are capable of being ambidextrous is problematic when operating in a political environment.

But to paraphrase Bob Dylan, when the times, they are a-changin', you must too.

## The Consequences of Interest Costs on US Debt
8/20/2022

Over the next thirty years, the fastest-growing category of government spending is projected to be interest on the national debt. That means the government will be shelling out hundreds of billions of additional dollars each year for interest payments.

The growth in interest costs presents a huge threat to the economy and to Americans' economic future. The long-term societal effects will be massive; it will be a painful reckoning when the bill comes due.

According to the 2022 Long-Term Budget Outlook of the Congressional Budget Office (CBO), the cost of interest on the national debt will surpass defense spending in 2029; Medicaid, Medicare, and Children's Health Insurance in 2046; and Social Security in 2048.

The CBO projected that annual interest costs paid to holders of Treasury securities would total $399 billion in 2022 and nearly triple over the coming decade to $1.2 trillion, growing from 1.6 percent of gross domestic product (GDP) to 3.3 percent in 2032, which would be the highest level ever.

If the Federal Reserve raises interest rates by larger amounts than the CBO has projected, costs may rise even faster than anticipated. Still further, interest costs are on track to become the federal government's single largest expenditure in 2054. By then interest costs will account for almost 40 percent of tax revenue and become the largest federal expenditure.

Rising interest payments are the result of escalating interest rates and debt levels that have risen like the blade of a hockey stick. Treasury yields have surged with inflation running hot and the Federal Reserve in an aggressive tightening mode, while the national debt has grown by some $6 trillion since the pandemic began. Pandemic-driven fiscal and monetary policies changed the debt situation considerably and for the worse.

The latest data show inflation at an 8.5 percent annual rate. It is reasonable to expect the Fed to keep tightening over a sustained period, trying to reduce aggregate demand, relieve pressure on consumer prices, and produce a hoped-for soft landing. In 2017 the national debt was $20 trillion; now it is approaching $30 trillion. Ten-year Treasury yields have climbed close to 3 percent, double what they were last December.

Increasing debt and high interest rates can crowd out important federal budget priorities and lead to a vicious cycle of even more debt, deficits, and interest payments. This means the government will be paying hundreds of billions dollars more each year on interest payments on top of other fixed costs that are also growing, such as health and retirement provisions for an aging population. This enhances the risk of a fiscal crisis.

As for those who hold on to the hope that folks in Washington will develop a long-term strategy to deal with the debt pile and deficits, it is likely time to label that as wishful thinking.

Congresses and presidents of both parties have long avoided making hard choices about the federal budget and failed to put it on a sustainable path.

In line with time-honored tradition, they prefer to just pop into the national arboretum of magical money trees and grab what they want. The phrase "often wrong, but never in doubt" is only a slight exaggeration when it comes to their behavior. The present commands their attention. The few lawmakers raising issues about the debt, deficits, and rising interest costs are an endangered species.

Of course, crises can provide the necessary cover to make tough, hard decisions. As Stanford Professor Paul Romer said in 2004, a crisis is a terrible thing to waste—a sentiment later echoed by former White House Chief of Staff Rahm Emanuel. Let's hope the United States doesn't waste this one.

## Revisiting the 2008 Financial Meltdown
9/9/2022

This month marks fourteen years since the 2008 global financial crisis. The demise of the investment bank Lehman Brothers on September 15 sparked an economic downturn that was felt throughout the world.

The crash led to the worst recession since the Great Depression. It illuminated the dangerous corporate culture that had existed in banking for many years, explaining something as tangled and multidimensional as the 2008 financial crisis is fraught with difficulty.

The meltdown was one of the most critical events in American history, and its aftermath saw plenty of hardship. It wiped out some $11 trillion of the nation's wealth and destroyed more than eight million American jobs by September 2009. It froze up the nation's vast financial credit system, leaving thousands of firms too short of cash to operate.

It also forced the federal government to spend $2.8 trillion and commit another $8.2 trillion in taxpayer funds to bailing out crippled corporations such as General Motors, Chrysler, Citigroup, Bank of America, AIG, and a host of other too-big-to-fail companies run by corporate panjandrums.

It cost millions of Americans their jobs, homes, life savings, and hopes for decent retirements. This was a cataclysm far worse than any natural disaster in the nation's experience.

The lack of accountability for the banks and other bad actors helped spur social movements from the left (Occupy Wall Street) and the right (the Tea Party), the heirs of which have made themselves heard during elections dating back to 2016. It appeared to many that there were two sets of rules: one for ordinary Americans and another for the rich and well connected.

After the financial crisis, there was no shortage of wannabe Cassandras who supposedly had been warning about this for years. They wrote about "casino capitalism" and "corporate greed" without saying a word about the quite specific causes of this very specific crisis. They have been vindicated only in the way a horoscope might occasionally come true.

In November 2008, just two months after the Lehman Brothers bankruptcy and the Western economy's descent into the abyss, the Queen of England asked a roomful of academics at the London School of Economics a disarming question: Why had they not seen it coming? They were all caught off guard.

In the years after, many economists and academics have attempted to answer her question, but few have come up with more than citing immediate causes, such as high leverage and a strong appetite for risk and failed to identify the deeper causes.

The Queen's question resonated with ordinary people, who were baffled at why politicians, bankers, and academics all failed to spot the financial storm on the horizon.

The Financial Crisis Inquiry Commission, created by Congress in May 2009, is often cited as the definitive source for information about the causes of the 2008 crisis. The commission was tasked with restoring trust in the banking sector by bringing to light the misdeeds and malfeasance that caused the Great Recession.

But the bipartisan ten-member commission could not agree on the underlying causes of the financial crisis. Instead it completed its forensic work and produced three conflicting reports in January 2011.

All the members basically agreed on the facts, but disagreements arose over interpretation. For sure, no single narrative or satisfying theory to explain the cause of the financial meltdown emerges from the mother lode of factual information surrounding the crisis, but the variety of conclusions is informative.

It may be decades before anything approaching real perspective about the crisis can be achieved. The situation is similar to the story in the Japanese film *Rashomon*, where different witnesses give conflicting accounts of a crime.

One lesson to be learned is that what can't be easily understood can't be easily controlled. So the question may be when, rather than whether, it will occur again.

## Insider Trading in Congress
10/6/2022

A *New York Times* analysis found that between 2019 and 2021, ninety-seven senators and representatives or their family members bought or sold stocks or other financial assets in industries that could be affected by their legislative committee work, violating a law designed to prevent insider trading and stop conflicts of interest.

Over the three-year period, more than 3,700 trades posed potential conflicts between lawmakers' public responsibilities and private finances.

For example, fifteen lawmakers tasked with shaping US defense policy actively invested in military contractors. Still further, senators, House members, and top Capitol Hill staffers who will help decide whether the government regulates cryptocurrency are themselves invested in Bitcoins and altcoins.

All this while ordinary Americans are losing their shirts, if not their entire wardrobes, dealing with the pandemic and the rising cost of living while lawmakers are making hay. Sure, consumers may be getting some relief at the gas pump, but they are having to dig even deeper to pay for groceries.

The price of eggs is up about 40 percent since this time last year. They are paying 20 percent more for milk, bread, and a staple in many Americans' diet—chicken. Many of these working-class individuals risked their lives on the frontline of the COVID-19 crisis to stock grocery shelves, work in hospitals, or deliver food to homes, among other things.

To prevent members of Congress from taking advantage of their positions for personal gain, the United States passed the Stop Trading on Congressional Knowledge Act, known as the STOCK Act, signed into law in April 2012, an election year. At a highly visible signing ceremony, it was said that the legislation would address the "deficit of trust" that divides Washington and the rest of America.

The STOCK Act prohibits members of Congress and senior executive and legislative branch officials from trading based on knowledge obtained as a result of their jobs. It increased transparency by beefing up financial disclosure requirements on stock trades and posting the annual financial disclosure forms federal officials file on a publicly available online database. A key provision of the law mandates that lawmakers publicly and quickly disclose any stock trades made by themselves, a spouse, or a dependent child.

But transparency only works if people abide by the rules. Congress and top senior Capitol Hill staff have violated the STOCK Act hundreds of times, but they face minimal penalties that are inconsistently applied and not recorded publicly. If they file their disclosure more than thirty days after it's due, they have to pay a fee, this being the US Congress, of no more than $200. And Congress has the discretion to waive the fines stipulated in the law.

Is it any wonder that the average American does not understand why elected officials do not play by the same rules as everyone else? The hard truth is that the American people simply do not trust the federal government. Only two in ten Americans trust leaders in Washington to do what is right, according to the Pew Research Center.

There are a variety of rare bipartisan proposals floating around the House and the Senate to tighten the rules on stock trading, and key details still need to be ironed out. The only way lawmakers can earn back trust is to hold themselves to a higher standard, starting with an outright ban on the trading of stocks and other financial assets, such as cryptocurrencies, by members of Congress, their immediate family members, and senior congressional staff.

Members of Congress should spend their time working for the American people. But persuading them to start putting the public ahead of their personal financial interests is like asking them to perform surgery on themselves. And you can take that to the bank.

## OPEC+ Decision to Cut Oil Production Will Affect Gas Prices

10/31/2022

Earlier this month the twenty-three-member oil cartel known as OPEC+ (Organization of the Petroleum Exporting Countries), of which Russia is a member and led by Saudi Arabia, announced it would slash production by two million barrels per day. The production cut is equal to 2 percent of the world's daily oil production. The cut was seen as a slap in the face to President Biden. The move by OPEC+ drew angry criticism from Washington, and the White House accused the kingdom of taking sides with Russia.

In response the Biden administration said it plans to reevaluate the United States' eight-decade old alliance with Saudi Arabia. It is hard to forget that during the presidential campaign in 2020, the president's money quote was he promised to make Saudi Arabia a "pariah" state. He said there is "very little social redeeming value in the present government in Saudi Arabia." He has criticized the Crown Prince for his role in the killing of *Washington Post* journalist and political opponent Jamal Khashoggi. All this while courting Iran, an archenemy of Saudi Arabia, in the hopes of striking a nuclear deal that would give Tehran billions of dollars to threaten the security of Gulf states.

Still for months the leader of the free world lobbied Saudi Arabia to help ease energy prices by pumping more oil into the market. These pleas fell on deaf ears. The administration urged the Saudis to wait for the next meeting of OPEC+ on December 4 before making a decision on production cuts. The administration wants to hold down gas prices to advance the Democrats' chances in the midterm congressional elections. Now the administration has announced it will sell fifteen million more barrels of petroleum from the nation's strategic reserve, aiming to ease gas prices. The White House said it was prepared for more sales of the $400 million barrels in the strategic petroleum reserve if there are further disruptions in the world markets.

Not only that, but the White House is starting to relax some of the sanctions on the authoritarian government in Venezuela, which sits atop some of the world's largest oil reserves to allow Chevron to resume pumping oil and exporting oil to the United States. There is an ominous sound of barrel scraping here.

Congressmen from both parties called for retribution against the cartel as well. Some called for taking direct action against Saudi Arabia, such as denying it access to military hardware and passing legislation allowing OPEC+ members to be sued under antitrust laws.

The Saudis rejected the accusation that it was getting in bed with Russia. They stated that the decision to cut output was driven purely by economic considerations and in response to future uncertainty about demand for oil. OPEC+ was doing what it usually does. They want to regulate the flow of crude oil to world markets in an effort to control prices. That is what the cartel is all about, full stop. They are seeking to protect their national economic interests, as has always been the case. The Saudis need money to provide for a decarbonized future and to fund its on-off war in Yemen.

The irony here is that according to the US Energy Information Administration in September 2019, the United States became a net exporter of crude oil and petroleum products for the first time since 1973. In 2022 the United States will again be a net oil importer. The administration's policy has been to wean the American economy off fossil fuels in favor of clean energy. Quite apart from bans on fracking, bans on drilling, the president's first act in 2021 was to scrap the cross-border permit for Canada's XL pipeline, which was projected to carry nine hundred thousand barrels of crude oil a day into the United States.

Events such as the coronavirus and the tragic war in Ukraine should have revealed the dangers of being dependent on unreliable regimes and geopolitical adversaries. These choices have left the United States in an untenable, vulnerable place.

## Is the Fed Changing Course on Interest Rates?
11/26/2022

There is a sliver of good news on the economy: Inflation may be moderating. For October the consumer price index (CPI), a key inflation barometer, came in below expectations. Though up 7.7 percent from a year ago, it's the smallest increase since January.

But members of the Federal Reserve would be wise not to repeat their earlier mistakes by reading too much into a single month of cooling numbers.

You don't have to be a professional economist to know that inflation is insidious for working Americans, as it erodes purchasing power. For example, in 1970 the average cup of coffee cost 25 cents; by 2019 it had climbed to $1.59. That's inflation, and it refers to price increases across the entire economy.

For decades central bankers led by the Fed have flatlined interest rates and created money out of thin air, first in response to financial emergencies and then to the coronavirus pandemic. What were once emergency measures became totally normal, certainly since 2008. In simple terms, over the first two decades of the twenty-first century, the Fed engaged in a long love affair with ultralow interest rates and printing money.

Easy money after the global financial crisis in 2008 produced several ill effects, including the creation of multiple asset price bubbles. As one market analyst put it, "Never in the field of monetary policy was so much gained by so few at the expense of so many."

But now Fed officials are walking back Fed Chair Jerome Powell's hawkish comments in his briefing that followed the November Federal Open Market Committee (FOMC) meeting. The Fed chair emphasized that it's "premature" to discuss a pause in rate increases. He said the goal was to get inflation back to 2 percent, as the Fed announced an unprecedented fourth consecutive three-quarter interest rate increase, taking the central bank's benchmark funds rate to a range of 3.75 to 4 percent.

This is the highest funds rate level since early 2008 and represents the fastest pace of policy tightening since the early 1980s, as the central bank tries to slow consumer and business demand and give supply a chance to catch up.

But multiple members of the Fed are now saying it looks like time to slow the pace of interest rate increases. For example, the president of the Philadelphia Fed recently said the central bank should "pause when it makes sense." Then the president of the Boston Fed said, "[T]he risk of overtightening has increased."

And the vice chair of the Fed says "soon" it would be appropriate to move to a slower pace on rate hikes. The FOMC gets to see one more CPI report before its next meeting on December 13–14 to decide if it is time to pull back on the level of interest rate hikes.

These dovish comments are coming from the same grand pooh-bahs who, eighteen months ago, claimed inflation was transitory as they sat on the sidelines and waited for it to abate. They ignored the alarm bells and missed a crisis in formation.

Then when inflation got out of control, the Fed finally tightened monetary policy. It was just a year and a half too late doing so. As history has shown, printing too much money causes inflation.

Still, Fed officials convinced themselves that inflation was a thing of the past. The threat of inflation has faded from public memory. All this was before Russia invaded Ukraine.

The takeaway from all this is that the Fed will likely dial down the pace of interest rate hikes to a 0.5 percentage point increase in December after the recent encouraging signs that October inflation cooled more than expected. If this is the case, then it raises the question of whether the Fed has the minerals to stay the course and crush inflation.

# 7

## 2023 Columns

### FTX Collapse Another Regulatory Failure
1/28/2023

Disgraced crypto tycoon Sam Bankman-Fried, also known as SBF, a young man with Promethean ambitions, has been arrested for his role in the collapse of FTX, the virtual trading app he founded. Prosecutors allege that he orchestrated "one of the biggest financial frauds in U.S. history," using customers' money to pay the expenses and debts of his hedge fund, Alameda Research.

The episode again raises troubling questions about the effectiveness of government regulators and the lack of regulatory oversight, despite many promises to bring crypto under their regulatory purview and avoid financial fraud.

Americans have gotten used to financial chicanery. They witnessed Bernie Madoff, who ran a multibillion-dollar Ponzi scheme that wiped out the life savings of thousands of investors. Then there was the 2008 financial meltdown that cost millions of Americans their jobs, homes, life savings, and hopes for decent retirements. Many Americans never recovered from this cataclysm.

A grand jury in the Southern District of New York indicted Bankman-Fried on eight counts, including securities fraud, money laundering, and making illegal political contributions. In total the thirty-year-old faces a combined maximum sentence of 115 years.

After his extradition from the Bahamas and release on a record-breaking $250 million bail bond, he has holed up at his parents' $4 million Palo Alto home with an electronic monitoring bracelet while he awaits trial.

Bankman-Fried is also facing a civil case brought by the SEC and possible civil actions by the Commodity Futures Trading Commission (CFTC) and state banking and securities regulators.

The house of cards collapsed when FTX filed for bankruptcy protection on November 11 with a reported $32 billion in debt. At the heart of the scandal lies a system for defrauding investors. Billions of dollars in customer assets have vanished, used to plug losses at Alameda Research, finance SBF's lavish lifestyle, make massive political contributions, and bankroll his speculative investments.

FTX was a platform that let users buy and trade cryptocurrencies, such as Bitcoin. The firm also minted its own digital currency called FTT and was big on environmental, social, and governance investments. SBF was a leading proponent of so-called "effective altruism," a theory that advocates using "evidence and reason" to do societal good. He told the media he planned to give most of his wealth away to make the world a better place.

SBF donated almost $40 million to political candidates and political action committees in the 2022 congressional midterm elections. He was the second-largest individual donor to Democrats, trailing only billionaire businessman George Soros in the 2022 election cycle.

Prosecutors said one reason he made those contributions was to influence policies and laws affecting the cryptocurrency industry. There may not be a criminal trial until late 2023, legal experts say, because the government will need to build an extraordinary case.

Legions of criminal and civil defense attorneys will make bank by the time the dust settles. Case in point, angry investors have already filed class action suits against prominent endorsers such as Tom Brady, Larry David, Steph Curry, and Naomi Osaka, who all received equity in the company for failing to do due diligence before marketing FTX to the public.

The firm's blue-chip investors included Sequoia Capital, BlackRock Third Point LLC, Tiger Global Management, Ontario Teachers' Pension Plan, SoftBank Group Corp., and Singapore's investment company, Temasek Holdings.

Can there be any wonder why public trust is on the wane? The plain truth is that regulators exist to protect the interests of the regulated. Surely another special counsel is needed.

Closely related, American should be asking questions of politicians in Washington who sit on key financial oversight committees that were beneficiaries of SBF's generosity. But that may be wishful thinking. Insulated from oversight and accountability, they will not be performing surgery on themselves anytime soon.

All of which brings to mind Honoré de Balzac's insight: "Behind every great fortune there is a crime."

## Inflating Away the National Debt
2/28/2023

Once again the federal debt is big news, as lawmakers grapple with bumping up against the US debt ceiling. The government has

347

reached its borrowing limit, and House Republicans claim they will not vote to raise the debt ceiling and allow further borrowing without real spending cuts, not reductions in planned increases.

High government debt is a significant problem. The higher the debt to GDP ratio, the harder it may be for a government to borrow by issuing bonds, and investors will demand a higher interest rate for what they view as a risky investment.

It's also a political hot potato, but quick fixes come with big downsides. Slow and steady may be the best solution.

The federal debt held by the public as a share of gross domestic product increased to 98 percent in fiscal 2022. For governments this metric is comparable with the debt-to-income ratio a lender usually wants to know before approving a loan. Think of GDP as the nation's income.

It is also a key metric investor use to measure just how creditworthy a country is. When the debt-to-GDP ratio is high, investors begin to question the government's ability to pay back the debt and start demanding higher interest rates.

The Congressional Budget Office forecasts that the federal debt will increase to 185 percent of GDP by 2052. Spendthrifts have been ramping up deficit spending for a crazy long time—US debt has increased more rapidly than national income for more than half a century. To be sure, monetary policy has contributed to the debt, providing cheap credit by keeping interest rates artificially low for more than a decade.

Federal government debt increased by $2.5 trillion in the fiscal year that ended on September 30, 2022, from $28,429 trillion to $30,929 trillion. Since the new millennium, the debt has increased from almost $6 trillion to nearly $31 trillion.

Governments have four tools to retire debt. One is to generate higher economic growth by focusing on GDP. Growth increases nominal GDP, driving down the debt to GDP ratio over time and reducing the risk of a debt crisis.

Another option is to reduce deficits by cutting government spending. This is politically unpopular in the best of times and therefore unpalatable to politicians. Taking away something the body politic regards as a "right" or an "entitlement" can be a career ender.

Raising taxes is somewhat less unappealing, especially on those the electorate views as "rich." The risk here is that raising taxes may reduce the incentive to work, causing tax revenue to fall, which would force government to borrow more and thereby exacerbate the debt problem.

One other option remains: inflating your way out of debt and debasing the currency through inflation. High inflation reduces the real value of the debt, allowing government to pay it off with money that is worth less than when they originally borrowed it. As prices go up, so does GDP. It's a bit like a snake eating its own tail.

Inflation makes old debt easier to pay off, but it also makes new debt more expensive. That means higher inflation can lead to spiraling hyperinflation. Trying to inflate debt away is dicey; it is by no means a silver bullet.

But compared with the other options, such as getting spending under control, slow, chronic inflation, as embodied by the Federal Reserve's 2 percent annual goal, may be the most politically palatable way to reduce the debt.

If all goes well, such an approach might produce the much ballyhooed "soft landing," or getting inflation under control without triggering a recession.

# Chatter About Stock Buybacks
3/13/2023

Before the 1980s corporations rarely repurchased shares of their own stock. But this year alone, S&P 500 firms are buying back stock at double the pace of last year. It is forecast that there will be at least $1 trillion in completed corporate stock buybacks by the end of the year.

All this despite a 1 percent tax included in the Inflation Reduction Act, which went into effect on January 1 and is designed to slow stock buybacks. Corporations that are awarded a piece of the $39 billion in grant money under the CHIPS and Science Act may also be barred from doing corporate stock buybacks.

Now the White House wants to further increase taxes on stock buybacks. In his recent State of the Union address, President Biden said the tax should be much higher. "Corporations ought to do the right thing. That's why I propose we quadruple the tax on corporate stock buybacks and encourage long-term investments. They will still make considerable profit."

That comment may have led the Oracle of Omaha, Warren Buffett, to weigh in on the hot-button issue in the Berkshire Hathaway CEO's annual letter to investors, touting the benefits of repurchases: "When you are told that all repurchases are harmful to shareholders or to the country, or particularly beneficial to CEOs, you are listening to either an economic illiterate or a silver-tongued demagogue (characters that are not mutually exclusive)."

Still, Buffett included a caveat: He says buybacks make sense only if they are made at "value accretive prices," that is, when corporation don't overpay.

Taking a step back, corporations have a number of ways to allocate capital:

1. Make capital investments designed to grow their businesses. For example, buying new machinery or pouring more resources into research and product development.

2. Acquire or merge with another company or business unit that the corporation believes could help grow its core business.

3. Pay regular cash dividends to shareholders that tend to be more reliable than stock buybacks, an actual real return of cash to investors.

4. Use the money to repurchase their shares—a stock buyback automatically increases earning per share and has a stronger short-term impact with little, if any, tax consequences for shareholders.

As with many things in finance, the answer to whether stock buybacks are good for investors is "it depends."

If a corporation sees its shares as undervalued and is flush with cash, a buyback could be a way to generate shareholder value. A share buyback reduces the number of the corporation's outstanding shares in the stock market, and, theoretically, its share price should rise. Shareholders will own a bigger portion of the corporation and therefore a bigger portion of its earnings.

In theory a corporation will pursue stock buybacks because they offer the best potential return for shareholders with relatively lower risk than other options for allocating capital. When a corporation announces a stock buyback, it makes sense to ask if the firm believes its stock is cheap or if there are other factors at play, such as senior management lining their own pockets in the case of a compensation incentive for executives based on stock price.

Also, investors are concerned if the stock buybacks are financed with debt, unlike dividends that are typically paid for out of cash flow, which makes the corporation's balance sheet less resilient. Of course, it is a good sign if senior management is also buying company stock for themselves.

The tricky part in considering corporate stock buybacks is making sure senior executives are focused on sustainable long-term growth opportunities rather than increasing stock prices and engaging in share price manipulation while prioritizing the short term.

## More on Stock Buybacks
3/21/2023

Few corporate policies have generated as much controversy in recent years as stock buybacks. If excessive compensation for senior managers is the most criticized use of corporate funds, stock buybacks may well take second place.

But like most controversial capital allocation decision, the details of stock buybacks are complex and nuanced.

Buyback opponents argue that the practice overwhelmingly benefits top executives. Conventional wisdom is that buybacks give executives the opportunity to manipulate the stock price and, as some have argued, "create a sugar high for the corporation."

Proponents of stock buybacks point out that share repurchases give companies the flexibility to return excess cash to shareholders. Moreover companies may believe its shares are undervalued and are confident in its growth, which would make repurchasing shares a smart move.

Companies have no obligation to complete announced share buybacks, nor do they have to say when they have halted buybacks. They just stop buying shares.

In a share repurchase, a company buys back some of its outstanding shares, typically at a price greater than the going rate for the stock. The shares are then retired or held as treasury stock.

Although there are several ways for a company to buy back shares, doing so through an open-market repurchase program is the most prevalent. There are three other stock repurchase methods. One is a fixed-price tender offer, where the company offers to repurchase a specified number of shares at a single specified price.

Another method is a Dutch auction, in which the price is set at the end of a tender process rather than at the beginning. The company offers a range of prices set above the current market rate at which it is willing to buy back shares. Shareholders submit their proposals by stating the lowest price they would accept and the shares they are willing to sell. The Dutch auction tender offer is executed at the lowest price that allows the company to repurchase the shares.

Finally, a company may contact one or more large owners directly and offer to buy back its shares from them. The share purchase price, in this instance, includes a premium.

In the past, companies rarely repurchased shares in the open market because of potential liabilities related to price manipulation. However, a 1982 SEC rule provides a "safe harbor" for US listed companies to repurchase their shares without being subject to liability for manipulation under the Securities and Exchange

Act of 1934. The rule proved to be the catalyst for increasing share repurchase activity in the United States.

Companies buy back stock for many different reasons. In addition to senior management believing the company's stock is undervalued, they may have more money than available investment opportunities. There may also be instances in which managerial compensation incentives such as earning per share may influence the decision to repurchase shares. Of course, this aspect of share repurchases is rarely mentioned by corporate executives and lends some credence to concerns expressed by opponents of share buybacks.

Lastly, share repurchases may be used to counter a hostile takeover or greenmail threats, where a corporate raider acquires a large stake in the company in the open market and then threatens a takeover. Companies may use share buybacks as a defensive action to reduce the possibility that a potential acquirer would get a controlling interest in the company.

Share buybacks, like any other capital allocation decisions, can be problematic when used to prop up the stock without regard for the value of the company, poorly timed, or designed to increase compensation for company insiders. All this is in contrast to dividends that are carefully considered and predictable. A whole lot of things have to go just right for share buybacks to be done properly.

## It's Déjà Vu All Over Again
3/30/2023

What's telling about the Silicon Valley Bank collapse is that no one saw it coming. On a visit to a London business school after the 2008–2009 global financial crisis, when the late Queen

Elizabeth asked why nobody saw it coming, no one had a clear answer. Why, in a financial world crawling with regulators, did no one realize that subprime mortgages were toxic and on the brink of falling apart?

It looks like the regulators dropped their guard again. Had they come to simply and blindly assume another set of false beliefs that ultralow interest rates, designed to help tackle recession, were here to stay?

Entire business models were built on this assumption. But then inflation returned, and interest rates shot up. And now we're learning just how many banks bet the house on the idea that rates would never rise again.

Regulators closed Silicon Valley Bank, which catered to the tech industry for three decades, on March 10. After an old-fashioned bank run, it did not have enough cash to pay its depositors. It was the biggest bank to fail since the 2008–2009 financial crisis and the second biggest ever, after Washington Mutual fell in the wake of the collapse of investment bank Lehman Brothers, which nearly took down the global financial system.

During the COVID-19 pandemic, Silicon Valley and other banks were raking in more deposits than they could lend out to borrowers. In 2021 deposits at the bank doubled.

But they had to do something with all that money. So they invested the excess in long-term ultrasafe US treasury securities and mortgage bonds. But rapid increases in interest rates in 2022 and 2023 caused the value of these securities to plunge.

The bank said it took a $1.8 billion hit on the sale of these securities and was unable to raise capital to offset the loss as their stock began to drop. The bank's client base, which included a lot of tech companies, exacerbated the problem. Venture capital firms advised companies they invested in to pull their business from the bank. This led to a growing number of the bank's depositors to withdraw their money, too. The investment losses, coupled with withdrawals, were so large that regulators had no choice but to step in and shut down the bank.

Despite being the sixteenth-largest bank in the United States, Silicon Valley Bank was exempt from many stress-testing regulations other banks were compelled to follow. It did its best to show it was one of the good guys. Last year, for instance, it publicly committed $5 billion in "sustainable finance and carbon neutral operations to support a healthier planet."

But how sustainable were the bank's own finances? It turns out its business model was hugely sensitive to interest rate hikes. It had tied up its money in government bonds, which decrease in value as rates rise.

Here again the Queen's question is relevant: Why did no one see it coming? In this case why was the bank so complacent in the year leading up to the crisis, when inflation was soaring? And what other problems are lurking in the banking system as interest rates move back toward historical averages?

Silicon Valley Bank's collapse highlights how blind regulators were to the scenarios that ultimately led to the bank's demise—large and rapid increases in interest rates. Do the Federal Reserve's bank regulators not talk with or read about what their monetary brethren are doing? Are the regulators fighting the last war, the last crisis?

More laws and regulations don't always help if regulators are incompetent. If they are, they should be terminated—along with the senior management at failed banks.

# The Next Banking Crisis
4/17/2023

When markets are in a "seek and destroy" mode, like the last drag-on in *Game of Thrones*, it's fruitless to guess where they might attack next in search of weaklings. But their next focus, alongside the impact of fast-rising interest rates on bond portfolios, may be commercial property and commercial real estate loans.

Concerns about a commercial office space crash have followed the collapse of Silicon Valley Bank, Signature Bank, and the regional banking crisis that began in early March. Federal Reserve officials have stressed that the collapse of these two banks had nothing to do with commercial real estate.

So often used for investment purposes, higher interest rates are making the commercial office property sector far less enticing. Fast increases in the Federal Reserve Bank's benchmark interest rate have led to significant shifts in customer behavior. Institutional investors are shunning real estate for higher yields at lower risk on government bonds.

Fragility in parts of the banking system has not stopped the Federal Reserve from pushing up interest rates to subdue stubbornly high inflation. The Fed recently voted to raise the benchmark borrowing rate by a quarter of a percentage point, the ninth increase over the past year. That brought the fed funds rate to a target range of 4.75–5 percent, its highest level since late 2007. Another part of the motivation to raise rates might be to show—rather than simply tell—that the central bank has faith in the banking sector.

As property deals become more expensive to finance, the appetite for them wanes, which means fewer projects being built. Across the sector, the Green Street Commercial Property Price

Index is down 15 percent in a year, with the biggest drops in urban office real estate, where space stands empty as working from home takes permanent hold and people predict the death of the office.

US office occupancy rates are between 40 and 60 percent of pre–COVID-19 levels, according to the real estate firm JLL. Further, almost a quarter of the mortgages on office building must be refinanced in 2023, according to Mortgage Bankers Association data, which will bring higher interest rates.

COVID-19 changed everything when employees were forced to work from home. While some companies have pushed for a return to the office, others have adapted to the change and are allowing their workers to stay remote. That is a bad sign for office owners. As leases come up for renewal, many companies that have embraced work from home as the new normal will opt to terminate the leases. That leaves some banks, especially regional ones, facing losses on real estate loans.

Consider that commercial real estate is a highly leveraged asset. When mortgages on these properties mature and owners have to refinance, interest costs increase and adversely affect cash flow. Higher interest rates and more vacancies also decrease the value of some office buildings. Indeed, some bank commercial office real estate loans may be threatened.

This is especially concerning for smaller banks because of larger exposure as a percentage of their assets. For example, before its collapse, Signature Bank had the tenth-largest commercial real estate book in the United States. Another bank in the news, First Republic, had the ninth-largest loan portfolio in the same market.

According to Fitch Ratings, "[T]he office sector faces asset quality deterioration, putting smaller banks at risk." It may turn out that the pretense that Silicon Valley Bank was a one-off is finished.

In 1992 Warren Buffett coined the phrase, "It's only when the tide goes out that you learn who's been swimming naked." Now that the flood of cheap money has drained away and interest rates are on the rise, there may be more unpleasant revelations.

It's unclear what the market dragon's breath may scorch next. But the next banking calamity may be commercial office real estate.

## Monetary Mischief
4/29/2023

The past two and a half years have been extraordinary. The unnerving combination of a global pandemic exacerbated by energy scarcity, supply chain disruptions, the return of inflation, rising multipolar geopolitical tensions, and a new monetary era has people wondering what certainties are left. Still, in times of rapid change, it's nice to know that some things stay the same.

Take the Federal Reserve for an example. The Fed does not learn from its mistakes. The Fed lost control of the money supply, causing inflation to soar. In the two years after the March 2020 COVID-19-induced recession, the Fed allowed the broad money supply to expand by a staggering 40 percent.

It did so by keeping its policy rate at its zero-lower bound and increasing the size of its balance sheet by almost $5 trillion through its aggressive purchases of Treasury bonds and mortgage-backed securities.

In 2021, not hemming and hawing, the Fed kept assuring the American public that the inflation they were experiencing was a transitory phenomenon. The Fed lost much credibility by failing to acknowledge inflation was surging back in 2021, and it is not obvious it has rebuilt its reputation. This despite warnings that the explosion in money supply growth would take the country back to the inflation of the 1970s.

Not to forget, the Fed effectively pursued a policy of zilch interest rates or free money for fourteen years since the 2008 financial crisis. Individuals and institutions happily adapted to a universe in which money was practically free. They forgot that free money turns out to be expensive. By failing to return the price of credit to something normal, the Fed was fueling greater risk-taking.

A sign of an intelligent mind is learning from one's mistakes. This is not the case with the Fed. The technocrats, the boffins, and the cognitive elites didn't know what they were doing. Worse than not knowing what they were doing, Americans suffered big declines in disposable incomes over long period as a result of their policy choices. The economy did not deliver to the great majority of Americans the sort of life they wanted and hoped for.

People bought houses they could only afford with tiny interest payments, companies borrowed to buy back their own shares, investors borrowed to buy stock in a can't-lose stock market, and politicians ran up national debts whose servicing was only possible if interest rates remained negligible forever, putting the country on an unsustainable fiscal trajectory.

Then in 2022 the wise men at the Fed started raising interest rates at the fastest pace in half a century: five hundred basis points in pursuit of lower inflation. That is a lot to cram through the economy in a year, and something just might break. And it did. March madness was the appropriate tagline applied to last month's scare provoked by the collapse of three US banks as a result of rate hikes poor management and the abject failure of regulators.

Of course, none of this would have been necessary had the Fed started tightening monetary policy a year earlier. The inflation was not transitory. It's a bitter solace to savers that they can earn a meager, say, 4.5 percent interest on their savings only now that, inflation being so high, their funds on an inflation-adjusted basis are still losing value and adding to the cost of living crisis for the ordinary American.

Ushering back in a new era of cheap money is by no means a requirement, but it would be a tempting one given how addicted to mass spending everyone has become. But if the Fed has learned anything, it would have serious repercussions.

It may well be that in God's newly automated earth, AI will offer a precious escape from the problem of setting interest rates, avoiding the friction, stress, and politics that accompany the development of monetary policy. Just as the intelligent ChatGPT is churning out poetry better than Milton, surely this new technology can design, plan, and execute monetary policy in the future. They are becoming quite good at that.

## The Fed's Recent Rate Hike
5/8/2023

So things really are different this time. The Federal Reserve Bank decided to raise its federal funds rate on May 3 by a quarter point, to 5.00–5.25 percent, despite a banking crisis that has seen three large banks fail in the space of six weeks, with remarkably little spillover into the economy at large. The misery mostly limited to shareholders in the banks concerned. This is where rates sat before the financial crisis hit in 2008.

This recent rate hike has caused plenty of controversy as fears grow that further hikes risk tipping the economy into recession. The inflation rate sat at 5 percent on the year in March, but core inflation (which excludes fuel and food) slightly increased, up to 5.6 percent. So the Fed raised rates once again in an effort to get price hikes under control, reiterating their focus on dragging inflation back down to earth even if it means tipping the economy into recession.

It should be noted that unemployment fell to 3.4 percent last month, matching the lowest reading since 1969. So far, historically high inflation, slowed economic growth, increasing interest rates, and banking turmoil have not cracked the still-hot labor market.

For the past two decades, this sort of thing didn't happen. Under the unwritten laws of the "Greenspan put," the Fed could be relied on to provide some form of stimulus at the first sign of financial trouble. It began with the collapse of the hedge fund Long-Term Capital Management in 1998, when the Fed put together a $3.6 billion bailout funded by a consortium of banks, and it carried on long after former Fed chair Alan Greenspan himself had departed the scene.

Greenspan argued with monotony that "free markets are inherently self-regulating" (like foxes are inherently the best guardians of chickens). If markets wobbled, if banks got into a spot of trouble, an interest rate cut, or quantitative easing, was never far behind. He took the Fed in a direction quite different from the previous ruling guideline expressed by William McChesney Martin, Fed chairman from 1951 to 1970, who was famous for supposedly having said that the Fed's job is "to take away the punch bowl just as the party gets going." Or words to that effect.

Investors formed an expectation that the Fed would always help. It was an Alice in Wonderland world, where bad economic news often became good—good because investors calculated that the Fed would respond with a stimulus package. By such means the country ended up with the bubble economy of the past twenty years.

But this time around, the Fed has failed to oblige. True, until the collapse of the Silicon Valley Bank, the Fed had been expected to raise rates by half a percentage point compared with the quarter point increase announced May 3. But by raising rates at all, the Fed has signaled that yes, it really did mean it when it said it was going to tackle inflation. Not even falling US inflation has persuaded the Fed to take a break from its tightening program. The Fed officials have said they want to see sustained evidence that inflation is moving toward their 2 percent goal.

The Fed finds itself in a tricky situation, having failed to act on price rises early on, so now they are playing catch-up. They were too late to the game to keep prices under control—having suffered a hit to credibility, they have had to keep hiking rates, putting a damper on economic growth. The Fed is clearly hoping this is the end of the line.

It softened its language in its statement after the May 3 hike, no longer preparing investors for further rate hikes but rather noting that a myriad of factors—including economic growth—would feature in the "extent to which additional policy firming may be appropriate." In other words interest rates may still rise, but it is by no means certain. Ergo, only a naive or ignorant person who say the worst is over.

# Pay Me Now or Pay Me Later
5/30/2023

Maintenance is often seen as the stepchild of infrastructure. It easily slips from public notice in the face of more glamorous new construction.

Yet delayed or poorly executed maintenance can add billions of dollars to the private and public costs of infrastructure. In addition, deferred maintenance hastens the need to replace assets by years, if not decades. Many urban transit systems are testament to the high cost of inadequate maintenance.

Infrastructure spending has traditionally been divided into two categories: capital and operations and maintenance. But such a breakdown can be misleading and is too simplistic to serve as a basis for allocating resources. A more useful approach would be to think along functional lines. So capital spending can be split into new capacity and rehabilitation and operations and maintenance divided into its two components:

- **New Capacity**—expenditures for the engineering design or construction of new facilities or for plant and equipment that significantly expand existing capacity.

- **Rehabilitation**—capital-intensive activities that extend the useful life of a facility more than two years.

- **Maintenance**—expenditures on routine schedules to repair or maintain the good working order of existing facilities, plant, equipment, or rolling stock that neither adds new system capacity nor extends the life of facilities beyond two years.

- **Operations**—expenditures incurred on a routine basis for labor, utilities, engineering, and other overhead activities that support the day-to-day delivery of services.

For certain, a rigorous breakout of spending into each category is difficult. It is particularly easy to confuse maintenance and rehabilitation. For example, the two-year criterion used to differentiate between them is somewhat arbitrary. The key is that "pure" maintenance focuses on short-term improvements (filling potholes), while rehabilitation has a longer-term impact.

Similarly, rehabilitation work and new capacity are often combined. A road may be resurfaced at the same time that additional lanes are added. Maintenance and operations also overlap.

In many ways these four activities represent a continuum that, taken as a whole, could be called life cycle costing. In other words inattention to one aspect increases the cost of all the others. Finding the most cost-effective combination of spending, as opposed to focusing exclusively on building things, is one of the keys to effective infrastructure management.

Proper maintenance of infrastructure assets is important for two reasons. First, there is a direct link between the quality of current services and the performance of the nation's infrastructure. Second, public perceptions of the overall quality of infrastructure services depend on good routine maintenance.

Just to be clear, lack of maintenance spending affects long-term infrastructure costs. Effective maintenance reduces rehabilitation costs or delays the time when such spending is required.

Although maintenance spending plays an important role in life cycle costing, it is not always an obvious part of the infrastructure decision-making process. This can result in maintenance being ignored or afforded neither adequate attention nor funding.

Since local governments own and operate most infrastructure assets, they also bear the heaviest financial burden for maintaining those assets. Yet local governments do not always possess the financial resources or have the institutional flexibility to implement innovative maintenance programs. Consequently, they must be the main focus of efforts to ensure adequate maintenance.

Maintenance of infrastructure assets is surely not a politically compelling category of public spending. That adds to the dilemma of getting it properly funded.

Putting maintenance on par with other categories of infrastructure investment is not a simple matter, especially given the temptation to defer maintenance when the much higher costs it causes would likely hit on somebody else's watch. That explains why elected officials all too often put the politics of new construction ahead of maintaining existing infrastructure.

## Playing Let's Pretend
6/5/2023

One definition of intellectual dishonesty is the practice of ignoring reality when it interferes with what you want to believe about the way the world works. The bipartisan deal President Biden signed on June 3, after months of political brinkmanship to raise the debt limit for two years and increase the amount of money the federal government can borrow, is an example.

Cynics might be forgiven for insisting there is a great deal to be said for intellectual dishonesty in American society. They would remind us that the body politic is much more likely to enjoy an adequate supply of the public goods and services that are so vital to the national welfare if Americans can convince themselves that "someone else" is paying for them.

Whenever we admit to ourselves that the cost is coming out of our pockets, we inevitably try to cut corners or do things on the cheap and ultimately deprive ourselves of much that is really needed.

Many Americans would argue that the government has played a major role in this national con game since the early days of the republic. By cleverly manipulating things such as tax rates, deductions, and public accounting practices, the government has made it easy for Americans to convince themselves that "the other guy" is paying most of the bill for the things we need. All of which has helped make the United States great—in the sense of becoming the world's most ostensibly successful national economy for the moment.

The national debt has soared, nearly tripling since 2009, forcing the US Treasury Department to borrow more to pay for government spending. The legislative curb on this borrowing is known as the debt ceiling. When Treasury spends the maximum amount authorized under the ceiling, Congress must vote to suspend or raise the limit on borrowing.

The latest deal includes caps on federal spending, additional work requirements for food stamps and welfare, and reforms to build energy projects more quickly. But the caps would not actually reduce spending. The end game is to make it grow more slowly, say more slowly than the rate of inflation.

Divided government is never pretty. But if you are of a Panglossian persuasion, you will rejoice that this deal enables both sides to claim a win of sorts.

Neither wants to be responsible for a catastrophe, so each pretends it is a win-win deal. Republicans can say they cut spending since it will grow more slowly than it might have otherwise. Democrats can argue that they prevented actual cuts. In theory everyone wins, and politicians insist they conducted themselves in an intellectually honest fashion.

But the American public, not elected officials and government bureaucrats, is to blame for this. They insist on receiving more from government than they're willing to pay for, and they don't ask any serious questions about the charades and fiscal shenanigans necessary to sustain the illusion of a free lunch.

The United States is up to its neck in debt—$31.4 trillion as of January 2023. Since it cannot increase its income in the short term, it needs to exchange new debt for old debt, leaving no choice but to raise the debt ceiling to avoid global economic chaos. The annual federal deficit has averaged nearly $1 trillion since 2001, meaning the government spends that much more money than it receives in taxes and other revenue.

To make up the difference, the government has to borrow to finance payments that Congress has already authorized. Even with the debt limit raised, the best way to repay the debt is to figure out how to revive the economy.

Good government types and fiscal moralists may be outraged by these shell games and urge Americans to stop acting like children. But Americans have a long and pragmatic tradition of believing that fiscal morality, like religion and the law, is great as long as it doesn't get in the way of anything really important.

## The Future of Roadway Pricing
6/17/2023

The need to find a better way of managing public roads in metropolitan areas is painfully apparent to many Americans each morning when they drive to work.

It is easy to conclude that the United States has made a series of wrong-headed choices about how to finance its all-important metropolitan roadway systems. The results of these mistakes are ubiquitous and take several forms.

We have insufficient roadway capacity where it is most needed, as evidenced by severe traffic congestion on many critical roadway links in important metropolitan regions during increasingly long portions of the day.

We are chronically unable to build new roadway capacity to keep up with demand, to the point that blindly chanting "we can't build our way out of congestion" too often replaces serious discussion of how to overcome obvious capacity shortfalls.

We insist on "saving money" in government operating budgets by reducing needed roadway maintenance, which causes roads to wear out faster and reduces long-term capacity.

To move beyond these mistakes, transportation policy-makers must recognize the potential of recent technological breakthroughs that enable effective, market-oriented roadway financing systems that can dramatically improve how the United States manages, maintains, and pays for existing metropolitan roadway systems.

In simple terms technology can now allow access to metropolitan roadway capacity through the same kind of marketplace mechanism traditionally used to distribute access to a host of private sector goods and services.

We can charge motorists directly for access to each roadway in a metropolitan area without requiring them to stop or slow down. Prices can be based on the distance they travel on that roadway and can be differentiated based on the "popularity" of each route as measured by the number of vehicles per hour traveling on them.

Prices can also be differentiated based on vehicle type, so trucks and other heavy vehicles that cause more wear and tear on pavement pay higher prices than small vehicles that cause less wear. Charges can be adjusted frequently to reflect changes in the number of vehicles traveling on a roadway.

Frequent price adjustments can also be used to guarantee motorists a certain minimum average speed on a particular route. Charges can be raised or lowered to maintain a target maximum number of vehicles on the roadway.

Intelligent use of these new technologies narrows the often considerable gap between a roadway system's theoretical capacity and its functional capacity. This is achieved by applying the classic economic principle of using price to control the demand for scarce resources. It also results in better service for all roadway customers in a metropolitan area.

Note the term "customers." A customer is a willing buyer of what you have to sell at the price you are charging. What makes someone a willing buyer is a personal judgment about whether the value they are getting is greater than the price charged.

Suppose a driver can use two different lanes to reach their destination. One lane charges a price per mile but promises an average speed of 60 mph. The other charges nothing but moves at less than 10 mph. If the driver is on their way to an important business meeting and can't afford to be late, they may decide that the value of time saved by using the priced lane is greater than the cost. But if they are simply making a discretionary trip to the mall, they may opt to use the free one and put up with the additional travel time.

Put simply, roadway pricing lets you create value for drivers by offering them shorter travel times for high-priority trips. Drivers determine the priority of their trips, making personal judgments about which are the most important and how much they are willing to pay to reach their destinations faster.

Using price to distribute travel demand rationally at and raise resources for roadway maintenance? Now that would be something to write home about.

## Inflation, Interest, and the Fed
6/21/2023

Interest rates play a crucial role in the economy, influencing savings, investment, consumption, and overall growth. Central banks around the world cut benchmark interest rates sharply after the 2007–2009 financial meltdown that tanked the global financial system. In many cases the nominal interest rate was cut to zero, close to zero, or even negative territory.

It was thought that these aggressively low interest rates helped stimulate economic activity, although there remain uncertainties about the side effects and risks.

Distressed, or "zombie," companies feasted on cheap credit. These firms tied up resources that could have been better allocated to more productive and efficient businesses, hindering overall economic growth.

For example, companies such as Bed Bath & Beyond earned just enough money to continue operating but were unable to pay off their debts as interest rates rose. As rates have risen, many of the loans banks made to these firms have turned out to be stinkers, as borrowers miss payments or default.

Indeed, cheap credit, by way of low interest rates, was allowed to persist for an improbable fourteen years—much too long in the minds of many analysts. What was initially seen as a blessing turned out to be a curse.

When continued for too long, cheap credit effectively inspires excessive borrowing—some of it speculative. And bubbles do eventually burst.

A lot has happened since the 2007–2009 financial crisis. Recently inflation has returned with a vengeance. The Federal Reserve and other central bankers are trying to stop surging prices by raising short-term interest rates, which is not necessarily a boom for the stock market or the economy.

Rising interest rates help control demand for credit, soften growth of the money supply, and therefore help control demand. In theory higher mortgage rates may slow housing price inflation and help make property more affordable over time.

Others argue that today's rate hikes threaten to push up tomorrow's housing costs amid high prices for materials and loans. This creates a threat of future housing shortages that could lead to more inflation.

High interest rates prevent a misallocation of capital, goosing the price of the riskiest assets in the shares casino. Then there are investment projects, often vanity projects, that only proceed because of cheap capital.

As interest rates rise, they incentivize savings in contrast to the recent near-zero interest rates that made savers—including many retirees—feel like fools.

Finally, high interest rates give central banks room to cut interest rates in the event of a negative external shock. In sum they act as a deterrent to excessive borrowing and spending, curbing inflationary pressure and preventing the formation of bubbles.

But higher interest rates also bring with them the risk of significant slowdowns in consumption. They might choke off much-needed business investment in new home building and renewable energy capacity, for example.

Rising interest rates may cause the dollar to appreciate, making exports less competitive and leading to an export slowdown and perhaps a worsening trade deficit.

Higher interest rates certainly make government debt more expensive, sending debt costs soaring and eating up a bigger share of public budgets.

Finally, higher interest rates might lead to a broad-based economic slowdown that could hit stock prices, pension fund assets, and dividend incomes.

In recent months inflation has been as persistent as gravity. A cold dish of truth is that it is unclear when prices will moderate. The Fed took a break from raising interest rates at its June meeting after a string of ten consecutive rate hikes in just over a year. Still, the benchmark rate could go a bit higher in the near future.

The Fed is taking some time to assess the effects of its prior rate hikes on inflation and the overall economy, as well as the impact of other economic activity—namely the collapse of three banks this spring. Improvisation is clearly the order of the day.

## Cancel Culture and the Chinese Cultural Revolution
6/26/2023

It's not news that Americans live in a new Age of Magical Thinking. The Enlightenment is seen as the start of hate speech, feelings must always overrule facts, and transubstantiation has taken on a whole new meaning. Men can become women simply by wishing it so.

Over the last several years, much ink has been spilled about whether there are similarities between cancel culture of the twenty-first century, particularly in Anglosphere countries, and

China's Great Proletarian Cultural Revolution. Pundits warn of the dangerous implications of cancel culture.

Both social media and real-life mobs target people who dissent, aiming to ruin their reputations and sometimes getting them fired, all while toppling statues of the Founding Fathers and looting in the name of social justice.

Contemporary events come nowhere near the scale of violence and repression associated with the Cultural Revolution. Thankfully, social ostracism and unemployment are not the same as firing squads and gulags, but they are still harmful, especially to those committed to free speech.

The ordinary American lives in an age when they witness "high-tech" lynching, to borrow a phrase coined in 1991 by then Supreme Court nominee Clarence Thomas. The core features are public smears and ridicule, along with the moralistic mob forcing victims to publicly recant their sins.

Between 1949 and his death in 1976, dictator Mao Zedong directed a radical transformation of China. He grew increasingly suspicious of government apparatchiks and Chinese Communist Party intellectuals, leading him in 1966 to launch a stunning attack on the establishment in the form of a Cultural Revolution.

He encouraged youthful Red Guards, his shock troops, to destroy the "four olds" (old ideas, old culture, old customs, and old habits). In practice this meant widespread beating, denunciations, and mob-instigated "trials." Red Guards roamed the country, attacking establishment elites, including government officials, managers, intellectuals, and former members of the bourgeois class. The goal was to purge the country of anyone who was insufficiently leftist.

Today America and other Anglosphere countries are going through an admittedly more genteel cultural revolution of activists preoccupied with identity politics and cancel culture preaching the same old shibboleths. As under Mao, people suffer disproportionate consequences for small ideological heresies.

Cancel culture involves public shaming, boycotts, online harassment, and calls for removing people from positions of influence because of perceived offensive comments or behavior. It can lead to reputational damage, loss of employment opportunities, and social isolation without due process. Canceling people who disagree with you is straight out of the playbook of dictators and cults.

For example, when former NFL quarterback Drew Brees stated he could "never agree with anybody disrespecting the flag of the United States of America," citing his grandfathers' military service, he was accused of violating contemporary social justice dogmas. Acquiescing to the pressure less than twenty-four hours later, Brees issued an apology on Instagram. He soon followed up with another apology. Then his wife apologized. Any wonder why public figures spend their days walking on eggshells?

It remains to be seen where America goes next in its nascent cultural revolution. Where this trend goes and how long it lasts will ultimately depend on whether Americans stand up for their convictions or cave before online mobs. Maybe nothing permanent will come of it, despite the best efforts of today's Red Guards. It may well turn out that the worst harm from legitimization of censorship and cancel culture may befall those on the right or the left who wield these weapons.

We would do well to remember the words of John Stuart Mill: "He who knows only his side of the case (argument) knows little of that. His reasons may be good, and no one may have been able to refute them. But if he is equally unable to refute the reasons on the opposite side, if he does not so much as know what they are, he has no grounds for preferring either opinion."

# Ford Motor Co. and Industrial Policy
7/8/2023

The US government is giving the Ford Motor Co. a $9.2 billion loan, by far the biggest infusion of taxpayer cash for a US automaker since bailouts during the 2008 financial crisis, to build three battery factories in Kentucky and Tennessee. Neither Ford nor the Energy Department (DOE), which provides loans at far lower interest rates than those available in the private market, has revealed details about the loan.

The United States is taking a page from Beijing's playbook. China has a top-down industrial policy, with serious government planning and support of target industries. China's sustained industrial policy has yielded the world's largest battery manufacturers. Between 2009 and 2021, the Chinese government poured more than $130 billion of subsidies into the EV market, according to a report last year by the Center for Strategic and International Studies. Today more than 80 percent of lithium-ion battery cell manufacturing capacity is in China.

Simply put, industrial policy means that centralized agencies formulate national visions and programs to develop specific industries. It has been a toxic phrase in American politics.

As Gary Becker, who won the Nobel Prize for Economics in 1992, said, "The best industrial policy is none at all." It has long been associated with pork barrel politics, picking winners, and crony capitalism. The political rhetoric has been that the free market works best and is closely associated with freedom and democracy. The history of the United States does not square with this perspective.

On the surface Ford would seem an unlikely party to receive the largest loan ever extended by the department's Loan Programs Office. Just last month Ford touted having almost $29 billion of cash on its balance sheet and more than $46 billion in total liquidity. It is worth nothing that one of the best known loans made by the DOE was $465 million to Tesla in 2010 to support the manufacturing of the Model S.

Ford aims to close the gap with Tesla on electric vehicles, just as the United States aims to close a similar gap with China. Ford told investors early last year that it would put $50 billion into its EV manufacturing efforts. By the end of 2026, the company wants to make two million EVs a year.

Alexander Hamilton, the first Secretary of the Treasury, outlined a strategy for promoting American manufacturing both to catch up with Britain and provide the material base for a powerful military. Hamilton's *Report on the Subject of Manufactures* promoted the use of subsidies and tariffs. Similar practices have been expressed in various forms throughout American history.

During the nineteenth and twentieth centuries, the government played an active role in promoting economic growth, using policies such as high tariffs to protect strategic industries, federal land grants, and subsidies for infrastructure development. The federal government has sometimes backed failures, but it also has remarkable success stories, such as nuclear energy, computers, the internet, and building the interstate highway system.

These days industrial policy is viewed more positively, spurred by bipartisan concerns about the competitive threat China poses. US programs are now underway to cover semiconductor production, development of critical technologies, to secure key domestic supplies and support industries that are considered strategically important.

For example, subsidies from the Inflation Reduction Act and Infrastructure Investment and Jobs Act are spread across the EV value chain and are carpet bombing the entire automobile industry. There are tax credits for sourcing critical minerals within the United States or friendly countries, for manufacturing or assembling the batteries and EVs they go into, for the consumers who buy the vehicles, and even for anyone building the public chargers needed to keep those vehicles moving.

The debate over industrial policy will continue because it gets to the long-standing controversy over the role of the government in our economy. One thing is clear: The rosy rhetoric about the United States not engaging in industrial policy is contradicted by the country's history.

## Bankers Once Went to Prison in the United States
7/24/2023

Once upon a time in America, bank executives went to prison for white-collar crimes. During the savings and loan (S&L) debacle, between 1985 and 1995, there were over 1,000 felony convictions in cases designated as major by the US Department of Justice.

In contrast no senior bank executives faced prosecution for the widespread mortgage fraud that contributed to the 2008 financial apocalypse, which precipitated the Great Recession. Not a single senior banker who had a hand in causing the financial crisis went to prison. Rather than reining in Wall Street, President Obama and Congress restored the status quo ante, even when it meant ignoring a staggering white-collar crime spree.

Indeed the Department of Justice did not prosecute a single major bank executive in the largest man-made economic catastrophe since the Great Depression. They went after the small fish, not the mortgage executives who created the toxic products or the senior bank executives who peddled them.

The S&L crisis was arguably the most catastrophic collapse of the banking industry since the Great Depression. S&Ls were banks that for well over a century had specialized in making home mortgage loans. Across the United States, more than 1,000 S&Ls had failed, nearly a third of the 3,234 savings and loan associations that existed in 1989. It is estimated that by 2019, there were only 659 S&L institutions in the United States.

In 1979 the S&L industry was facing many problems. Oil prices doubled, inflation was in double digits for the second time in five years, and the Federal Reserve decided to target the money supply to control inflation. This not only let interest rates rise; it also made them more volatile.

As inflation continued to soar, S&Ls, with their concentration in home loans, found themselves squeezed by an interest rate mismatch. The thirty-year mortgages on their books earned single-digit interest rates, but they either had to pay depositors double-digit rates or lose them to competitors. Overnight long-term depositors turned short term. Funding long-term assets like mortgages with short-term liabilities like deposits is a risky formula, and in a high-inflation environment, it quickly makes insolvency inevitable.

For sure there are several parallels between then and the failures of Silicon Valley Bank and other banks over the last several months. Just as many S&Ls went bust because surging interest rates increased their costs as mortgages brought low fixed rates of interest, many of today's banks face similar balance sheet problems.

The changing economic and financial environment ruined the "3-6-3" business model that had served thrift executives well for decades: pay 3 percent on savings deposits, charge 6 percent on mortgages, pocket the difference, and play golf at 3:00.

In 1982 lobbying from the S&L industry led Congress to permit them to make highly leveraged investments far removed from their original franchise to provide mortgage funding. In response the federal government also enacted statutory and regulatory changes that lowered the capital standards that apply to S&Ls.

For the first time, the government approved measures intended to increase S&L profits, as opposed to promoting home ownership. The premise underlying the changes was that deregulation of markets could let the S&Ls grow out of their insolvency. Instead the crisis culminated in the collapse of hundreds of S&Ls, which cost taxpayers many billions of dollars and contributed to the recession of 1990–1991.

And some S&Ls contributed to the development of a Wild West attitude that led to outright fraud among insiders. Many S&Ls ended up defrauding their depositors and speculating on high-risk ventures, including illegal land flips, accounting fraud, and other criminal activities.

The S&L crisis teaches at least one important lesson: There is no ending financial chicanery without holding senior bankers accountable for their wrongdoing.

# Is 2 Percent the Right Inflation?
8/3/2023

People the world over have been facing a poisonous new economic reality, as inflation has emerged from multidecade hibernation. And many of the people dealing with it are too young to remember when inflation was last a serious issue. It is economically damaging, socially corrosive, and extremely difficult to bring down.

Both the US Federal Reserve and the European Central Bank appear dead set on getting inflation back to their 2 percent target. Why did these and other banks, such as the Bank of Canada, Sweden's Riksbank, and the Bank of England, gravitate to this 2 percent figure?

In January 2012, a thousand years ago in internet time, the Fed, under Chairman Ben Bernanke, formally adopted an explicit inflation target of 2 percent. This marked the first time the Fed ever officially established a specific numerical inflation target. The 2 percent target was seen as a way to provide clarity and enhance the effectiveness of monetary policy.

Bernanke's successor, Janet Yellen, and current chair Jerome Powell maintained the 2 percent inflation target. While Powell has a laser focus on the 2 percent target, the Fed has recently moved to a more flexible 2 percent average over time. This means the Fed would tolerate some periods of inflation above 2 percent to offset periods when inflation was below that level.

The 2 percent target was not established based on any specific formula or fixed economic rule. Despite its widespread adoption by central banks, there is little empirical evidence to suggest that 2 percent is the platonic ideal for addressing the Fed's dual mandate of price stability and maximum employment.

This inflation target is an arbitrary number that originated in New Zealand. Surprisingly, it came not from any academic study but rather from an offhand comment during a television interview.

During the late 1980s, New Zealand was going through a period of high inflation and inability to achieve stable economic growth—the financial equivalent of a bloody nose. In 1988 inflation had just come down from a high of 15 percent to around 10 percent. New Zealand's finance minister Roger Douglas went on TV to talk about the government's approach to monetary policy.

He was pressed during the interview about whether the government was satisfied with the new inflation rate. Douglas replied that he was not, saying that he ideally wanted inflation between 0 and 2 percent. This involved targeting inflation, a method that had kicked around in economic literature for years but had not been implemented anywhere.

At the time there was no set target for inflation in New Zealand; Douglas's remark was completely off the cuff. But the inflation target caught the attention of economists around the world and went viral, becoming a kind of orthodoxy. The approach gained recognition and, as noted, was subsequently adopted by many other central banks, making inflation targeting a widely used monetary policy strategy—a classic example of how ideas spread within the small priesthood of central bankers.

The hard truth is that many economic luminaries have tried to come up with what is thought to be the optimum inflation rate but with little success.

All things considered, the 2 percent target was seen as a kind of sweet spot for inflation despite the lack of serious intellectual groundwork. Simply stated, there is nothing magical about 2 percent. It is low enough that the public doesn't feel the need to think about inflation but not so low as to stifle economic growth. That's how it goes but not so much more.

## Can Machines Think?
8/12/2023

In 1950 Alan Turing, theoretical mathematician responsible for breaking the Nazi Enigma code during World War II, who is considered the father of modern computer science and artificial intelligence (AI), posed a fundamental question: "Can machines think?"

Today we are on the verge of answering Turing's question with the creation of AI systems that imitate human cognitive abilities, interact with humans naturally, and even appear capable of humanlike thinking. These developments have sparked a global discussion about the need for comprehensive and coordinated global AI regulation.

Implementation would be a tall order. Even if regulations could keep up with the pace of technological change, passing a framework acceptable to countries that would view it through the lens of self-interest would be a daunting task.

Turing was just forty-one when he died from poisoning in 1954, a death that was deemed a suicide. For decades, his status as a giant in mathematics was largely unknown, thanks to secrecy around his computer research and the social taboos about his homosexuality. His story became more widely known after the release of the 2014 movie *The Imitation Game*.

Alan Turing played a foundational role in the conceptual development of machine learning. For example, one of his key contributions is the Turing test he proposed in his seminal 1950 paper, "Computing Machinery and Intelligence."

The Turing test is a deceptively simple method of determining whether a machine can demonstrate human intelligence. If a machine can converse with a human without the human consistently being able to tell that they are conversing with a machine, the machine is said to have demonstrated human intelligence.

Critics of the Turing test argue that a computer can have the ability to think but not to have a mind of its own. While not everyone accepts the test's validity, the concept remains foundational in AI discussions and research.

AI is pretty much just what it sounds like—getting machines to perform tasks by mimicking human intelligence. AI is the simulation of human intelligence by machines. The personal interactions that individuals have with voice assistants such as Alexa or Siri on their smartphones are prime examples of how AI is being integrated into people's lives.

Generative AI has made a loud entrance. It is a form of machine learning that allows computers to generate all sorts of content. Recently examples such as ChatGPT and other content creating tools have garnered a whole lot of attention.

Given the rapid advances in AI technology and its potential impact on almost every aspect of society, the future of global AI governance has become a topic of debate and speculation. Although there is a growing consensus around the need for proactive AI regulation, the optimal path forward remains unclear.

What is the right approach to regulating AI? A market-driven approach based on self-regulation could drive innovation. However, the absence of a comprehensive AI governance framework might spark a race among commercial and national superpowers to build the most powerful AI system. This winner-take-all approach could lead to a concentration of power and to geopolitical unrest.

Nations will assess any international agreements to regulate AI based on their national interests. If, for instance, the Chinese Communist Party believed global AI regulation would undermine its economic and military competitive edge, it would not comply with any international agreements as it has done in the past.

For example, China ratified the Paris Global Climate Agreement in 2016 and pledged to peak its carbon dioxide emissions around 2030. Yet it remains the world's largest emitter of greenhouse gases. Coal continues to play a dominant role in China's energy mix, and emissions have continued to grow.

It would be wise to be realistic about the development and implementation of global AI regulations. Technology usually does not advance in a linear fashion. Disruptions will occur with little to no foresight. Even if a regulatory framework can keep pace with technological advancement, countries will be hesitant to adopt regulations that undermine their technological advancement, economic competitiveness, and national security.

## The BRICS and the Almighty Dollar
9/3/2023

When the BRICS (Brazil, Russia, India, China, and South Africa) summit was held last month in South Africa, it highlighted both the group's main economic strengths and the divergent interests that make it difficult for them to leverage those strengths. Whether those differences can be resolved will have a major impact on the United States in general and the dominance of the dollar in particular.

Nearly two dozen countries formally applied to join the group. The bloc invited top oil exporter Saudi Arabia, along with Iran, Egypt, Argentina, Ethiopia, and the United Arab Emirates, to join in an ambitious push to expand their global influence as a viable counterweight to the West. This is certainly the goal of Beijing and Moscow.

Developing countries are increasingly the biggest and most dynamic parts of the world economy. This has resulted in both the shift of a vast amount of know-how from the West to the rest and the development of new know-how in the rest—not just in China but also in India.

The new BRICS members bring together several of the largest energy producers with the developing world's biggest consumers, potentially giving the bloc outsize economic clout. Most of the world's energy trade takes place in dollars, but the expansion could enhance the group's ability to push more trade to alternative currencies.

This is a win for China and Russia, who would very much like to undermine the dominance of the US dollar. This would be especially helpful to Russia, as its economy struggles with sanctions imposed after its invasion of Ukraine last year. China is looking to build a broader coalition of developing countries to extend Beijing's influence and reinforce its efforts to compete with the United States on the global stage.

Former French President Valéry Giscard d'Estaing called the dollar's role as the world's reserve currency "America's exorbitant privilege." Most Americans don't think about the value of the dollar. But for the rest of the world, its value on currency exchanges is a big deal.

US monetary policy is closely watched around the world because interest rate hikes by the Federal Reserve increase the dollar's value and make loans denominated in dollars more expensive to repay in local currencies. This is certainly an advantage for the United States.

But the dollar's unique position is under threat on several fronts and will likely experience a stress test in the future. The most immediate and unnecessary threat would stem from the self-inflicted wound of the United States defaulting on its debt.

One of the bedtime stories DC politicians tell themselves is that the dollar is unassailable. If Americans have learned anything from history, it is that there is no escaping it. Moving on from history requires some honesty and truth telling, but truth tellers are an endangered species among the political elite.

There are a growing number of countries, notably China and Russia, that resent the United States' weaponization of the dollar on global markets. Their de-dollarization efforts bear watching. Another threat arises from technology, as central banks around the world work to develop their own digital currency networks.

Though home to about 40 percent of the world's population and a quarter of global GDP, the bloc's ambitions of becoming a global political and economic player have long been thwarted by internal divisions and the lack of a coherent vision.

The BRICS countries also have economies that are vastly different in scale and governments that often seem to have few common foreign policy goals, which complicates their decision-making. China's economy, for example, is more than forty times larger than South Africa's.

Russia, isolated by the United States and Europe over its invasion of Ukraine, is keen to show Western powers it still has friends. Brazil and India, in contrast, have both forged closer ties with the West. Given these differences it is unclear how the group will be able to act in unison and enhance their clout on the global stage.

## Jack Welch and Strategy
9/26/2023

Everyone, it seems, is in need of a strategy these days. Luckily everyone is a strategist. The word is used promiscuously as a value-enhancing modifier—a strategy for tax preparation, a strategy for losing weight, a strategy for coping with stress, and the beat goes on.

Overuse has left the word "strategy" devoid of meaning.

As a practical matter, it is about using your limited resources to achieve the best outcome in situations that are both uncertain and contested. In the business world, books about strategy are legion and usually voluminous. These days, no company would dare to admit it lacks one.

One can argue that references to strategy in a business context started in the 1970s, as American companies became subject to increasing global competition and no longer enjoyed benign market conditions. In 1964, when Peter Drucker sent his publisher the draft of a new book called *Business Strategies*, the publisher changed the title to *Managing for Results*, believing that the word "strategy" was associated with politics and the military, not business.

The post–World War II boom in the United States was produced by the massive, global, industrial-scale war that was not fought on American soil and radically depleted the industrial capacity of America's most important competitors and potential competitors, including, but not limited to, Germany, Japan, and Great Britain.

The American economy benefited from the Marshall Plan and other spending to help rebuild these nations. They used much of the money to purchase American goods, and for several decades the United States had very few major global competitors.

For instance, post–World War II Japan relied on close ties with the United States to protect its territorial integrity and regional interests. This enabled Japan to focus its resources on education, economic development, and nondefense production that created competition for the United States.

America provided assistance to rebuild shattered economies in Western Europe and East Asia and opened up its market to their products. However, by the 1970s, these countries were competing against American corporations. By then, thanks to negative trade balances; higher oil prices; the combination of high interest rates, unemployment, and inflation; and a crushing defeat in Vietnam, American corporations and households were experiencing real distress.

In response, academics, management consultants, armchair strategists, and corporate executives such as Jack Welch, the CEO of General Electric, the Apple of its time, began to transform their business strategies to acknowledge that international competition was a serious threat. By then writing and consulting about business strategy had itself become a big business, offering magic bullet solutions such as "attack the competitor's strongest point," "swim in blue oceans away from the competition," as universally valid nostrums.

Jack Welch understood that large firms could use their scale and scope to deal with increasing foreign competition, leverage international opportunities, and exploit the shift from manufacturing to services in the emerging knowledge-based economy, all while managing to stay cool.

Fortunately for Welch, he came to understand that the strategic resource in the new economy was human capital. He realized that how strategy plays out depends on the operational effectiveness deployed by the Dilberts in the firm. This is one reason he was so insistent on learning and sharing knowledge and expertise throughout the organization. In sum he got the strategy right in the context of time and place, communicated it relentlessly, and monitored the strategy's execution.

He understood that it is easier to grasp strategy in theory than to put it in practice, not least because strategy is difficult to develop and implement. He likely subscribed to Yogi Berra's perspective: "In theory there is no difference between theory and practice. In practice there is."

## Strategy as a Way of Thinking
10/1/2023

Strategy may well be a disposition rather than a doctrine for practitioners. Strategy is a way of thinking about issues in the future tense that goes to the success or failure of an enterprise. From this disposition, certain positions follow, views of change and innovation key among them, along with a deep sense of situational awareness.

Strategy, while essential, is not everybody's idea of a good time. In a world clamorous with so many other demands on their attention, it is challenging for practitioners. Helpful as the various schools of strategy have been, successful practitioners are not intellectually hostage to any one school, consulting reality before embracing any of them.

On the other hand, the strong hand, for practitioners there are intelligent arguments on the debate for the superior strategy, and on the other hand, the shaky hand, it is hard to know who is right when little guidance is provided on which models and tools to use. Management theorists who seek the holy grail of the Great Single Solution to the problems of business are disappointed. Successful practitioners understand how each of the various strategies advanced works individually, as well as how they might be combined for best effect.

Behind closed doors, senior leaders embrace a number of approaches and tools to reach a decision about what their strategy should look like and what they should avoid informed by their own on the ground experience. Choosing a strategy to meet the specific demands of their competitive environment in mature, nascent, growth, and declining industries is a major effort. Ultimately, strategy is a way of thinking, not the mindless application of models and tools.

However, how and when to use the various tools and their limits is still an outstanding issue. How to use business strategies is settled only in the minds of the practitioners who know how to apply the art and blend the various schools. Should the firm in a mature industry pursue an innovation strategy trying to create new markets? Should it seek to dominate existing markets or perhaps use a hybrid strategy?

Also, strategy can be a strange and frustrating subject matter for students who frequently feel as though they are lost in a whiteout, paralyzed with boredom. Many students are none too enthusiastic to study strategy.

Part of the problem is that students are generally unprepared to receive knowledge that is not immediately useful or exciting, that won't free them from the financial wars and close the book on their debts. For many students taking the required course in strategy, time seems to pass more slowly than in a laundromat.

Strategy requires students to have well-stocked minds, which means having knowledge of cross-functional disciplines and acquiring a more than nodding acquaintance with history—in short, to be educated. That means having knowledge of literature, history, and philosophy. Sadly historical consciousness is no longer in currency, let alone in vogue.

Students need to think in interdisciplinary terms, invariably that means finding dazzling connections, for as historian Edith Hamilton put it, "to see anything in relation to other things is to see it simplified." Instead they struggle with trying to integrate and coordinate various functional areas. Reference to context is de rigueur when discussing and analyzing a particular case or scenario.

Students get caught sometimes between warring disciplines such as finance, accounting, marketing, and other functional subjects. This is especially difficult in an academic environment with the pressure to specialize and many students living exclusively in the present. Students who go into the real world and attempt to practice strategy will quickly gain a healthy respect for the myriad challenges it poses.

## Surfing for Strategy
10/8/2023

Does Justice Potter Stewart's quote about obscenity—"I know it when I see it"—apply to strategy? Is strategy some MBA type's interpretation of elaborate Excel spreadsheets that claim to define the shape of an enterprise's future? Is it a carbon copy of something that worked well for another enterprise at a different time, place?

Is strategy solely the product of stained glass rational thought uncontaminated by the hurly-burly of the real world? Is it something to fall back on when all else fails? Is it the ad hoc play-calling of a CEO whose gut instincts—or maybe just pure luck—have made them a Wall Street favorite so far?

The word "strategy" is beguiling, but do we really know what it means? The coining of a workable framework is a task fraught with danger. It has to be right enough. It must highlight the core of the subject.

Perhaps it is time to return to basics. Let's make a sharp right turn. Consider a somewhat different and perhaps slightly simpler perspective common to and underscoring all strategies used in the business world. For sure, stated in this rough and ready way, as well as in a manner that invites scholarly challenge, it underlies and accommodates a potentially wide variety of strategies.

Let's take the capacious model advanced by Arthur F. Lykke Jr., a military strategist who taught a generation of military leaders at the Army War College in the United States. He divided military strategy into a ends/ways/means/risk equation. It is a basic framework for discussing the particulars of a military strategy. For our purposes, focus on means and ends.

At its most basic, overarching level, strategy is the essential linkage that connects resources with a set of defined, prioritized, and feasible goals that fit the competitive environment. Usable resources are both tangible and intangible. Strategy demands the intelligent interaction and integration of all the firm's significant resources to achieve goals.

It aligns means with ends while reserving some resources for rainy days. It is the link between resources and goals, the scheme for how to make one produce the other. The alignment, like beauty, is in the eyes of the beholder.

Strategy may not be about asking who and why. The question that haunts every strategy maybe how. How do you get from means to ends? It is always the how before the who and why.

Strategy happens in the space between means and ends. It is the relationship that unfolds at the intersection of means and ends.

Strategy, according to this model, is a force multiplier when it provides value added to resources. This perspective can accommodate the various schools of strategic thought and plausible arguments about various definitions and their imperial claims that they are valid for all times and places. This vantage point may provide a unifying perspective among various strategies, a conceptual center of gravity covering competitive activities. All the relevant resources come together to create a center of gravity to bring to bear on achieving the goal.

Again, in this context, it is not the strategist's job to select goals, but they are obliged to contribute to the setting of goals by advising what is possible based on resources. Strategy frequently fails when the resources prove insufficient to achieve the goals. This can happen because the wrong resources are in play or because the ends are too ambitious.

The strategy adopted may frequently be dictated by the availability of resources rather than by desired goals. Executives quickly come to understand that strategy is unavoidably and inevitably about trade-offs. Making trade-offs means accepting limits—saying no to some customers, for example, so that you can better serve others.

## Still More on Strategy
10/16/2023

In business, trade-offs occur when companies have to make choices between strategies that are inconsistent. For example, senior executives' short-term focus on earnings per share may conflict with long-term shareholder value and derail the firm's strategy.

The pressure from financial markets can tempt executives to perform unnatural acts, such as managing earnings in a fashion that undermines a long-term strategy. They are motivated by the personal impact of the decision and fixated on the short term.

One downside of stock-based compensation for executives is that it incentivizes strategies that might benefit stock prices in the short term but could be detrimental to firms in the long term. So rather than repairing the unsafe roof on the factory in Toledo this quarter, they decide to postpone the work to meet investor expectations for the quarter.

This asymmetrical reality, coupled with the four- to six-year average tenure for a CEO, undermines the serious consideration of strategy. This is unfortunate since the stakes and therefore the costs of failure are high.

Limited resources force executives to carefully and wisely match the resources available to the problem or set of problems at hand. They must not only choose among resources but also integrate and rationalize their use.

One of the challenges in developing a successful strategy is to set goals that are realistic in the context of finite resources and not to confuse means with ends. Since executives can't have everything at once, they need a set of goals that recognize the firm's limitations. Goals should be feasible, not pipe dreams found in the wild blue yonder.

Closely related, since external circumstances are not static, resources that are valuable now may not be in the future. When this occurs, executives are faced with the interplay and trade-offs between internal and external considerations.

Keep in mind that executives are trying to perform all these tasks while trying to cope with the tyranny of day-to-day events and crises. Functioning in this intense environment inevitably affects the quality of the choices made.

Moreover, all strategies are contextual. Strategies are derived from and shaped by political, regulatory, sociocultural, economic, and technological forces. None of these contexts should be ignored. Context provides meaning to events.

Strategies should act in these multiple contexts. Successful executives analyze the varied contexts that affect strategy and the ways in which context and ideas act on each other from the time they are developing strategy through its implementation, a progression that will, in turn, give rise to further ideas.

While the definition of strategy may have changed over the decades, in a word, strategy remains consequential, and the stakes are huge. It involves long-term commitments, large allocations of resources, and the making of critical decisions—all in a fiercely competitive environment in which the path forward is often unclear. Executives need to maintain the ability to see the forest rather than the trees.

Strategy is an attempt to control the future. Long-term goals are translated into proximate goals for execution. Changing strategies is like the popular metaphor of changing the direction of an aircraft carrier—it doesn't happen quickly.

Despite all these complex variables, strategy should be kept simple. Simplicity does not guarantee success, but complexity begs for failure. There is a chain of events between resources and goals. A chain is as strong as its weakest link, and the more links in the chain, the higher the odds that something will go wrong. The sovereign role of chance in strategy must be respected.

# Postscript

**WITH THE PASSAGE** of time, both the world and I have changed. Many of the columns in this volume were written in the heat of a moment—when a policy debate flared, a market convulsed, or some new technology promised to "disrupt everything." Rereading them now, I'm reminded how fluid reality can be and how often certainties evaporate under new light. Opinions that once seemed etched in granite now look more like chalk on the blackboard I still use in class.

Time humbles even the most confident analyst. Experience teaches that history doesn't repeat itself, but it does enjoy rearranging familiar themes in new and surprising ways. The truths we hold most tightly often turn out to be temporary, shaped by context, circumstance, and our own blind spots. So while these essays reflect the convictions of their moment, they also trace an evolution in my own thinking—a record not just of what I believed but of how I learned.

Over these years the world I wrote about has grown noisier, faster, and less forgiving. Markets have become algorithms, industries have become ecosystems, and attention spans have become nanoseconds. Yet the underlying questions remain stubbornly the same: What constitutes leadership? How do societies balance growth and equity? What does progress really mean, and who gets to define it?

If these essays show anything, it is that theory and practice are dance partners, not rivals. The ideas that animate our classrooms gain their meaning only when tested in the messy choreography of real life. I've been fortunate to live in both worlds—the analytical and the applied, the reflective and the pragmatic—and each continues to inform the other.

When I wrote *Columns That Cut*, I saw it as a bridge between experience and reflection. This continuation is, in some sense, a map of how that bridge has weathered the years—repainted, reinforced, occasionally closed for repairs but still standing.

I've learned to regard change not as an admission of error but as a measure of growth. If, over time, my conclusions have evolved, it's because reality has too. And reality, unlike theory, never grants tenure.

I offer these columns as a snapshot of a moving target—a record of the questions I've asked, the arguments I've made, and the lessons I've had to relearn. The world has changed, and so have I.

The dialogue continues.

# Acknowledgments

**NO MAN IS** an island, and no book is written alone. Every page in this collection carries traces of conversations, collaborations, and kindnesses that have shaped my thing and my life. When a book is written in this fashion—bit by bit over several years—the thank-you list gets long. There are far too many people to mention by name, and for fear of overlooking someone who deserves to be included, I've chosen not to list specific individuals. Suffice it to say, I've been fortunate to work with people who were not just colleagues but teachers, friends, and fellow travelers—across the worlds of finance, government, and the academy.

In my years in investment banking, I hit the lottery when it came to mentors and colleagues. They taught me that success depends not only on numbers but also on judgment, trust, and timing. Some offered advice, while others offered reality checks—both were invaluable. Their lessons about risk, resilience, and leadership echo throughout these pages, often in ways they might recognize but would, I hope, appreciate.

In government, I was privileged to work alongside men and women for whom public service was not a slogan but a calling. Together we learned that policy is as much about executions as intention and that good ideas fail without discipline and follow-through. The strategic challenges of that world—balancing competing interest, managing uncertainty, and staying grounded in purpose—left lasting marks on how I think about leadership and responsibility.

The academy has been the longest and, in many ways, the most revealing chapter of this journey. I have been sustained by those colleagues who remind me that education is the long game, not the quick return. They keep alive the belief that ideas still matter and that teaching remains an act of faith in the next generation. Still further, understand that theory matters most when it illuminates practice and that the classroom, at its best, is where experience and theory met on equal terms.

My students deserve special mention. They have been both audience and inspiration—challenging assumptions, questioning orthodoxy, and forcing me to translate abstract ideas into practical guidance. They keep me honest and, occasionally, humble. Watching them find their footing in the world has been among the greatest satisfaction of the late-stage reinvention.

I also owe thanks to the editors and colleagues who gave my columns a home, sharpened my prose, and tolerated my deadlines. Their encouragement helped turn solitary writing into a shared dialogue with readers, improving my work in ways that only good editors can.

A big thanks to Paul Burton, my superb editor of this book, who helped considerably in arranging the columns into something resembling a coherent volume.

Looking back, I realize every career change, every column, and every classroom moment was really just another way to say thank you—for the chance to keep learning from people who made the journey worth taking.

www.ingramcontent.com/pod-product-compliance
Lightning Source LLC
Chambersburg PA
CBHW070408290526
45791CB00005B/1680